Confronting the Present

Global Issues

General Editors: Bruce Kapferer, Professor of Anthropology, James Cook University and John Gledhill, Professor of Anthropology, Manchester University.

This series addresses vital social, political and cultural issues confronting human populations throughout the world. The ultimate aim is to enhance understanding – and, it is hoped, thereby dismantle – hegemonic structures which perpetuate prejudice, violence, racism, religious persecution, sexual discrimination and domination, poverty and many other social ills.

ISSN: 1354-3644

Previously published books in the series:

Michael Herzfeld
The Social Production of Indifference: Exploring the Symbolic Roots of Western Bureaucracy

Peter Rigby
African Images: Racism and the End of Anthropology

Judith Kapferer
Being All Equal: Difference and Australian Cultural Practice

Eduardo P. Archetti
Guinea-pigs: Food, Symbol and Conflict of Knowledge in Ecuador

Denis Duclos
The Werewolf Complex: America's Fascination with Violence

Thomas Hylland Eriksen
Common Denominators: Ethnicity, Nation-Building and Compromise in Mauritius

Confronting the Present

Towards a Politically Engaged Anthropology

Gavin Smith

BERG

Oxford • New York

First published in 1999 by
Berg
Editorial offices:
150 Cowley Road, Oxford OX4 1JJ, UK
70 Washington Square South, New York NY 10012, USA

Berg is the imprint of Oxford International Publishers Ltd.

Library of Congress Cataloging-in-Publication Data

A catalogue record for this book is available from the Library of
Congress.

British Library Cataloguing-in-Publication Date

A catalogue record for this book is available from the British Library.

ISBN   1 85973 200 3 (Cloth)
        1 85973 205 4 (Paper)

Typeset by JS Typesetting, Wellingborough, Northants.
Printed in the United Kingdom by WBC Book Manufacturers,
Mid Glamorgan.

To Timothy

Ideas that have overcome our intellect and conquered our conviction, ideas to which reason has riveted our conscience, are chains from which one cannot break without breaking one's heart . . .

– Marx (1971: 48)

Contents

Preface and Acknowledgements   9

Introduction   1

>   **PART I**   17

Selective Traditions

>   CHAPTER ONE   19

Politically engaged social enquiry and images of society

>   **PART II**   51

Cultural Differentiations

>   CHAPTER TWO   53

The production of culture in local rebellion

>   CHAPTER THREE   88

Secret agents, hidden meanings: domination and resistance
re-examined

>   **PART III**   131

Modernity and New Socio-Economic Forms

>   CHAPTER FOUR   133

Knowing their place: regional economies and the social
construction of place in Western Europe

CHAPTER FIVE 167

Towards an ethnographic method for the study of 'informalized' regional economies in Western Europe

PART IV 193

Disciplined Practices

CHAPTER SIX 195

Overlapping collectivities: Local concern, state welfare and social membership

CHAPTER SEVEN 228

The dialectics of history and will: The Janus face of hegemonic processes

References 271

Index 291

Preface and Acknowledgements

This is a book of reflections by an anthropologist who comes home and finds none. Perhaps two stories set alongside one another will say more about this than I can explain in any straightforward way. Midway through fieldwork, some years ago, I took a break. I had met a fellow student and her father said I could stay at their country place just outside Lima. As I later recorded, it was a disturbing experience:

> *This was the pause I needed and did not want. A country house loaned. A pile of disorganized and fragmented notes. The company of bright, crisp people. Certain reckonings. The tension uncoils like a fist. Or a snake.*
>
> *The gardener, Pardo, is cleaning the swimming pool. He stands in the empty, sloping pit pushing a broom up the stained walls. His arms are covered in burns from the chloride. Paulina, his partner, is walking towards the front door of the house. She sees me, pauses, and changes direction. She is walking towards me. She has something in her arms. A child? I wait for her but she stops. Quite far off. Does she want to talk to me?*
>
> *A pleasantry: 'Buenos días, Sra Pardo. ¿Qué tal?'*
>
> *'Ningun problema, Señor,' she says. 'It's just the child, Señor.'*
>
> *Is the child sick, I ask. Well, perhaps just a little sick, yes, she says. I get up and come over to you, Luisa. What are you? A child? A shrunken mummy from a Nazca grave site? A newborn infant? This is the house of a rich man. One of the richest of them. What are you? How do you come to be here on this finely cut lawn, with the swimming pool there, just so. And over there the stables. And here the wrought-iron garden table and the parasol. Wasn't this to be the pause? Isn't the filthy city down there?*
>
> *Little Luisa. So little. Just twelve-and-a-half pounds and two-and-a-half years old for all that. Two hospitals we took you to simply refused to waste their time. At the Anglo-American Clinic there happened to be two students visiting from Johns Hopkins University who were here to look at chronic forms of malnutrition. You were interesting. They take you in. I am asked to sign papers saying that I am responsible for you (your bills?). So I mention the name of my host. It turns out he is a governor of the hospital. Why don't you call him? I do. A voice sounds different on the phone. It is absurd and embarrassing to take the child to such a hospital. Paulina has five other children; this one will*

either die, after costly treatment, or survive and be mentally deficient. He wishes that I had consulted him first.

We return to the house. Paulina has left her children in the care of another employee of my host. When we arrive, she goes off to her own house. We are back on the lawn now. I talk to Paulina about where she gets her food. I hope I do not understand what all this is about. I hope that there is a terribly clever and convoluted explanation of how I can be confronted with a child suffering from extended third-degree malnutrition living in the garden of the president of IBM, Peru. I am also thinking about how much money I have left for moving into a rooming house down in the city. The neighbour returns. She has another baby in her arms. This I cannot believe. She uncovers the child, but before I can look at his face, she passes the bundle of rags into my arms. Then Paulina is there. She says, this one is no problem, Señor. This one is dead. The other woman says we must bury him. Yes, I say, trying to keep within the ordered logic of events. But we must report it, says the old woman. To whom? To the Guardia Civil.

The police. The old pick-up truck with the ragged bundle on the boards in the back. (I am looking through the rear window. Nobody comes with me this time.) The morgue. The morticians handing out their business cards . . .

Luisa is in a tent at the clinic. Paulina is back in her shack at the end of a rich family's garden. Pardo has finished the pool. Now I am standing at the counter of a shanty-town stall drinking warm Cristal. This is where the second piece of fieldwork will begin. Trickier than the first part. Dispersed. Working through the barriadas *and* coralones. *How can I get people to talk? They don't know me so well here. The tension begins to coil into a fist inside. It's all starting again. What respite?* (Adapted from Smith 1979a.)

About a year after I wrote this, I paid a visit to the village in Britain where my parents lived and I had grown up. I had left when I was seventeen to go to Canada. Like most migrants, I had returned occasionally, sometimes for visits, sometimes because I intended to stay: 'to settle', as they say. Now I was over thirty. Things had changed. There had been the incident of Luisa, for example. I thought *I* had changed – a touch of hubris quickly dispelled in the village pub, to which I had taken myself to regale childhood friends with my adventures. The publican came over behind the bar, looked into my face, unremarking, and said, 'The usual?' He didn't even have to embellish this evidence of enduring local memory by adding my first or last name!

Leaving Luisa, I had expected to leave as well the tugs of politics made extreme by poverty and marginality. Some years later I was to replay the irony of this sentiment, when I saw the Costagavras film *Missing*, which ends with the same absurd sense of closure I had felt when I returned to 'my' village. Having gradually and reluctantly discovered that the murder and corruption he found in Chile were not so a much a function of local culture as of American political agendas, Jack Lemon returns to hometown Chicago. As we see the plane touching down 'back home', we can almost feel the audience around us breathing a sigh of relief that they are back again in the safety of the good old USA and things that are familiar. It's a closure that works against the entire spirit of the movie. And it repeated the one I felt then as a took my first tug of beer in the village pub.

Yet when *I* had touched down ... This time in Heathrow. I had called my brother, who greeted me with the news that my mother was 'ill'. 'What kind of "ill"?' I had asked. As far as I could remember my mother, who daily rose early to skim the milk in the larder, made breakfast, cleaned up, made her famous huge lunches, cleaned up, made tea, cleaned up, made her ceremonial suppers, cleaned up . . . and was, without pause for doubt, or for remark, to be found sort of asleep in an armchair, her glasses fallen along her nose, her blue-veined shamefully rough hands resting on some 'mending' covering her lap . . . and this *is* how I remembered her then. . . . My mother had never been 'ill-in-her-life' as my family were wont to say proudly of themselves.

A book small and thin enough to carry easily in a pocket and terrifying enough to be guaranteed to distract under most conditions, a book, in other words, well suited to travelling, and one I thus had with me as I spoke to my brother, was R. D. Laing's *The politics of experience and the bird of paradise*. In retrospect I suppose it was in fact two books, but over the years I had come to take the title as all one. For me the politics of experience seemed somehow bound up with a bird of paradise, a caged experience and then flight. Never having seen a bird of paradise it was always simply a bird just beyond reach, just flown. The cage door left open. The bird, in the morning gone.

So it was, that I had this book of Laing's with me as I spoke to my brother, a book that made it quite clear to me that the kind of 'illness' my brother was describing had as much to do with politics as Luisa's ailments, yet now much closer to home. Indeed *in* the home. A home that apparently had made me and, in the process, destroyed my mother – un-noted; in this at least, a contrast to my melodramatic annotations of Luisa's case. My father kept a diary, filling a full page every day of his life, from the age of 21 (exactly) to three weeks before he died. This makes it possible to record that my mother's path to catatonia went uncharted.

What we have here is a juxtaposition. And, as with other, similar vignettes, stories, cases and so on, it says a lot more than I can say *about* it. As I say, put bluntly this book is about coming home and finding none. Migrants do this all the time. Like so many other words to do with places, words like 'community', like body, so the word 'home' has a physical and an abstract meaning, at least for the migrant. These are quite distinct. The one could be destroyed and leave the other standing, possibly regnant in all its glory. The one means 'a centre'. It resembles the tethering iron to which a goat is tied. In this way the animal's movements are restricted for its own safety. The other means 'the place I go to be me'. Neither of these senses has a very firm relationship to reality. Indeed, both are best thought of as more or less captivating fictions. Most of us are migrants, and so for most of us, there is no centre; the old meadow in the woods where once we grazed is no longer recognizable.

And anyway, much earlier on, as the backdoor from the kitchen slammed shut and you found yourself out in the cold backyard with hours to kill, it soon dawned on you that the self you left behind in there by the warm hearth was, as Lévi-Strauss said in reference to something else, 'vraiment une bricolage' – not an especially secure 'me' to return to. We get patched together in there, brutally, thoughtlessly, fitfully, just as much as we get patched together and pulled apart later on. There's more than one migrant who studiously avoided politics 'out there' only to return home to the most bitter and savaging political engagement. For anthropologists such sentiments can be reversed too, as they gain a vicarious high from the politics they see performed abroad, and then allow that preoccupation to occlude what they might see or do at home.

Like many people then, I went away to grow up: to see the world, an expression with special resonance for anthropologists, for whom there has long been a sense that because we cannot see what is obvious to us, it therefore follows that we *can* see what is not. And there is much of this sense in the book: first becoming aware of the politics that lay behind the malnutrition of Luisa in Peru, then using it to stoke up the fires of indignation being quenched by age, only to return to some pre-imagined centre of my life to find there too a gloved politics lying beneath my mother's mental and emotional malnutrition.

The essays that follow, then, are motivated by these tensions between distance and proximity, vision and blindness. And across this tight cord dances always the fascinating figure of politics. While I was in Peru I went to see the film *Read: Mexico Insurgente*. One scene in that film – my friends now tell me I have imagined it – threw me off a lot when I returned to my fieldsite. It still haunts me. There's Read, sitting on the floor in an abandoned building with a contingent of peasants in Villa's army. They have some hooch and they are drinking it. Read begins to tell his momentary friends of his home, his youth and, increasingly – his anguish. They listen – perhaps out of curiosity, perhaps courtesy – as he relates a garbled story of a tunnel from his father's house to some place else and ends by talking about the Wobblies' strike taking place right this moment in his home state of New Jersey. I can't remember if we are left to ourselves or if a peasant says it, yet clear as day is another one of those juxtapositions: what the hell is Read doing in Mexico if there's a political struggle closer to home he could as well be engaged in? In any event Read passes out, to awaken the next day at the end of a battle, and staggers out to discover the bodies of his erstwhile friends strewn about like fieldstones on the dusty earth.

Encaged or engaged, at home or abroad? That seemed to be the choice. At least the one that made anthropology attractive to me. There was the dross of home, at least as I saw it then, something one wanted to get disengaged from. And there was the *need* of the marginalized, for which I felt a far greater responsibility than I did for my mother (who I scarcely saw from seventeen to twenty-seven), a need that called up in me a sense that I could not remain *disengaged*. It is hard now to disentangle this desire for engagement with the desire for excitement, whose opposite was the torpor and contentment that afflicted my life at the centre. The vicarious prurience of all this is captured by a poem Philip Larkin wrote when I was about fourteen, at about the time I was beginning to be so stirred:

> Sometimes you hear, fifth hand,
> As epitaph:
> *He chucked up everything*
> *And just cleared off,*
> And always the voice will sound
> Certain you approve
> This audacious, purifying move.

And they are right, I think.
We all hate home
And having to be there:
I detest my room, its specially-chosen junk,
The good books, the good bed,
And my life, in perfect order
So to hear it said

He walked out on the whole crowd
Leaves me flushed and stirred,
Like *Then she undid her dress*
Or *Take that you bastard;*
Surely I can, if he did?
And that helps me stay
Sober and industrious.
But I'd go today,

Yes, swagger the nut-strewn roads,
Crouch in the fo'c'sle
Stubbly with goodness, if
It weren't so artificial,
Such a deliberate step backwards
To create an object:
Books; china; a life
Reprehensibly perfect.

Much of recent reflection in anthropology has to do with this phenomenon; indeed, Larkin's 'deliberate step backwards' has perhaps an especial meaning for those whose travels to the periphery were closely associated with their beliefs in social evolution. But I think another reversal has occurred. Increasingly, engagement at home (instead of the kind that attracted me) has meant a certain kind of political engagement – an engagement with 'my' identity politics and a disengagement from all that is not immediately of mine and me, a squeamishness *vis à vis* responsibility to others which, I believe, is ethically acceptable only in the most private of scholars. So this set of essays is at least partly to do with bringing engagement back to a home that I find does not, never did, exist. It is not just, then, about what happens when we try to turn the ethnography of travel into ethnography *in situ*. It is about this *and* the stickiness of political engagement – a word that forms a centrepiece of this collection.

It will quickly become obvious that there is little said sympathetically in this book about the postmodern turn; and yet there is one element of the postmodern spirit exemplified here. These are essays in the literal sense: attempts, journeys, reflections and so on. They emerge out of conversations with many different people, different *kinds* of people, and they continue as conversations. Occasionally they go back to see where we have come from; at other times they try intentionally to cross thin ice toward a new, possibly false outcrop. They eschew conclusions, or at least settle only for temporary ones, and often one essay takes up a strand left behind by an earlier one. One thing I think I learned from the people of highland Peru who shared their lives with me is that strongly felt disagreement combined with the willingness and ability for conversation can be the basis for powerful collective solidarity, and that is what I feel about the people to whom I owe so much in this book – the combination of their strongly held views, their ability to voice and share them, and their commitment to conversation. And so, as once before, I do not relieve them of their responsibility for this book; I simply thank them.

I am for ever in debt to the numerous people who will not read this English version in Peru, and in Spain, and as the years go by I look in the chest of secrets and find that my debt to them has grown and goes on growing. Students in senior undergraduate classes and an intimate bunch of graduate students have been plundered, battered and confused into allowing me to slip in and glide away with many of their ideas. I need especially to thank a number of them for their very specific contributions to the ideas in this book: Pauline Barber, Vasilios Dirlis, Leslie Jermyn, Belinda Leach, Albert Schrauwers, Claudia Vicencio. If most of these people are no longer students it just shows how slow my digestion of their ideas has been. I would also like to thank the students in the graduate seminar in the Department of Anthropology of the University of Barcelona that I have taught, as well as participants in a couple of City University of New York graduate anthropology seminars, a seminar at the University of Padua to which Enzo Mingione invited me, and a seminar organized by the Canadian World History Society at the University of Victoria in 1995. I would like to thank members of the Colegio de Michoacan in Zamora for inviting me to spend time there on two occasions. I owe especial thanks to Claire Belanger, Simone Ghezzi and Enzo Mingione for their help in Italy. And I would like to thank the Social Sciences and Humanities Research Council (Canada) and the Connaught Fund at the University of Toronto, for their support of the research on which this book is based. A special thanks to Kathryn Earle and John Gledhill for their editorial encouragement as well as an anonymous reviewer for her/his helpful suggestions and to Annette MacDougall for the index.

The interventions and conversations of a number of people in Spain have given character to this book. They include Joan Bestart, Jesus Contreras, Joan Frigole, Gonzalo Sanz and Ignasi Terradas at the University of Barcelona, as well as Josepa Cuco, Primitivo Pla, Enric Sanchis and Josep Ybarra. I would like to extend special thanks to Jesus Contreras for his energetic support of my work in Spain, for his hospitality and for his kindness. In France I would like to thank Maurice Aymard for his thoughtful help and insight and for allowing me to spend time at the Maison des Sciences de L'Homme, and also Daniel Nordman, who has shared his research interests with me. A great number of people have read and commented on various drafts and papers that now appear as chapters here, and my gratitude to them for their time, their kindness, their generosity of spirit, and their energetic engagement really knows no bounds. On various chapters I would like to thank Jonathan Barker, Micaela di Leonardo, Glynis George, Meric Gertler, John Gledhill, Gaston Gordillo, Philip Gulliver, Michael Lambek, Blanca Muratorio, Marilyn Silverman and Eric Wolf. One or two especially masochistic friends have tussled and tugged with me over pretty much everything that appears here, and these I need to thank for fear of what they might do to me next time. They are Malcolm Blincow, of course, whose integrity as a person and knowledge as an anthropologist I would like to emulate, Dipankar Gupta, who manages to bring together cool intellect with the warmth of friendship, Gerald Sider, whose sheer passion and insight make him a comrade I am proud to have, William Roseberry, whose quiet critique and careful scholarship conceal a warmth and caring for people that rubs off on them, and Susana Narotsky, an inspirational anthropologist and a friend who has shown me dimensions of the world and living in it that make it all worthwhile. I have learned so much from Winnie Lem that I don't know where to begin to thank her; if love were coinage mine would make you rich.

Chapter 2 originally appeared in Jay O'Brien and William Roseberry (eds) (1991), *Golden ages, dark ages: imagining the past in anthropology and history*, University of California Press, Berkeley. An earlier version of Chapter 5 appeared as 'Toward an ethnography of idiosyncratic forms of livelihood', *International Journal of Urban and Regional Research* Vol. 18 (1) (1994).

Introduction

What follows is a series of reflections by a person whose political views took him into anthropology. Yet, confronting the present, I find that many of these political views have to be rethought and, with them, my understanding of what anthropology is or ought to be. It is this that connects up the chapters; and yet they can be read independently, though in truth, each is an *essay* rather than a self-contained and nicely concluded piece. Ends left loose in one chapter tend to be taken up, albeit in a different register, in another.

Each essay arises from reflections on a problem encountered while doing ethnography. 'Doing' ethnography in at least two senses. First in the sense of observing, listening, reading ancient handwriting in archives, scrawling notes, eating, drinking, getting sick, being puzzled and feeling embarrassed somewhere 'else' than the university or the study in my house. Second in the sense of doing pretty much the same things while 'writing up' back at my place of work – on campus and at home. I'm aware that I cannot locate myself very perfectly in the labyrinth of assumptions and purposes that constitute my particular perspective on the world; but it's fair to say that the puzzlements I have felt arise from a twofold commitment: to study contemporary society ethnographically and to do so from the perspective of historical realism.[1] Perhaps if I were not so committed to these two things the puzzles would be less, or at least different; and, for that reason, readers who feel vastly different commitments may find my concerns misplaced, easily resolved or better abandoned. Yet before they walk off and close the door, let me call over their shoulder that herein are elements of a conversation; one which even – no, especially – when disparaging, impatient, or angry, is aimed at keeping the conversation going, to entice or threaten you back from the threshold.

Ethnography has changed. It has changed in shape and in purpose as its practitioners have engaged with different intellectual challenges and as the world they study has groaned, rolled over, and assumed a different posture in the bed of history. For my part, in most of my work I have tried to relate different forms of livelihood to varieties of collective political expression, and this interest continues throughout the book, but is now extended from the Andes to include more recent research in Spain and Italy. In Peru my original interest had been to study the ways in which rural people organized a local rebellion: but as questions accumulated, I was drawn more and more into studying the relationships they engaged in to make a living. This in turn drew me from the rather remote setting of the community of Huasicancha to the market stalls of the provincial town of Huancayo, the streets of the smelting town of La Oroya and the shanty towns and inner-city dwellings of Lima. Nevertheless, across this wide compass, people always referred to themselves as 'Huasicanchinos', and would be quick to point out to me the 'cultural' features that they shared among themselves and that distinguished them from others.

Later on, when I felt the desire, as a European, to do anthropological work in Europe, it was the discovery of the importance of livelihood relationships in shaping collective political action that led me to a particular fieldsite in Spain. There I sought out a setting where people had a 'working-class' experience in industry; but unlike what one might be led to expect by more conventional views of the working class, their 'factories' were small and dispersed through the countryside (not the city), and they frequently retained one foot in agriculture. The dispersal of production in this way had the effect of making the region itself take on some of the trappings of a factory – as though factory divisions of labour were now sorted out across this wider geographical setting. Yet it was almost as though this dispersal of workplaces also meant a kind of dispersal of cultural identity. This area of Spain to the south of Alicante could be, and was, referred to as 'a regional economy'; but people's sense of local-ness, of cultural distinctiveness having to do with place, was far more diffuse and plastic than I had encountered in Huasicancha. The juxtaposition of these rather different research experiences reflects in some measure the challenges that many anthropologists today feel with respect to doing ethnography. It has effectively pressed hard on the shape of my ethnographic enquiry, contorting it sometimes almost out of recognition (as 'ethnography'), tearing it apart into small disconnected rags, stitching it together to make a different but not necessarily a better fit.

To begin with, it seems to me that in so far as anthropologists study other people they worry about it. While loath to give up entirely the connection of anthropology with a focus on 'others' (in contrast to sociology, for example) they have begun to acknowledge that there is something suspect about a professional desire to make one's politics always somewhere else and to do with persons characterized as in some way 'different' from ourselves (Smith 1994b). Yet, if they were once protected by a distance, whether geographically real or intellectually constructed, they are now unable to stand aloof from the people they study, raising the question of what the nature of the anthropologist's political engagement should now be and how this might affect the way she or he does ethnography.

As old forms of difference and distance melt and shrink, other forms of difference arise, and anthropology's subjects themselves become highly mobile. An older world imagined – rather conveniently in the case of our discipline – in terms of the 'Third World' or the 'South' in contrast to the 'West' or the 'North' has to be rethought. The centre does not hold. One effect is that as anthropologists reconfigure this way of formulating the world for study, one that has been so fundamental to the discipline's identity, so anthropology loses an older kind of monopoly from which it traditionally drew a great deal of its authority. Finding themselves today doing fieldwork in places that are the stamping grounds of other disciplines, anthropologists can no longer confine their professional discourse to their own guild, employing a code that keeps them insulated from other disciplines, or treating local scholars with patronizing condescension. Rather, the very issues that are of pressing concern for anthropologists turn out to be of long-standing concern to colleagues in cognate disciplines. Questions of the changing role of place in people's sense of collective membership or of different forms of citizenship in social identity, become central to the issues anthropologists must now address. They are hardly foreign to other disciplines; they may indeed have been of central concern for a very long time. In this context these essays can be seen as a dialogue with one or another discipline tackling a similar issue: from social history to cultural geography, from economic sociology to political theory.

These are essays, then, often forays into unfamiliar territory where I no doubt have read the maps wrongly and returned with more riddles than trophies. As I say, like any essays, they are attempts in a conversation; each remains incomplete; none stands alone, innocent of resonances from the others. Yet the sand in the ointment is of a particular kind: unlike many of my anthropological colleagues I cannot dispense with the sediment of realism. Tempted at a party, or before the rounded eyes of my seven-year-old son's breathless friends, to finesse with a show of 'quelque chose extra-ordinaire et d'anthropologie' I find myself uneasy, as though I know that, like a conjuring trick, the hey presto effect only works by concealing the strings. Usually these are the strings of a real world of forces and conditions unreached by the immediacy of ethno-graphic fieldwork – historical processes and connections whose exposure would deflate the anthropological afflatus that makes for such good story-telling and such elegant evocations of 'culture'. As somebody who started his professional career on Wall Street I am only too tempted to run from this past by making no more than a token gesture toward the movements of capital, the complexity of regulation theory or the sheer mundaneness of 'economics'. But I firmly believe that intellectual honesty and political responsibility do require anthropologists to situate their interest in culture within the frame of historical realism.

Yet even as I resort to the term, I admit that I find it hard to say just what I mean by *historical realism*. Certainly for me it means more than a being a corrective to the way in which anthropologists feel the need to produce the *frisson* effect (Wolf 1990: 587) to get attention – the professional equivalent of the fisherman's yarn of how big was the fish and how thrilling the catch. Nor am I advocat-ing a realism that is simply an empiricist rejection of that body of thought that wishes to stress the constructedness of truth and to foreground the apparently renewed power of ideas, of desires, of experience in a supposedly 'information society' peopled by 'con-sumers'.

Let me try to evoke what I am getting at by comparing different ways of talking about dreams and possibilities. In Richard Fox's edited book, *Recapturing anthropology: working in the present* (1991) Arjun Appadurai reflects on the shape of a possible 'transnational anthropology'. He argues that,

> More persons in more parts of the world consider a wider set of 'possible' lives than they ever did before. . . . Until recently, whatever the force of social change, a case could be made that social life was largely inertial, that traditions provided a relatively finite set of 'possible' lives, and that fantasy and imagination were residual practices . . . [Now] this weight has imperceptibly shifted . . . even the meanest and most hopeless of lives, the most brutal and dehumanizing of circumstances, the harshest of lived inequalities is now open to the play of the imagination (1991: 197–8).

We need to note here the particular characteristics Appadurai selects out of the past and the present in order to make a case for a radical break between now and then. He contrasts an older world of finite possibilities where imagination was a 'residual practice' to a present world having a plurality of possibilities. Here we find the anthropologist reflecting on 'globalization' in what other practitioners could easily understand to be a distinctively anthropological way: a global *culture* that, through the reach of its media and the diaspora of the people it has unleashed, opens the way for possible worlds unimaginable to many before. Yet while I find it pleasant and congenial to imagine such a world, I find it troubling to think that an entire discipline might devote itself to the study of just this dimension of it. I find myself obliged to think of people trying to make a living; and once I do, I begin to find radical distinctions between the past and the present much harder to draw.

Here I need to draw on some pretty everyday experiences of my own. I often spend time in Southern France, where my partner Winnie Lem has been doing fieldwork. For many years people in this region have responded to most external pressures to change their form of livelihood with the Mediterranean equivalent of the raised finger, a firm clap of the right hand on the opposite upper fore-arm, accompanied by a forceful upward movement of the left fist: Phwam!

'Tear up your old low-grade wine stocks and plant new varieties.'
Phwam!
'Replant your vines so as to get bigger machinery down the rows.'
Phwam!
'Well, how about moving into some other fruits, to broaden your base.'
'We're wine-growers. That's not just what we do; it's what we are.'
Phwam!

When I first encountered this view of possibilities it struck me as quite different from the people I knew in the area where I have worked in Spain. There for many years a person (and I use the singular intentionally) has had to deal with external pressures to change of the greatest whimsy and caprice imaginable. In response he or she was one year working in irrigated agriculture, the next abandoning it or relegating it to a lower priority, while taking up small artisan production in the back patio; then being forced out of that and into migrating to find work in Northern Europe; still another year abandoning that for subcontracted homework; then abandoning that for agriculture again, but now (owing to pollution and drought) dry cropping . . . and so on.

Different horses; different courses, no doubt. Different places, different histories, different people, possibly (dare I say it?) different cultures. Yet there is something about Appadurai's quest for new-ness, something about his confidence in a new 'cultural' fix for anthropology that seems to me too much, too terribly much what a lay-person expects an anthropologist to talk about. Somehow his imagery of 'globalization' has already been politically sanitized before we get to the anthropologist's task. Yet we need not abandon the role of the imagination to endorse a more realist kind of anthropology. Alessandro Portelli, for example, has spent some time helping us to understand the role 'possible worlds' play in ordinary people's lives. Working with the contemporary equivalents of the chap books and balladeers that E. P. Thompson wrote about or on conversations with miners, ship-builders and low-level political organizers in Italy and the United States, Portelli is especially insightful as he moves across the terrain of personal struggle and collective expression (1985, 1991). At one point in his writing he has organic intellectuals, like Togliatti, the leader of the Italian Communist Party just after the Second World War, accepting the conditions imposed on Italy through the 'tactical compromise'. And he juxtaposes these figures to 'the dream of another possible world' that lower-level organizers continue to hold.

Something in Portelli's text kept worrying at my mind as I thought of the French wine-growers and the Spanish *bricoleurs*. He writes of the way people he talked to in the Italian shipbuilding town of Terni narrate their lives when they have become used to tying the dream of a different personal life to 'the dream of a different collective history' . . . and that history fails them (Portelli 1990). Faced with the two very different experiences in France and Spain

I began to become aware that the way in which people tied their personal histories to the maintenance or fulfilment of collective possible histories was quite different. And this difference had distinct political consequences. While the French wine-growers' response to threats to their way of life took the form of collective political strategies, the Spanish pluri-active families responded with individual 'flexible' economic solutions.

How are these examples to be interpreted both in terms of political agency and of Appadurai's image of an increase in ordinary people's imaginative possibilities? For me, they come together only in the realities of the quite troubled marriage of the experienced world and the more elusive processes of its social reproduction. This is especially clear in the way I understand the militant particularism of the Huasicanchinos. Much of this book is the product of a shift I made in my own geographical focus of attention: from the highlands of central Peru to the 'flexible' regional economies of the European Union. The Huasicanchinos, in Peru, were like a considerably more stroppy-minded version of Winnie's companions in France. It is hard to imagine any adults from Huasicancha who were not taken up almost through every waking hour with the imagining of a different possible world for themselves. Perhaps, as Appadurai suggests, to some extent we all are; but, to return to Portelli's imagery, this 'dream of a different personal life' has for them long been tied to 'the dream of a different *collective* history'. Yet this collective history has been unwaveringly place-oriented – in a word: local – in its utopian vision. This draws me back to Appadurai's reflections:

> What a new style of ethnography can do is to capture the impact of deterritorialization on the imaginative resources of lived, local experiences. Put another way, the task for ethnography now becomes the unravelling of a conundrum: what is the nature of locality, *as lived experience*, in a globalizing, deterritorialized world? (1991: 196, *italics mine*).

Like Appadurai, I am convinced that present reality should call anthropologists to ask much more about the nature of locality than they have in the past (Appadurai 1995). Unlike Appadurai, and here is an element of the realism I want to stress, I don't restrict the re-thinking of ethnography to what we might call, rather facetiously, a revised celebration of empiricism – now not reality as experienced by the analyst, but as the lived experience of others. Both advocates of the explanatory power of a narrowly *cultural* anthropology on the one side and those who seek to trace the hidden hand of global capitalism through ever more elaborate number-crunching on the other side, need to recognize the immense distortions they risk by so limiting their professional problematic. Simply understanding the Huasicanchinos' militant particularism *in its own terms*, even sympathizing with it as a political strategy, is not enough. The celebration of place, and the collective identification with locality, that characterized the Huasicanchinos' perceptions, was absolutely essential to the success of their campaign; yet its strength came partly from its myopia, and its form was greatly influenced by the unfolding of historical forces and relationships that are by no means to be understood in terms of 'experience'. A realist anthropology requires that we interpellate such perceptions with an *explicit and detailed* exposition of mechanisms of social reproduction that are only misleadingly referred to as 'material conditions', since they are neither necessarily material, nor simply 'externally' restrictive conditions. Neither the world as experienced phenomenologically nor the world as produced through historical fields of force has a greater 'reality' the one over the other; yet their analysis does require quite self-conscious shifts of attention and of technique on the part of the analyst.

And that is where the conundrum for ethnography begins in this book. To some extent we might suggest that the balance reached between different lines of enquiry will be determined by the analysts' political agenda. Yet if it is so that our purposes impose horizons of relevance on what matters to us, what happens when that purpose becomes obscured? Social theories have always been tied to projects, and increasingly central to theories that called themselves 'social' was the idea that their refinement would lead to a better society; for many this meant, literally, social-ism. Yet socialism as a viable alternative to political liberalism and economic capitalism is in a state of hiatus, making it difficult to produce coherent social theory (a source of rejoicing, of course, in some quarters). What then can help us to identify what should be relevant to our social enquiries once bereft of this particular modernist purpose?

An answer that has become attractive to a certain kind of anthropology that sees itself as pre-eminently political is to say: only by getting as clear a picture as possible of people's self-understanding can we hope to discover what should be relevant for theory in the first place (see also Escobar 1992b: 63). But what if people's knowledge is the outcome of power differentials? Then their understanding should be thought of not so much as though it were local knowledge pure and simple, but also as a kind of knowledge peculiarly shaped by power – not even the insidious kind of power to which Foucault refers, but something more mundanely simple: the control of how such people get to know things, the control of what they know, what constitutes knowledge, what seems worth knowing. What *then* does it mean to base what is relevant for theory – how we set our intellectual priorities – on people's 'self-understanding'?

This doesn't mean abandoning the interpretative task of getting at people's self-understanding, but rather suggesting that such understandings arise in a particular historical setting, so that characterizing those settings in quite rigorous terms becomes an important component of our work. In Chapter1, for example, I suggest that the way in which certain intellectuals understood their roles had much to do with the state of working-class politics at the time. To illustrate a more recent shift in which 'society' itself is understood as inherently oppressive and disciplining, and the facilitating role of social institutions is downplayed in favour of a kind of social enquiry that goes directly for the voice of the individual, I refer to Raymond Williams's discussion of modernist novels of the city (1973). Speaking of the 'malaise of modernity' Charles Taylor (1991) reflects on the fact that while we rely on other people to endorse our own personal authenticity as *particular* kinds of people – special, individual, even a little idiosyncratic in our ways – we can only believe in such a freely self-constructed Self by *denying* the extent to which we have thus been socially formed. Williams takes up the same issue from a different angle by use of James Joyce's insights on urban life. He notes how personal understanding of an especially 'artistic' kind arose not through recognizing the self's identity within a knowable social community, a recognition of our embeddedness in social institutions, but by leaping over any particular identifiable community to a personal feeling that one's acute sense of the true Self lay in the realm of the universal and metaphysical, and, as such, *against*, *beyond*, 'society'. Here we are given insights into the particular character of people's self-understanding; but this is not confined to an attempt to find a technique to reflect, or properly to translate other people's experience. Instead, people's self-understanding is *problematized*, and it is problematized in a quite specific way: subjectivities are understood within the frame of the historical development of quite specific kinds of social relationship. This seems to me to be the beginning of a way to tie interpretative method to a historical realist view of the social world.

It does, however, require the careful characterization of the form and purview of institutions under different historical conditions. It is not enough to reduce social relations to something called 'practice', a term that seems as fuzzy and comforting as its (identical?) twin 'experience'. It is at this point that the popularity of Giddens and Bourdieu can be explained, for superficially at least, both appear to tie agency/practice to institution/structure; and both match their social phenomenology with a respectful bow to Marx. The relationship between 'subjectivism and objectivism' (Bourdieu 1990: 123) is one that both wish to collapse in favour of 'ontological complicity', in a phrase famously coined by Bourdieu (Bourdieu and Wacquant 1992: 20).[2] And we can expand and contract the role we want 'culture' to play in their formulas. It can be a residue of habits, possibly even experiences that mediate between 'mechanical rules' and 'statistical rules'. In Bourdieu, for example, this links subjective phenomenology to statistical patterns by producing a kind of elective affinity for behaviours that generate clusters, or what Bourdieu would call 'classes'. In a slightly different formulation, culture itself becomes a type of practice, as in 'cultural practices' – individual or collective. In either case, though, the term 'culture' in these contexts serves as a cover for historical refusal – an old sociological foible: a squeamishness with respect to history precisely because its specificities get in the way of the sweep of theory. Yet the sorts of social identities that Williams and Taylor are referring to can only be comprehended by reference to sets of historically constructed structures that vary from one setting to another. This means that the 'interpretative quest' needs to be underwritten by very careful historical anthropology of the kind practised by Wolf (1959, 1982) Roseberry (1983), Mintz (1985), Sider (1986), Comaroff and Comaroff (1991) and Nugent (1993). It seems too to be a strong case for the value of ethnography, as against grand theory.[3]

A realist ethnography needs to deal with experience then, just as it needs to deal with practice: the one – experience – calls for the need to find means of investing interpretative methods with ways of comprehending power and the situatedness of cultural perception, i.e.: the social distribution of knowledge; the other – practice – calls for the need to embed social practices and relationships in the historical shaping of institutions: not just institutions as the outcomes of accumulated practices or agency, but institutions in terms of the very inertia and concreteness of their existence. In prisons, in armies, in lawcourts and hospitals, we see evidence of the kind of concreteness to which I refer.

Yet despite this concreteness we have to resist the temptation to see these phenomena as static and as 'things', a temptation that is especially strong when we use the idea of structure and contrast it to agency. Once we understand institutions in terms of social reproduction, we are able to see them less in terms of things and more in terms of forces, or at least in terms of a geography of society in which we understand institutions as bridgeheads of power – facilitating certain practices, often by means of 'order' and regulation, and, just as surely, preventing other practices, closing certain social spaces, and inducing disorder and deregulation.

> When we encounter some sonorous phrase such as 'the strong ebb and flow of the trade cycle' we must be put on our guard. For behind this trade cycle there is a structure of social relations, fostering some sorts of expropriation (rent, interest and profit) and outlawing others (theft, feudal dues), legitimizing some types of conflict (competition, armed warfare) and inhibiting others (trade unionism, bread riots, popular political organization) – a structure which may appear, in the eyes of the future, to be both barbarous and ephemeral (Thompson 1968: 224–5).

These kinds of processes taken together, I refer to as *concrete abstractions* (borrowing the term from David Harvey 1985). As Thompson's example makes clear, they are neither necessarily material (though they can be) nor accessible through empirical observation. Because they are often 'off-stage' there is a sense in which they are occluded, though even here we need to take care.

Most images of society conjured up by social analysts give us an idea of those elements of the social world that are immediately available for study and of others that are obscured. We are all of us aware that our views of the world are selective, highlighting some elements – the way people express themselves, for example, and

downplaying others – their material well-being, for example. But
this is not quite what I am saying here. Rather, as we think about
society, we don't just become selective in our focus, we also
configure society in terms of what we take to be easily perceived
and what we take to require a more critical acuteness and attention.
All ways of drawing metaphors of society rely on some version or
other of hidden transcripts. Writers like Marx, Freud and Lévi-
Strauss, for example, are frequently accused of being essentialists.
The argument is that they made a distinction between surface
features of society, the person, or culture, and less accessible
features, which needed to be known for the better understanding
of capitalism, neurosis or kinship. Because they appear to use this
geological analogy, as Lévi-Strauss called it, their theories can be
accused of explaining the multiplicity of surface phenomena as
simply the manifestations of deeper relationships and forces, that
is to say, their more essential reality. Perhaps because I don't think
this is a proper interpretation of these writers I am not making a
case that concrete abstractions provide us with the determinant
underlying laws of motion of social reproduction. Yet in their
historical particularities from one time and place to another they
do configure social forms. This means fighting against the strong
current in today's social thought that ceases to problematize
capitalism, seeing it instead as something to be taken for granted,
treated as natural and, in the end, the only way societies can be
made to work.

Each of the chapters that follows represents my attempt to think
through the puzzles laid out in rather abstract terms here. Chapter
4, for example, 'Knowing their place' is an attempt to explore
precisely the implications of the kinds of historical processes I have
just referred to for thinking about the way localities come into being
and are reproduced through time. In Chapter 2, on the other hand,
I lay very little stress on concrete abstractions, and try instead to
explore the relationship between interactive practices in the context
of collective action and the dialogical, open-ended constitution of
local culture.

    In order of appearance, then: in Part I, 'Selective Traditions',
the book opens with an essay that uses historical materials to discuss
how political concerns have tended to give priority to particular
sociological questions. In doing so, I suggest that contemporary
prioritizing of the interpretative dimension of social enquiry should

not work to the exclusion of concern with problems of organization. Yet I do take the view that the earlier interest in organization was seriously flawed by a lack of interest in ordinary people's own perceptions, and that this was reflected in methodological limitations. I suggest that Gramsci was, in this regard, a threshold figure. After the various explorations of the intervening chapters, the issues no more than broached in this opening chapter are taken up again and expanded in the final chapter.

Part II, 'Cultural Differentiations', brings together two pieces in which resistance and culture are juxtaposed. In Chapter 2, 'The production of culture in local rebellion', with evidence from Peru I use my understanding of Raymond Williams's 'keywords' to suggest that under conditions of intense political pressure, through a group's internal dialogue crucial elements of their cultural expression were subjected to forge-like heat and thereby dialogically battered into new shapes. I follow this in Chapter 3 'Secret agents, hidden meanings', by exploring the extent to which a variety of more recent authors have advanced on Hobsbawm's and Wolf's studies of 'domination and resistance', referring to the contribution of James Scott and the Subaltern Studies school, on the one hand, and what I call expressivist studies of collective political resistance, on the other.

Part III, 'Modernity and new socio-economic forms' draws on my recent work on the salience of regions for the reconstitution of capitalism in Western Europe. In Chapter 4, 'Knowing their place', I explore recent work in the new economic sociology and in 'postmodern' geography, as well as David Harvey's work on the geography of capitalism, to see how these might help us to understand the role of place in contemporary society. In doing so, I find that the use made of the notion 'culture' in recent geography and economic sociology is confused and, more important, prevents these people from going on to more critical insights, because 'culture' acts as a surrogate for a more analytical kind of history. In Chapter 5 I suggest that the world of people engaged in the heterogeneous and plasticine social relations of an ever more informalized economy acts as a critique of existing sociological categories for our understanding of capitalism. This essay ends with a number of suggestions for the design of a kind of ethnography that retains much of the rigour associated with realist views of social reproduction, while seeking more sensitivity to interpretation embedded in social practices.

Part IV, 'Disciplined practices', contains two essays that arise directly from my attempts to think out the role of anthropology in studying the shifting shapes and rhythms of this world of tenuous order and induced fear of disorder. They are both about dispersed and overlapping fields of social regulation. The first of these, 'Overlapping collectivities: local concern, state welfare and social membership', ties social membership mediated through 'culture' to the ways in which different states have attempted to form 'social citizenry'. I argue that anthropologists need to do a far more thorough historical reading of the way different states constitute proper social membership. Local claims, often studied in terms of older anthropological notions of culture, are likely to be strongly influenced by these differing state and civil interpellations. Chapter 7, 'The dialectics of history and will: the Janus face of hegemonic processes', is an attempt to explore two rather different components of hegemony, with a view to working out how to operationalize these elements for ethnographic method. After exploring the way hegemony takes form through history, I try to think more about the ways in which hegemonic processes are vital in understanding dispersed forms of social regulation in the present.

What it means to be politically engaged as an anthropologist has shifted for me over the years, a shift moreover in the opposite direction from what I take to be the current in anthropology – away from experience as the measure of authenticity in politics. The line of connections seems to go like this. Being politically engaged is intimately tied to political practice. Political practice is a certain kind of experience, so one should not deny or push aside the importance of experience in politics. And I do not deny this. But it seems to me that what might be a healthy corrective change of course for such social sciences as economics and geography, may in fact be more of the same for anthropology. The stress on fieldwork has inevitably made experience almost a magic key for entering the world of adulthood among anthropologists, and indeed explains the present attraction of ethnography among other disciplines like social history and cultural studies. But for anthropologists this highly intense and often quite anguished moment can mislead us into thinking that this exhausts the entire quotient of the social engagement required of us.

Much harder for us is the move in the opposite direction – toward engagement with systemic and historical forces that, in Marx's words, lie behind the backs of people. It is a move we fear to make lest we have to abandon *something*, something usually rather unarticulated: a kind of contact with the other that is exclusively ours. This I think explains the easy dismissal by many cultural anthropologists of any move *away from experience*. Yet political praxis seems to urge us towards engagement with the gears of system as well as to a pledge to experience, so I hope that what follows demonstrates my attempts, albeit limited and incomplete, to tramp the muddy boots of experience across the patterned carpet of system.

Notes

1. I prefer the expression 'historical realism' to the term 'political economy' which has come to embrace a very wide variety of approaches in contemporary cultural anthropology (Roseberry 1988; 1989: 145ff.). In the United States in the 1950s 'political economy' was used among anthropologists as a code word to refer to those whose work was informed by their socialism, and for that reason I continue to use it. But we should be aware that the term rarely has this radical association outside the discipline, and that, albeit in different eras and for different reasons, two major influences in anthropology developed their theoretical positions *against* the political economists: Marx and Durkheim.

   Gaston Gordillo has pointed out to me that a writer such as Gramsci was especially critical of realism, which he associated with positivism. Terms such as *critical* realism have been coined to address this issue, but I prefer *historical* realism. Gramsci once noted that in the term 'historical materialism' it is the 'historical' that should carry the greater weight. My use of the expression 'historical realism' partly reflects the need to understand society entirely in historical terms, and partly reflects the need to emphasize the realness of history over its constructedness.

2. Despite Giddens's and Bourdieu's claims to the contrary, I remain unconvinced that they have succeeded in superseding what Philip Abrams (1982: 227) refers to as 'The weight of two and half millennia of treating dualism as the obvious basis for thought . . .'. See especially: Archer 1995; see also Held and Thompson 1989 for Giddens, and Calhoun, LiPuma and Postone 1993 for Bourdieu.

3. This is a case that Bourdieu has often made himself. Brubaker has argued that Bourdieu is a much better ethnographer than social theorist (Brubaker 1985).

PART ONE

Selective Traditions

CHAPTER ONE

Politically Engaged Social Enquiry and Images of Society

> It is because alternative and irreconcilable views of human order – one based on mutuality, the other on competition – confronted each other between 1815 and 1850 that the historian today still feels the need to take sides.
>
> — E. P. Thompson 1968: 225–6

> Granted the importance of the subject, one might ask why anthropology seems to have relinquished the study of organization, so that today you can find the topic more often discussed in the manuals of business management than in our publications.
>
> — Wolf 1990: 590

I want to begin the series of essays in this book by going over old ground, exploring moments of political engagement for social analysts, but doing so with certain assumptions. These start from the proposition that there is always a certain urgency to our work, which acts as a selection process. What we see to be the most important political priority affects what we see to be the most useful ways of studying social reality, highlighting certain characteristics of the social world and occluding others. Yet really this is only a useful way of *beginning* the journey over old ground. Social analysts are particular kinds of social agents, but social agents never the less. And, as with all agents, there is a dialectical relationship between the formulations they produce to figure 'society' and the currents and forces prevailing at the time. I argue that if we collapse the issues and concerns of an earlier generation of scholars into a kind of historical vacuum that permits us to make comforting moral and political judgements of them, we run the risk of ourselves believing that *our* urgencies, concerns and anguish are in some way above and beyond history and society.

19

Much of an earlier kind of writing on the part of politically engaged and progressive social analysts was framed within a perception of what Ernesto Laclau (1977) has called 'the national popular'. I attempt here to give a historical sense of this notion for the case (mostly) of England, and to show how the images that emerged of society and history were dialectically linked to real forces and the real concerns of ordinary people, albeit highly contoured and unevenly expressed; dialectically linked in the sense that these currents gave form to intellectuals' images of society, and then intellectuals' images of society materially affected social currents and political possibilities. An especially powerful image, for example, was one that understood society in terms of *production* broadly conceived, and this gave rise to particular configurations of questions, methodologies and narratives. To a great extent *this* image has been elbowed aside by a *spatial* image of society, which employs metaphors of fields, of within and without and so on. But, as we might expect, there are always loose ends and uneasy fits whatever the root metaphor, and as the essay progresses I draw on a number of writers whose own studies have encouraged them to take a sideways glance at elements of the world tangential to the lens of dominant views.

An especially interesting element for anthropologists here is that of 'experience'. Along with anthropologists of a wide range of persuasions I strongly endorse the need for social science to address the way in which the social world is experienced by people; and yet I argue that there is a danger that a particular kind of selectivity might result – one that extracts the social subject from the organizations and institutions of society. Again, not surprisingly, this is because of the dialectical tension between analysts' *incorporation* into prevailing discourses on the one hand, and their *critical attention* to the stresses and limitations in such discourses, on the other.

Of course the first thing we need to note is that not all professional social scientists would subscribe to the view that the issues that interest them and the ways they study those issues are (and should be) a function of a quite self-conscious and explicit political agenda; yet this *is* to be my question: how our often rather technical and apparently nitpicking preoccupations with methods and concepts are the product of a broader political project, and hence seek to contribute to that project.

There's an old joke that anthropologists can be divided into two kinds: those who believe that human beings can be divided into two kinds and those that don't (see for example Keesing 1994). Here the joke varies according to the relevant debate of the moment: those that believe there is an 'other' and those that don't; those who believe that human experience can't be reduced to one universalistic formula, versus those who believe that ultimately there is only one 'human condition'; those who seek to capture the last remnants of a disappearing pre-capitalist, pre-contact world and those for whom the world is inescapably a world capitalist system.

But I think there is another, more important and less well-articulated sense in which professional anthropologists can be divided into two groups. There are those for whom the political project of anthropology is a persistent concern – to stress its more extreme form: those who *agonize* over what they are doing, or should be doing, as anthropologists – and those for whom such a concern, while always important, should not get in the way of the often difficult intellectual questions argued within the discipline. Indeed, for the latter, the trumpetings and alarums of what in another age would be described as 'the enthusiasts' smack strongly of self-importance, even a purposeful distraction from the finer distinctions of difficult intellectual concerns (see, for example, D'Andrade and Scheper-Hughes 1995).

There is, then, a certain rancour among many of those who *do*, with those who devote much ink and paper to *why they/we do it*. This is certainly one way in which anthropologists might be divided into two groups. Yet *within* what I call here the politically engaged group there is another binary division. The blood pressure gets especially high when these two moieties, both concerned with the politics of anthropology *as critique*, find themselves facing off. This is often expressed as an argument between 'materialists' and 'postmodernists', but to use such terms is to cast the distinction in such extreme terms that the argument appears settled before it is engaged. I prefer to argue that there is a (possibly irresolvable) tension between a body of anthropologists with a realist epistemology whose interests are grounded in social relations and another body of anthropologists whose epistemology is constructivist and whose interests pre-eminently have to do with culture and its various modes of expression. Following the title of Marcus and Fischer's (1986) book, I refer to the latter as 'cultural critics'.

Debates between 'materialists' and 'postmodernists' or 'new ethnographers' are often infused with a sense of resentment that those in the other moiety are taking the moral high ground and

proclaiming monopolistic and exclusionary rights to the determining of where an engaged anthropology might go in the new
millennium, each side accusing the other of a disingenuous, overly
gross, reading of its key texts (or no reading of them at all). Either
a vendetta ensues, with blood-letting mounting apace, or the two
sides disengage and go their separate ways, each comforted in the
warm blanket of their own discursive fields. But, by re-formulating
the distinction as I have done, I want to point to a far more fundamental difference within anthropology than is captured in the easy
name-calling of 'postmodernist' versus 'empiricist, materialist' and
so on.

Few on either side want to give up their claim to Gramsci as a
token of their political authenticity – either explicitly or through
extensive use of his notion of hegemony; and I suggest here that
this is not entirely surprising, since Gramsci occupies a threshold
position, his career taking him from concerns with organization to
concerns with consciousness and interpretation. I end this chapter
therefore by a discussion of his changing sense of urgency in respect
to political priorities, and I end the book as a whole with a chapter
in which I try to render some of Gramsci's figurations of society
and history more operational for the purposes of anthropological
ethnography.

Political Priorities and Images of Society

I agree with Grimshaw and Hart that modern anthropology 'should
be understood above all as a response to the rise and visibility of
ordinary people as a force in history' (1994: 236; see also Bourdieu
1990: 150–6). Yet the principles of such a project are now called
into question by what I call here 'cultural critics': those who feel
that what constitutes a distinctively *anthropological* critique of the
present is a critique that highlights the *culture* of modernity through
juxtaposition with cultural difference and expressive alterity. Part
of such a critique has to do with the way we should characterize
'ordinary people'; but also, locked more deeply within this critique,
there is a shift in emphasis with respect to a crucial leftist idea:
that of 'ordinary people *as a force in history*.'[1] It is useful therefore
to pursue the shift away from centre-stage of the proposition that
the purpose of an engaged intellectual was 'to give men and women
the means with which to exercise *a real popular self-determination for*

the first time in history' (Anderson 1980: 22): that ordinary people, acting as collective agents, were the motor for radical change in the structure of society. When and how did this shift occur?

To answer this we need to be aware of two powerful images of 'society', one associated with production, the other with space. We will return to the second later. As for the first – the idea of *production* – we need to recognize that in its association with *energy*, this image of society implies a twofold understanding of social *power*.

It is conventionally argued that a Marxist view of society is based upon the view that the social subject is formed by her/his position in the relations of production and division of labour. Although it is true that theories influenced by Marx tend to be quite explicit about the causal role of a 'production process', the fact is that virtually all modernist theories of society in the Marx–Weber–Durkheim pedigree assume (often implicitly) *some* relationship between actors' engagement in material production and their perceptions of the world, be it Marx's class consciousness, Durkheim's *conscience collective*, or Weber's entrepreneurial spirit. It is not the emphasis on *material* production that is distinctive about the influence of Marx. It is the image of society itself as an ongoing historical formation, ever in the process of producing and reproducing its component parts. This is neither an image that depends on 'material causality'[2] nor one that substitutes 'structure' (as in 'social structure') for human agency:

> The act of [social] reproduction itself changes not only the objective conditions – e.g. transforming village into town, the wilderness into agricultural clearing etc. – but the producers change with it, by transforming and developing themselves in production, *forming new powers and new conceptions, new modes of intercourse, new needs, and new speech* (Marx 1965: 93, *italics mine*).

It is his or her position in *this* process that matters – which is just another way of saying that subjectivity is profoundly and inescapably *social*. Yet the word 'position', too, is misleading, for it suggests an unwarranted stasis. We are not talking of a moment but of a *historical process* in which the contemporary subject is caught: there is no 'environment' that does not come to us through history and hence no environment that is not thoroughly socially mediated – subjectively (in the way we see it) and objectively (as material conditions given to us from the agency of those who came before) (see Chapter 5).

Because this image of society refers to energy and because energy is about power, so power is imbricated in its entire language. Power understood in this light takes on an especially pervasive sense, for once society is understood in terms of production and reproduction, so increases in power can refer to the kind of power that inheres in *the organizational capacity to produce energy* and also to the ways in which unequal *power is distributed through society* so as to give some control over others. The one is closely tied to the other; but they are by no means the same thing. We do not have to be especially sophisticated theorists to accept the Machiavellian proposition that some societies can be more powerful than others (and hence dominate them). Yet modernism is and was precisely about a social design to produce such an effective society and components therein – intellectuals moving from gamekeepers to gardeners; from patrollers of the royal prerogative, to cultivators of the social garden – in Bauman's imagery (1987: 51–67); from prohibitive power to 'a productive network which runs through the whole social body, much more than as a negative instance whose function is repression' (Foucault 1980: 119). Not just the footloose indigent gathered into the discipline of the workhouse, but the workhouse transformed into the factory and the discipline directed toward ever greater productivity. Not just the power of machines, but the measure of humans in terms of their social 'productivity'. 'The wealth of the nation being nearly synonymous with its health,' wrote a reviewer of the Report on the Sanitary Condition of the Labouring Classes, in 1842, 'it is evident that the labouring poor of the British people is a machine which it is the duty as well as the interest of the state to protect' (quoted in Corrigan and Sayer 1985: 117).

Yet historically this productively powerful society arose through the unequal distribution of power through the social whole – not just incidentally but inevitably. Marx was just as impressed by capitalism's 'power' in the sense that I have just described it – human capacity becoming so great as to free up time for other activities – as he was by its inherent necessity to generate differentials of power. Ironically, human potential had achieved its maximum productivity through being dichotomized into two spheres of private ownership: the private ownership of means of production on the one hand, and the private ownership of the capacity to work on the other. This process simultaneously therefore created the conditions for free time ('freedom over necessity'), while denying the distribution of that free time to workers in proportion to the rate of productivity that made it possible. Put another way: the potential *agency* of workers was expanded, while the *structure* of capitalist society in practice delimited it.

Out of such an image of society and history Marx and Engels linked social enquiry to the purpose of facilitating the struggles of those whose human potential (in contemporary jargon: potential *agency*) was thereby so denied them. It is not difficult to see how such a view might appeal to the radical anthropologists who became increasingly articulate in North America, Britain and France in the 1960s and 1970s. Yet in the vast majority of cases, it was the *spirit* of the Marxian project – that the collective action of subordinate groups should play a decisive role in social change – that provided their inspiration. It was a very small minority, especially in the United States, who attempted to apply Marx's method to anthropological issues.[3] Yet, since the unarguably noble, ethical project of more general radical anthropology is not itself any different from the ethical justifications of cultural critics – both in anthropology and in cultural studies we need to go back and contextualize historically the distinctive perspective of students of nineteenth-century English capitalism.

In fact, anthropologists whose stock in trade hinges on cultural diversity should have little trouble recognizing the social world of early nineteenth-century England, a world in which a pot-pourri of working and unemployed people shared little in common, from highly respectable *master* craftsmen (*sic*), to consumptive women and children, to roaming destitutes – ('migrants' as they would be called today) shot of their rural communities and yet not integrated into the burgeoning urban world of 'industry'. From our present perspective it is hard to get a sense of the way history was seen midway through the last century, to sense the uneasy balance between its inevitability and its unpredictability (Cowen and Shenton 1996: 12–42). Indeed, it sometimes escapes our notice that 'determinist' texts like Darwin's were read precisely at a moment of social upheaval, a fear of disorder and puzzlement about the future perhaps no less deeply felt then than it is today. Moreover, the industrial revolution as it unfolded into that century affected these different groups in vastly diverse ways: the forming of a common 'working class' out of the processes of *industrialization*, that is, processes that involved the designing of machines that increased the productivity of one particular production task (but, by the same token, could not handle a large variety of tasks); the regimented large-scale factory, the urban concentration, the changing role of the state in working people's lives – none of these was in any way *inevitable*. Least of all were they seen to be inevitable by those who lived at mid-century.

The growth of large-scale factory production, for example, may indeed have heralded a deathblow to small, rural textile craftsmen and their families; but the dominance of the factory was a far slower process than is usually thought, and anyway its rise did not have this effect on *all* small-scale or even all rural manufacturing:

> [I]t will not do to explain away the plight of weavers or of 'slop' workers as 'instances of the decline of old crafts which were displaced by a mechanical process'. ... The suggestion to which [such a statement] leads us is that these conditions can be somehow segregated in our minds from the true improving impulse of the Industrial Revolution – they belong to an 'older', pre-industrial order, whereas the authentic features of the new capitalist order may be seen where there are steam, factory operatives, and meat-eating engineers. But the numbers employed in the out-work industries multiplied enormously between 1780–1830; and very often *steam and the factory were the multipliers* (E. P. Thompson 1968: 288, *italics in original*).

By 1870, Britain's dark satanic mills may have been more visible than those in France, Italy or Germany, and may have got more bad press too, but this should not obscure the fact that, even then, the vast majority of working people in Britain were *not* engaged in factory work (Samuel 1977; Hobsbawm 1984b: 179, 1984c: 196; Berg 1994: 13–33), still less in continental Europe (O'Brien and Keyder 1978; Zdatny 1990). Moreover, if we were to look, not at a moment in any one year, but at the trajectory of working people's lives, we would find that, even for those with long experience of factory labour, the factory did not constitute the only, or in many cases even the most significant, working experience of their economically active lives.

This is not to deny the bourgeois *project* during this period, of increasing societal 'productive power' through various techniques of regulation: the breaking down of those human variations that got in the way of better disciplining of the labour process (inside the factory and out). But this should not obscure the fact that, even where this project was steadily and dispiritingly grinding away at one segment of working people, there were others who resisted it and still others who felt the effect of industrialization in terms of growing variety and 'freedom' in the horizons of their lives (Bauman 1982). It was precisely *because of* this set of uneven dynamics that a counter-project of equal 'inevitability', determination and regulation was required for the agenda of progressive intellectuals.

Let me reiterate what I am suggesting. I believe that the traditions of engaged anthropology, one way or the other, draw their inspiration from people who wrote about nineteenth-century subordinated groups from a *parti pris* point of view, viz: for the betterment of their conditions through aiding in their empowerment. The key figure here has been Marx, and a variety of engaged anthropologists have drawn inspiration from his spirit, if not his method. Yet it is not *just* Marx and Engels' *interpretations* that are crucial for understanding ourselves as intellectuals; it is how they understood their *relationship* to the ordinary people that engaged their attention; an understanding that was itself the outcome of quite particular organizational features of the society they sought to study – a dialectic that especially exercised Gramsci:

> The process of development is tied to a dialectic between the intellectual and the masses. The intellectual stratum develops both quantitatively and qualitatively, but every leap forward towards a new complexity of the intellectual stratum is tied to an analogous movement on the part of the mass . . . (Gramsci 1971: 334).

Then as now, therefore, the methodological priorities that emerged were dialectically tied to the changing cultural phenomena to which intellectuals directed their attention.

We need to remember then, that Marx and Engels were not writing about any society or any group of subordinated people; they were writing about emerging groups of industrial working people in Europe – principally, but not exclusively in England – in the first two-thirds of the last century. We see, in the unfolding of their writing and in the broad movement of intellectual thought of the period, that what they were both describing and saw themselves contributing to was a shift from working-class culture *as pattern and figuration* towards working-class culture *as institutional organization*. For anthropologists, E. P. Thompson has come to be associated with a particular kind of history of subaltern groups that lays emphasis on their 'culture' (understood here in its common-sense usage, as patterns of values and norms). He is held up against others who supposedly stress more 'mechanistic' views of subaltern

collectivity. Yet to take this view is to read his intense engagement
with a quite particular historical period and mood as though it were
the universalistic theory-building that Thompson so energetically
loathed, for Thompson was actually writing about the making of
this first kind of working-class culture – one particular form of
cultural collective identity. It was one that was to fail, for want of
organizational resources, between 1848 and the 1880s. (cf. Nairn
1964). Another was the kind of working-class culture that emerged
thereafter, one in which 'forgetting' was at least as important as
'memory' (cf. Smith 1991b), and in which institution-building
became paramount.

Let us look at this more closely. What we find is an early period
of 'making' – one in which diverse historical memories come
together and are exchanged in the forge of actual political conflicts.
Culminating in the decline of Chartism by the end of the 1840s,
this is the period of 'making' we associate with the 'culturalist
approach' of Edward Thompson, through whose careful and
vigorous readings of plebeian expression we have come to learn a
great deal of what it must have felt like to be among the diverse
variety of 'ordinary folk' at that time. There is a sense in which the
everyday lives of working people in this period *were* accessible to
the writing classes: apparently knowable communities. There was
a proximity and a familiarity that gave these writers a sense of
'representative articulacy' – in the records of their festivals and fairs
(Thompson 1993) or in the rural novel (Williams 1973).[4]

There followed a period in which the social and geographical
position of working people became more isolated from the experience of the kind of person who wrote for or about them. By the
1840s Benjamin Disraeli was already writing about *the Two Nations,*
and, as the century crossed the threshold of middle-age, what we
see of working people's culture is largely from some distance. There
arises a strange mix of the social survey (newly emergent) on the
one hand, and on the other of writers for whom 'the major part of
the worker's life – his [*sic*] daily labour – was entirely unknown . . .
Disraeli in *Sibyl* (1844), Mrs Gaskell in *Mary Barton* (1848) and *North
and South* (1855), and Dickens in *Hard Times* (1854) – [who] remain
horrified, outside the gates behind which the actual labour of the
working classes took place' (Hobsbawm 1984b: 177).

Besides, evocative novels were no more synonymous with good
politics then than evocative ethnography is today (cf. Starn 1994).
By the time the Great Depression began, around 1873, it became

clear that, without a labour *movement per se*, the uneven development of British capitalism would continue to generate greater difference than common cause across regions, industrial sectors and working people's statuses. What this meant was a need for organization, and institution-building beyond – sometimes even against – culture-as-historical-memory. We should be neither romantic about this diversity, nor squeamish about the need to forge a less faulted steel through the application of heat and hammer.

Nor should we forget the contradictory forces that were operating. True, disciplining power was effectively effacing the historical differences among people at the lower end of the working class, rendering them daily less articulate and respectable, even – perhaps especially – in their own eyes. Yet while the steamroller of industrial society was flattening out the hills and valleys of an older order, this was *still* not a homogeneous mass of collective workers. For one thing, before the turn of the century the consumer goods that workers themselves required were provided by small 'penny capitalists' from among their own, and, as the number of factory workers increased, so too did their provisioners (Benson 1983; Hobsbawm 1984b: 184). For another thing, it was not just a middle class that was emerging, but also a growing army of petty bourgeois clerks intoxicated by Victorian respectability and the need to distinguish themselves from the manual classes (Stedman Jones 1983: 179–238). This had its effect on the old semi-skilled manual workers, who on the one hand were forced into the ranks of the working people and on the other drew upon a tradition of collective institutions for self-protection that were to become the basis of the labour movement, and whose ideals lay in 'the basic *collective idea* and the institutions, manners, habits of thought and intentions which proceed from this. Bourgeois culture, similarly, is the basic *individualist idea* and the institutions, manners, habits of thought and intentions which proceed from that' (Williams 1965: 327, *italics added*).

Eric Hobsbawm is quite explicit on this point, and it is worth quoting him at length:

> The ... aspect I wish to discuss concerns the relation between class consciousness and organization ... Bourgeois movements were based on a very powerful class consciousness ... However, they were rarely *explicit* class movements ... [claiming] to be all-embracing even when they were visibly not ... The bourgeoisie ... consists essentially ... of

people who can make things happen *as individuals* or in small numbers
. . . On the other hand, the working class, like the peasantry, consists
almost by definition of people who cannot make things happen *except
collectively* . . . Without a formal organization . . . they are unlikely to be
effective . . .' (1984a: 25–6 *italics added*).

Such a project was forged, then, out of the historical memory of a
selective component of working people in tandem with the political
analysis of intellectuals increasingly impressed (positively or
negatively) with the organizational resources of modern industry
and the state.

The dialectic between late nineteenth-century intellectuals and
ordinary people, therefore, was one in which semi-skilled workers'
traditions of mutual aid societies, cooperatives and guilds survived
the down years of mid-century to become the central pillar of
working-class culture. As a result, the way we understand this
experience *as a culture* must shift from the looser one of patterns,
figurations and memory to one that lays emphasis on *collective*
representations and social *organization* – because that's the way the
natives themselves saw it.

Or at least those who claimed to 'represent' them. For it seems
especially obvious in this case – perhaps more so than most of the
imagery of 'other people' that produced the more conventional
anthropological views of 'culture' – that we are talking about a
struggle for dignity, identity, and social praxis, in short: cultural
survival. This was not a culture 'handed down since the darkest
mists of time', but one above all of *selective tradition*. And to the
extent that such a collective form of identity was to come into being
and be resilient, to the extent it was to become an everyday and
holistic culture (as opposed to the more individual and specialized
'artistic' culture of the bourgeoisie) – that is to say, to the extent to
which working-class culture became synonymous with some kind
of strength-through-unity – it owed this to the labour aristocracy,
which

> saw itself as a working class, even in some respects as the spokesmen
> and leaders of the rest of the manual workers. And necessarily so,
> because its economic advantages and status *depended on the capacity to
> organize* – in trade unions, in consumer cooperative societies, in societies
> of mutual aid and insurance (Hobsbawm 1984b: 183, *italics mine*).

As left intellectuals, then, began to evolve a political strategy for and with the working class, that strategy directed their sociological methods toward institutions and toward the organizing of working people for the articulation of their collective identity. What they felt themselves to be working *against* can be heard in the words of a Dundee factory boy: 'The great mass of men and women are like corks on the surface of a mountain river, carried hither and thither as the torrent may lead them' (quoted in Vincent 1981: 69).

Or of Ian Jack, son of an Edwardian steam mechanic:

> The class conflict as I often heard it expressed was not so much between classes as internal to each of them: it was 'decent folk' versus the rest . . . A strict application of socialist theory would mean that our natural allies were the Davidsons (crash, thump; 'Where's ma fuckin' tea?') and that we would be bound to them for life. And bound not only to the Davidsons but to another heart of darkness in our family's past . . . the chaos and poverty which my father had caught the last whiff of as his family completed the last trek through the volcanic industrialism of Victorian Scotland (quoted in Joyce 1991: 334).

Even so, we should not let this powerful focus on organization mislead us into ourselves making a radical distinction between institutions and organization and *the ability to articulate*. After all it was at least in part precisely because of the visibility of their collective institutions, their role as beacons, that *organized* labour became the voice of the working people across the class divide. And, far more important than *just* the articulation of political and working-condition demands, these collective institutions from pub to union hall were the locales for interaction, amusement, security and self-help (cf. Carbonella 1992), in short for all the kinds of things we would normally associate with any 'culture' worthy of the name.

Rightly or wrongly, then, the pre-eminent concern of those whom we might term engaged intellectuals at the turn of the century was with the means for achieving some kind of empowerment of working people through the building up of their *collective agency*. Experience – of the skilled craftsmen at any rate – taught that such collective power depended on the proper organization of institutions for the aid and protection of working folk. Moreover, what listening was done – what 'interpretative work' in our own jargon – was focused on a few spokes*men*. There is no question that we can now, from our privileged perspective in the present era, exercise the savagest of criticisms against these our progenitors for their lack of interpretative sensitivity. Indeed, as the new century began, it was intellectuals from our own discipline who, with the new methods of ethnography, gathered more detailed data on the daily lives of 'ordinary folk' in the distant corners of empire than did left social enquirers at home. Moreover, we can link this interpretative absence to the way they thereby excluded major segments of ordinary folk, most strikingly, of course, women. As Swindells and Jardine argue, 'very late-nineteenth-century culture, which Williams identified as such a potentially positive (oppositional) source of values for a specifically working-class consciousness, confines women to the domestic, the family – uses women to *give* value to the working man, via the family and the home' (Swindells and Jardine 1990: 151).

Yet it is important to stress that the expressions of an Ian Jack or the Dundee factory boy *were not absent or silent* or even unrecorded – we should be more discreet in our use of these highly evocative accusations; we would not have either statement to hand, had not somebody written it down and somebody else printed and published it. Rather, these expressions were not taken up as relevant or given priority in terms of any political project of the time, and this was a function less of misplaced scholarship *per se* than of the dialectic between ordinary people's attempts to forge some kind of vindicative, collective 'culture' and those who wrote for and about them.

We see this dialectic quite clearly as those working people who had established for themselves organized institutional spaces thereby became visible to intellectuals. As a result these intellectuals, who imagine society in terms of historical production and reproduction, then give high priority to issues of organization and institution-building, for, as I have said, such an image embraced not just power in its distributional mode, but also social power in the peculiarly modernist sense in which society is understood as a more or less well-oiled machine.

But society as a process of production and reproduction is not the only image we might hold, and here we can turn to the second dominant image to which I referred earlier, that of space. Thus Touraine (1992) sees a shift in the imagery of society. He talks of the decline in an understanding of society as a life of production, which 'defined the social actor by his position in a social progress opposed by the forces of conservatism and of reaction . . . the representation of social life as, simultaneously, a set of cultural representations through which society reproduces itself and all the aspects of a central social conflict' (1992: 125–6). In its place Touraine discerns an image in which the populace is understood in terms of the degree of its *participation* in 'what some call values and others systems of social control' (ibid.: 129). Subordination is understood in terms of exclusion, marginalization, the inability to articulate needs. 'It is as if the nineteenth century believed that the oppressed could liberate themselves, whereas twentieth century thinkers are primarily impressed by the weakness of particular actors *vis-à-vis* the capacities for domination and manipulation of both absolute power and mass culture' (ibid.).

As with the metaphor of production, so here, too, we need to comprehend the re-ordered prioritizing and urgencies induced by this spatial image of society. Here the individual is no longer seen as pre-eminently emerging out of a dialectical relationship with historically identifiable social forms – characteristic kinds of social relationship, social organization and social institutions. Rather, the intellectual imagery now reflects a newer dialectic between the intellectual and the object of her/his gaze (note the spatial metaphor here too). The selectivity now responds to different urgencies, reflecting the Western individual's desires to affirm herself or himself in terms of personal experience felt as a vindicating struggle *against* the social itself (Elias 1991; Taylor 1991).[5] Thus Touraine, in an injunction that evokes an earlier project of Albert Camus (1956), goes on 'Let's call 'subject' the individual's effort to construct him or herself as an individual, rather than as a subordinate in a logic of order, *whatever that order may be*' (ibid.: 141, *italics mine*).

Cultural critique sits far more comfortably within *this* kind of discourse of inclusion/exclusion, with its imagery of society itself ('whatever that order may be') being the source of power against which or beyond which a liberating project might lie. Far from being manifested through a dialectical relationship to historically identifiable social forms, expression is sought in experiences that resist society by denying 'the social'. Hence democracy becomes a question of inclusion and participation rather than organization – if you like, of sound rather than orchestration – and while 'old' social movements were interested in the idea of revolution (note the imagery of reproduction/transformation), today's 'new' social movements are interested in democracy and participation – hence inclusion[6] (see Chapter 3).

Such new metaphors help to redraw the map of history, aiding us in seeing landmarks we missed before. But with this brief excursus into nineteenth-century English social history, I have tried to suggest that we run the risk of collapsing a whole period of struggles and counter-struggles, of disputes and counter-disputes, between working people and their representatives, between their representatives and the middle-class intelligentsia, and of all these among themselves. The handicap of such a view is that it limits our ability to go further; amidst celebration of dialogics, it seems to deny them here. Instead, I have tried here to contextualize an unfolding set of priorities within the historical circumstances that called them forth. This does not pre-empt critique. The prevailing images of society became so dominant they attained a materiality that worked against their critical acuity. A perceived need for organization, for example, led to a growing stress on organizations, which gave rise to serious omissions in perceptions of the relationship between individual experience and collective identity.

Experience Within and Beyond Collective Organization

I want now, therefore, to take some instances where, it seems to me, we do have the opportunity of exploring this space *between* the language of the subjective body experienced as unique and individual, *and* the actual organizations and institutions that configure the particularity of these sentiments – both mediating and facilitating them and constraining and suppressing them. In doing this I seek to expose a quite other set of problems that appear to arise from the agenda of contemporary cultural critique, where there is a danger that identity becomes too thoroughly enmeshed in 'experience'. Studies of the present then prioritize methods for *evoking* this experience, while studies of the past focus too much on institutionally decontextualized biography. The writers I discuss briefly now therefore appear to me to be exploring the difficult line of tension between a set of methodological priorities that effectively rendered the disquiet of an Ian Jack or the Dundee factory boy distractions to the programmatic task of organizing, and another set of methodological priorities concerned with the supposedly 'silenced voices' of these folk, stripped of all sociological characteristics.

We begin with the observations of the anthropologist A.W. Metcalfe, working in Australia

> Early in my fieldwork I was befriended by a man I will call George Hare, a mild and affable mine pensioner, who startled me one day by remarking that mine bosses cared more about the safety of pit horses than miners. When next we met, George repeated the remark. But when I asked him whether he really meant what he said, he seemed embarrassed and replied that the claim was 'just a saying', and not true of any bosses he knew, all of whom liked him.
>
> Looking over my field notes later I realised that it was characteristic of George to make [such an] assertion and then back away from it (Metcalfe 1988: 13–14).

Elsewhere, Metcalfe tells the following story:

> When a student wrote to the newspaper of an Australian coalmining town in 1970, asking people for help with his research, he objectified their humanity in the way common in the discourse of his discipline. His offence was pointed out by Jim Comerford, a miner and politically radical union leader: 'I would advise Mr Wallschutzky not to continue to use the phrase about miners' "propensity to strike" . . . Miners do not possess any more propensity to strike than any other section of the working population. *What they do is to react to the circumstances of their working and living environment*, as would people engaged in any other walk of life' (Metcalfe 1990: 46, *italics mine*).

What I am interested in here is the way in which people both associate their personal experiences with the relevant collectivities involved and at the same time draw back, withhold themselves as unique individuals, from those specific collectivities[7] – George Hare, who thinks bosses treat miners worse than pit horses, but then draws back from including himself in that condition. Or Jim Comerford, who rejects the association of miners specifically with a propensity to strike, and instead calls attention to an open-ended reaction to the circumstances of their working life, and then not just to the circumstances of their *working* life, but as he adds too, of 'their living environment'. There is nothing special about miners, as he sees it, that makes them prone to strike; rather their reaction comes from very much the same pot-pourri of lived experiences as would that of 'people engaged in any other walk of life'.

To my knowledge no recent writer has addressed this issue more sensitively than the social historian Alf Lüdtke. What makes

Lüdtke's work distinctive are his attempts to link the arena of
personal experience to the formal political arena – insistently,
persistently, and yet in a heterodox fashion. For Lüdtke 'everyday
life' is not itself simply an area of silence lost to history that we
must therefore find a means for recovering. Rather, the spontaneity
of everyday life must be continually situated *vis à vis* a whole
spectrum of fields of power that impose order on one set of arenas
– from the factory to the party to the police at the door – and
thereby induce disorder, or at least confusion, in other arenas. Seen
from this perspective, the ways in which working people asserted
and lived their daily life implied 'a striving for time and space of
one's own' (Lüdtke 1985: 305) within and against the 'forces of
order'.

In 1917 the turners in machine construction factories in Germany
were what we might think of as conventional unionized workers in
heavy industry at a time of heightened worker politicization.
Though not involved in big strikes, they concentrated on shop-floor
actions aimed both at improved working conditions and at critic-
izing the government's war policies. Lüdtke remarks that 'all
assessments of the political attitudes and actions of machine
construction workers, and especially the turners, insist to a
significant degree on their *consistency* and *homogeneity*. This implic-
ation is as strong as to seem unquestioned' (1986: 72).

Yet we should be cautious about the 'consistency' and 'homogeneity' of the working experience. We should note the sense of
isolation workers felt *within* the context of their work and collective
action. Paul Gohre, a pastor who spent six weeks in the sewing-
machine factory, was especially impressed by the extent to which
factory work forced these people to live together literally for long
hours. 'Almost unintentionally,' he wrote in his diary, 'these contacts
became close and intimate' (Lüdtke 1985: 310). Yet interchanges
during coffee-breaks were not, Gohre noted, quite what you would
call evidence of collective solidarity:

> More than anything else these people teased one another, scuffled and
> tussled . . . the slipknot of an apron was untied from behind, the plank
> of a seat was pulled away while a fellow worker took a break . . . But to
> be sure, especially favoured among older workers at the end of the
> week was another form of horseplay: 'beard-polish'. Shaving was a once-
> a-week affair. . . . By the end of the week, the worker whose beard had
> grown in would grab the head of a chap with more tender cheeks, lips

and chin, and would rub his face against the youth's face, a process which of course had a quite painful result . . . Among those who knew one another nobody was excepted. Even age made no difference (ibid.: 310).

The task then, for Lüdtke, becomes one of querying every minute expression of daily life from practical jokes to dressing habits *within the conditions of the prevailing fields of power* laid down by organizational politics. And, conversely, understanding the limitations that arose in actual, historical political organizations *in terms of the way they interfaced with these everyday expressions* of what Lüdtke calls *eigensinn*.

Lüdtke understands workers' perceptions and practices of *eigensinn*, like everyday life itself, to be by their very nature contradictory and ambivalent. *Eigensinn* was a way of being oneself, autonomous and self-willed, while not thereby denying or confronting the organizational fields within which such behaviour was practised. *Eigensinn* was an alternative to order, possibly within an organization, possibly beyond it. For the male, *eigensinn* found its most frequent daily practice on the factory floor:

> *Eigensinn* was expressed and reaffirmed by walking around and talking, by momentarily slipping away or day-dreaming, but primarily by reciprocal body contact and horse-play – in short it was 'being-with-oneself' and 'being-with-the-others'. Thereby workers neglected, *but mostly did not directly interfere with* the ongoing work process or the factory's regularity as it was conceived by management (ibid.).

What Lüdtke begins to describe is a space released from order, be it the order of management or, possibly, even the order of one's fellow workers.

Such spaces of release were to be found beyond the factory as well, and Lüdtke stresses how leaders of formal left-wing political parties were as concerned about this disorder in the streets as were the bourgeoisie and the police (1985: 313). He notes the rigid hierarchy of the German SPD and the military precision they imposed on their public meetings. 'Such military practices infiltrated the party functionaries' very notion of alternative social organizations; even more, they influenced the daily practices of the rank and file' (1985: 316). Yet, what Lüdtke reveals is that such strategies on the part of party leaders – 'the speaker(s) faced the crowd; the crowd's role was to listen quietly' (ibid.) – effectively *created* the social spaces of organization on one hand and *eigensinn* on the other. Noting that, with such organization, it would be extremely doubtful that people at the back of the crowd could even hear the speakers, Lüdtke uses photographs to show that, for workers, these were times less for didactic political education, than for expressing comradeship with workers from different factories. Once again showing the ambivalence and distancing 'let it be-ness' of *eigensinn*, Lüdtke suggests that the photographs show a kind of mixture: on the one hand a declaration of their loyalties (to the party and to one another); and on the other 'a Sunday outing, to be attended in proper Sunday clothes [i.e. an expression of *eigensinn*]' (ibid., cf. Stedman Jones 1983: 201).

In the practice of his own work, Lüdtke does not succumb to a celebration (and hence depoliticization) of the everyday *for its own sake*, such that simply discovering some hitherto lost daily practice becomes in and of itself a good thing; rather he sees the everyday and the personal within the historically specific fields of force that constitute them as such. Hence the world of Lüdtke's extremely complex studies reveals simultaneously the limitations of interpretative approaches devoid of an organizational dimension and of institutional approaches that lack more than a gesture toward interpretation. Lüdtke's entire project rests precisely at this point of articulation. As such he confronts the relationship between the *organizational element* of politics and the *'expressions'* of workers.

'Politics' traditionally refers to the formulation, achievement, and sustained *organization* of collective interests . . . Forms of expression that do not meet these criteria are usually labelled as 'private' . . .

In contrast to this traditional formula, I propose to examine the articulation and expression of both individual and collective needs as forms of political behaviour . . . I wish to transgress and then blur the usual boundaries between political and private.

Let me offer [an example] of what such blurring can teach us. Meat was not part of workers' daily diet in Imperial Germany: if, by some good fortune, a pork chop or rib was available, the wage-earning males in a given household got the lion's share, if not all of the meat. The implied scorn of wage-working (and house-working) women and girls – even the bite of hunger they suffered – was not, however, simply a family matter. Slowness in demanding a general suffrage, quite apart from the readiness of men and women to accept or justify lower wages for women, relied on, and, in part, stemmed from precisely this kind of daily patriarchalism. In turn, the generally accepted or publicly approved standards of appropriate treatment of male wage earners, and of men generally, reinforced seemingly 'private' forms of discrimination against women and 'others'. Thus, public perceptions about the fair apportionment of society's resources were reconstituted in private and intimate interactions as well as public and organized ones. Politics was always at stake . . .

. . . In all such cases, the search for the political in seemingly private actions and expressions *demands that we come to terms with the intricate connections between the spheres of production, reproduction and consumption* in working-class life. At the same time, meanwhile, we must recognize that expressions of self-reliance – commonly known as *Eigensinn* – could not abolish the sphere of organizational politics (Lüdtke 1985: 303–5, *italics mine*).

There is no question that what we see in these cases is an instance of self-expression *against* the regulatory power of the social. Yet we cannot place these cases in some ahistorical world of 'the everyday' or understand them by studying hitherto obscured personal biographies as though beyond the social, for it is clear that they make little sense beyond a wider set of historically constituted power relations specific to the Germany of that time. *Eigensinn* must be understood specifically in the aftermath of the nineteenth century, in which 'the power of official bodies (like the police and welfare agencies) to intercede in private life increased' (Lüdtke 1985: 305) to such an extent that by the beginning of the present century 'interference from above was part of the private life of the workers and their families. Rigorous enforcement of order in the factory, on the streets, or in the schools and offices constituted the daily experiences of children, youngsters and adults alike' (Lüdtke 1986: 86). Physical violence on the part of the state was not, in this case, so much an alternative to hegemony, but part of it, and the interrelationship between *eigensinn* and collective organization would have to take account of such a reality. The fact that the German Left failed in 1914 and 1933 to do so does not invalidate collective organization, it simply argues for the greater interpretative role of intellectuals. It was not German workers who cast *eigensinn* into the realm of the private, or limited its possibilities for an alternative politics, but the institutional conditions within which they lived.

We have seen in the work of Lüdtke, then, that by the beginning of this century 'interference from above' had become part of the private life of ordinary people in Germany. In such a setting there is a sense in which *eigensinn* is the statement of the individual craftsman against such interference. As also against simultaneously the de-skilling and dehumanizing of the capitalist workplace *and* the unions that tried to provide an oppositional setting for workers. Yet, ironically, in England at the end of the last century it was precisely these kinds of skilled workers who provided the vanguard for labour *organization*. It is hard to escape the conclusion that the historically and locally specific texture of 'the social' calls forth certain kinds of subjectivities. Put another way, the forms and imperatives of the social collectivities pertinent to any particular subject at a given time and place, are likely to vary immensely – from neighbourhood to factory, from 'community' to family, from union to beer-parlour – and with such variance different issues regarding political expression need attention.

The Socially Mediated Individual

As we move across different social terrains, therefore, we see different tensions, expressed in very different ways, between the sense of the autonomous person and the person's experience of social collectivities. We have seen, with Lüdtke, the way in which this is played out in the *presence* of regimentation in the workplace and then in its conjoining sites through *eigensinn*. I want now to explore the way in which this tension was picked up in another set of circumstances, which were experienced as an absence of collectivity, and gave rise to something perhaps like the flip side of *eigensinn*; and the setting is not the factory, but its wider purview – the urban world: 'The growth of towns and especially cities and a metropolis; the increasing division and complexity of labour; the altered and critical relations between and within classes: in changes like these *any assumption of a knowable community – a whole community, wholly knowable – became harder and harder to sustain*' (Williams 1973: 165, *italics mine*).

Williams goes on to allude to a process analogous to the one Lüdtke wishes to capture with the term *eigensinn*, and yet evokes a different setting. Williams expressly wishes to emphasize the importance of the social and the ideological character of the idea that the individual's authenticity lies in his/her resistance to real and present social collectivities. He does this through a discussion of Joyce's *Ulysses*. Quoting Thomas Hardy's observation of London –

'each individual is conscious of *himself*, but nobody is conscious of themselves collectively' (ibid.), he then turns back to Joyce:

> Given the facts of isolation, of an apparently impassable subjectivity, a 'collective consciousness' reappears, but in an altered form. . . . In and through the intense subjectivities a metaphysical or psychological 'community' is assumed, and characteristically, if only in abstract structures, it is universal; *the middle terms of actual societies are excluded as ephemeral, superficial, or at best contingent and secondary*. Thus a loss of social recognition and consciousness is in a way made into a virtue: as a condition of understanding and insight. A direct connection is then forged between intense subjectivity and a timeless reality: one is a means to the other and alternative terms are no more than distractions. The historically variable problem of 'the individual and society' acquires a sharp and particular definition, in that 'society' becomes an abstraction, and *the collective flows only through the most inward channels* . . . a whole range of techniques of self-isolation are then gathered to sustain the paradoxical experience of an ultimate collectivity which is beyond and above community. . . . There is a language of the mind – often more strictly of the body – and there is this assumed universal language. Between them, as things, as signs, as material, as agents, are cities, towns, villages: actual human societies . . .
>
> In the twentieth century there has been a deep and confused and unfinished conflict between this reappearance of the collective, in its metaphysical and psychological forms, and that other response, also within the cities, which in new institutions and in new social ideas and movements offered to create what Hardy and others had seen as lacking: a collective consciousness which could see not only individuals but also their altered and altering relationships, and in seeing the relationships and their social causes find social means of change (ibid.: 246–7).

Here Williams both allows us a very vivid sense of the *modern* social subject, and also makes us realize that we acquired these ideas from an imagery of the social world in which 'the middle terms of actual societies are excluded as ephemeral, superficial, or at best contingent and secondary'. Moreover, he makes it clear that social respectability depends on our denying, raising ourselves above, these 'middle terms of actual societies'. A loss of recognition by society is made into a virtue: as a condition of understanding and insight. Precisely, in fact, what we found Touraine advocating earlier in this chapter.

Williams then critiques this position – 'There is a language of the mind – often more strictly of the body – and there is this assumed universal language. Between them, as things, as signs, as material, as agents, are cities, towns, villages: actual human societies.' The task of the engaged intellectual becomes one of inserting their methodological priorities precisely *between* the language of the subjective body experienced simultaneously as specially individual and still yet naturally universal and *the actual organizations and institutions that contour the particularity of these sentiments in a given period and place* (Elias 1978: 260ff.). Hence the choice, he suggests, lies between the reappearance of the collective in metaphysical forms and another response, which uses new but actual, *real* institutions and movements to find social means for change.

Williams captures as no other social analyst does the complex tensions that arose at this crucial period. Clearly they were tensions felt differently from place to place and – especially – between classes. Thus Hobsbawm's crucial point about the role of collective agency for working people is taken up again by both Thompson and Williams in their understanding of the distinctive characteristics of working-class culture. Moreover they, like Hobsbawm (but in different language), contrast this kind of 'whole culture' with bourgeois individualism and the corollary: an intellectualized personal culture, cut off from the social. It is *this* distinction that Williams is alluding to in the alternatives he presents at the end of the previous quote; it is *this* distinction too that we find Thompson making in the opening epigraph of this chapter.

It is here that Gramsci's development as a political analyst becomes important, for it was tensions such as these that motivated his shift from an urgent concern with organization and discipline to far more interpretative preoccupations. He therefore occupies a watershed position as an engaged social enquirer, between on the one hand the productivist view of society and the organizational priorities of the late nineteenth century and on the other hand the (dis)integrationist view of society and interpretivist priorities of today's cultural critics. It is not, therefore, surprising that he acts as a key legitimating progenitor for engaged social enquiry along a variety of fronts. Yet, once again, it becomes important neither to collapse his views into those of his last years of confinement, nor to decontextualize them from the interplay between intellectual development and ordinary people's culture that, as we have seen, he himself most strongly urged.

Gramsci's views shifted from a stress on the organizational role of the factory councils in the earlier writings of *L'Ordine Nuovo*

(1977), to more extensive interpretative work aimed at the construction of a collective will 'which will put an end to the internal divisions of the ruled' in the *Prison Notebooks* (1971: 259).

In so far as in his younger years his interest was in the goal of a 'regulated society' Gramsci followed Marx's view of history as exemplifying increasing regulation through the wage nexus and the commodity form. Yet the uneven nature of Italian development and the failure of the Left in the wake of Mussolini's assumption of power in 1922 forced Gramsci to kick against any deterministic tendencies in such 'laws' of history as may exist. Once the existing perceptions of working people could no longer be seen as merely a transitional stage in history ultimately leading to revolutionary consciousness, then those perceptions became a persistent preoccupation for political organization. For Gramsci this meant an expansion of what constituted 'the political' into the realm of culture and everyday life.

But this came later. In his early career, with his contributions to *L'Ordine Nuovo* of 1919 and 1920 Gramsci placed his emphasis almost entirely on the role of organization in determining people's attitudes. Bourgeois forms of organization provided both the basis for workers' consciousness as a collective and also the target for revolutionary praxis. Capitalism produces a concentration of working people in which the principles of combination and solidarity form the mentality of workers and peasants (1977,v.I: 71). At one point Gramsci illustrates the importance of the spatial concentration of people and the role of discipline by contrasting the tiny number of elemental feelings of peasants dispersed over the countryside, with no understanding of organization and discipline, with the experience of recruits in the Great War:

> the war meant that individuals who had previously been scattered over a vast territory came into contact with each other. It meant that humans were concentrated together uninterruptedly for years on end . . . under a uniform and uniformly ferocious discipline. The length and duration of such conditions of collective living had profound psychological effects. . . . Selfish, individual instincts were blunted; a common united spirit was fashioned; feelings were universalized; the habit of social discipline was formed (ibid.: 84–5).

Large-scale factories of course had a similar effect; but in Italy the traditional institutions of the workers, specifically the socialist unions, he saw to be inadequate to the 'task of disciplining the forces' (ibid.: 77) against the influence of these bourgeois-regulated forms of organization. So, while he felt that these older forms should continue, Factory Councils should also be set up parallel to them, in a system of dual power.

For Gramsci the line between organization and *influence* was pretty much taken for granted at this stage:[8] just *how* certain forms of social organization gave rise to certain forms of consciousness was not deeply interrogated. As he saw it, the institutions that were developed for the production of material wealth likewise produced 'men's intellectual awareness', and if these objective conditions change, 'then there is a corresponding change in the totality of relations that regulate and inform human society and a change in the degree of men's awareness' (ibid.: 75). This, young, Gramsci seems a long way removed from the person who inspires so many of today's cultural critics.

The later Gramsci became steadily more aware of the need for people such as himself to attend more closely to working people's own perceptions of the world. Yet for Gramsci a particular set of perceptions could only be interpreted *as they occurred within quite specific (political) projects*: both ordinary people's perceptions and the way intellectuals interpreted them could only attain coherence in terms of identifiable 'concrete aims'. This meant, of course, that, while Gramsci shifted his ground from an almost singular concern with organization, discipline and 'propaganda' to interpretation, he continued to understand collective expression in terms of the institutions that made expression possible.

In fact, the first step in Gramsci's shift came in the form of his recognition that his social analysis had played insufficient attention to what today we would call human *agency*, what Gramsci called *will*. In the *Prison Notebooks*, Gramsci undertakes this interrogation by contrasting a sterile 'sociology' with what he called 'political science'.[9] He contrasted the deterministic failures of social evolution and the limitations of positivism with a political science devoted to understanding humans as pre-eminently *socially* formed. The fact that people in any given place or historical period were socially formed meant for Gramsci that social reality could only be under-stood through the study of specific *historical* conditions. Then, in its reformed sense he sees sociology to be redeemed through the addition of will into its vision, 'the will and the initiative of men themselves cannot be left out of account' (1971: 244).

Once, of course, the initiative of men (and women) cannot be left out of account, it becomes necessary for intellectuals to develop a methodology for interpreting this expressive component of the social world, and this became Gramsci's concern. Yet throughout his writings, politically, *the everyday* contains within it two inter-connected challenges. One is *organizational* – how to pull people from the small world of family and farm into the theatre of politics; the other is *cultural* – how to relate the interests and aims of the world appropriate to the everyday and mundane, to the historical and what Gramsci would call 'the universal, concrete aim' (Gramsci 1971: 71): *seeing the historical problems flashing on the screen as connected to my own.* The hegemonic project that politically engaged intellectuals are caught up in requires keeping these *organizational* and *expressive* components firmly attached. Rather than *just* focusing on the successes and failures of one or another kind of political organization or collectivity; rather than *just* focusing on the intimacies of the personal and biographical – it means a continual shifting of focus and a perpetual interrogation of the way the one presses itself against the other, suffuses it, diverts it, and sustains it.

Conclusion

In this chapter I have sought to suggest (with Gramsci) that there is a dialectical relationship between the images intellectuals evoke for their understanding of the social world, and the collective and individual projects of the people they study. The forming of a working-class collective culture was dealt a severe blow in England in the middle of the last century. As more systematic and pervasive forms for rendering the population docile took shape, and as older forms of collectivity such as craft guilds and rural communities either fell away or were made to serve new and different purposes, so the question of collective *organization* became more self-conscious. Yet the very pervasiveness of discipline and order, on both sides of the social battlefield – in factories and unions – as well as the exclusion of large sectors of ordinary folk from the principal agenda of the organized left, provoked an increasing concern with questions of 'consciousness', which I have condensed in the person of Antonio Gramsci.

Once again we see today the falling away of older forms of collective defence, as the concentration of labour in factories is no longer a principal form of capitalist relations *in* production (Burawoy 1985). We see too that 'discipline' has become a far more sophisticated bourgeois project – making 'culture' a pervasive form of social regulation and, logically therefore, a pivotal yet plasticine mould for the shaping of difference to that order (see Chapter 6). It is these kinds of institutional forms, these kinds of overlapping collectivities, these lines of force and counterforce, alliance and conflict, that provide the sociological basis for the kinds of fragmented and floating social subjects that fascinate those anthropologists I have referred to as 'the cultural critics'. This sociological basis therefore becomes as much in need of critical analytic attention does experience and expression. Indeed, I have used Williams's discussion of Joyce to argue that cultural critics' attempt to promote a notion of *experience* unmediated by – indeed as resistance *against* – a regulating society is less a position of *critique* than a position that uncritically *reflects* this late modern project, much as an older body of analysts had too quickly accepted the success of more regimented forms of social regulation. The effect of a project that suggests that a subject can express her/himself only by denying the social institutions in which they are historically embedded is to give subjects the feeling that their only form of community is in the realm of something that can only be imagined in quite metaphysical forms of 'culture' – not the cultures of various forms of organized social communities, but vaguer notions of popular culture, national culture, ethnic culture, and so on.

Rather than seeing conditions such as these in terms of radical breaks with the past, I have tried to use evidence – from nineteenth-century England, from early twentieth-century Germany, from the preoccupations of Joyce in *Ulysses*, etc. – to suggest that the not uncommon tension between personal autonomy and the demands of collective membership evolved in the context of changing historical forms. And we can learn something from understanding the detailed complexity of this process. The sources of failure were many, but at least one of them was the failure of left intellectuals to relate interpretation to organization: to discover the character of the sectional interests that arose out of the various projects that concerned ordinary people and then to *make connections* (see Chapter 7). I have tried also to suggest (with Gramsci) that such intellectuals can only do so through a dialectical relationship with people *who themselves recognize the limitations of their own experience.*[10] Limitations not just in terms of limited horizons and partiality, but also a recognition that experience is socially mediated and historically produced.

These issues I return to in the final chapter of this book. Certain experiences, and still more so certain expressions, articulations and practices, can occur only in the institutional space that makes them possible. The lesson from the British labour movement of the late nineteenth century is not *just* that the voice of an organized and project-oriented labour aristocracy drowned out the interests of other working people; it is also that they attained this voice precisely *through their organization and their single-minded pursuit of specific political projects*. Yet there was a profound and hollow emptiness as the marching bands drowned out the voices and eventually even the sight of other elements of ordinary folk. The specific interests and sectional concerns of others were left uninterpreted and hence isolated.

The connections, therefore, that engaged intellectuals make must be both interpretative connections between sectional meanings and the social connections that make possible the organizational field through which meaning as truth can be turned into reality in practice. This requires an uncomfortable shifting backwards and forwards in our methodological priorities, attending to the concrete abstractions of interest rates and capital flows at one moment; to the habitus where practice meets institutional channelling in family or workplace at another moment; and to the articulated expressions and silenced occlusions of culture at still a third moment. The chapters that follow bear witness often to an emphasis on one or another of these 'lenses'; yet throughout, I try to manacle insights along one line of vision, to the imperatives of the others.

Notes

1. This is not to say that 'ordinary people' have been abandoned by cultural critics, but rather that their ordinariness is, for them, problematic. Though cultural critics dismiss the charge that they are prone to 'exoticize' the 'others' they study, the fact that these kinds of anthropologists continue to feel wounded by the charge suggests that they continue to see the *differentia specifica* of anthropology as the study of cultural *difference*. On the second point, a scholar's concern with ordinary people, however much filled with concern for their lot, need not mean that he or she subscribes to the idea that they are, might be

or should be 'a force in history'. Nor does the contrary view – that ordinary people should be a significant force in history – necessarily mean the endorsement of a proletarian revolution. For an especially facile caricature of this latter position, but one that often provides the starting-point for a postmodern critique of 'the traditional left', see Jenkins 1997.

2. This is not to say that Marx and Engels did not have their own take on the role of material causality. My point here is simply that an understanding of society in terms of production does not itself rely on such a position.

3. Herman Rebel captures the position of the anthropologists I refer to here: '"Postmodern" anthropologists' claims to the contrary, the political economy approach has, with exceptions, on the whole never been given to "the typically Marxist relegation of culture to an epiphenomenal structure" (Marcus and Fischer 1986 cited in Roseberry 1988: 139) and it has not, for that matter, ever been entirely under the spell of Marx.' (1989: 131).

4. By *representative* articulacy I mean to allude to the distinction between representative and participatory democracy. I should make clear that I am not suggesting here that proximity did, or does, lead to better or more intimate knowledge of 'others' and hence a written work that 'represents' their perception. As Williams points out, 'a knowable community, within country life as anywhere else, is still a matter of consciousness . . . Neighbours in Jane Austin are not the people actually living nearby; they are the people living a little less nearby who, in social recognition, can be visited. . . . and through the holes of this tightly drawn mesh most actual people are simply not seen' (1973: 166).

5. The similarity of Elias's observations in the 1940s and Taylor's today are provocative in this regard. In *The society of individuals* Elias comments, 'Today the primary function of the term 'individual' is to express the idea that every individual in the world is or should be an autonomous entity, and at the same time that each human being is in certain respects different to all others, and perhaps ought to be different. In the use of this term fact and postulate have no clear dividing line' (1991:156).

   Taylor sees the modern person as a peculiar marriage of Rousseau and Herder: '[For Rousseau] It is a standard of freedom that obviously goes beyond what has been called negative liberty, where I am free to do what I want without interference from others because that is compatible with my being shaped and influenced by society and its laws of conformity. Self-determining freedom demands that *I break the hold of all such external impositions, and decide for myself alone*' (1991: 27, *italics mine*). He goes on, '[For Herder] It [is an ideal that] accords crucial moral importance to a kind of contact with myself, with my own inner nature, which it sees as being lost, partly through the pressures toward outward conformity, but also because in taking an instrumental stance to myself, I may have lost the capacity to listen to this inner voice' (ibid.: 29; see also Taylor 1989).

6. Thompson's work on the formative experience of struggle among early nineteenth-century English folk notwithstanding, it is argued that a distinctive feature of contemporary social movements (one which warrants classifying them as 'new') is their self-reflective concern with issues of identity, of finding new forms of living together and so on, the earlier movements being concerned only with instrumental goals. (e.g. Jelin 1987; Escobar 1992a, b). Yet we must be careful not to let our newer images of society to allow us simply to rewrite history. Were struggle in nineteenth-century England *not* about democracy, it would be hard to understand why the established order responded by expanding the electorate. Nor should we lose sight of relationships *between* forces in society. Social movements throughout Europe in the last century weren't 'revolutionary' or 'radical' just because Marx, or Proudhon, wanted them so, nor simply because ordinary people held such views beyond any real political context. The recalcitrance of the dominant powers, of different quantity and quality from one time and place to another, were a crucial part of the equation then, as they are today.

7. This is taken up along a different set of dimensions of individual/ collective; experience/practice in Chapter 7.

8. Somewhat later, but still before he had developed a more sensitive understanding of the hegemonic process, Gramsci noted how the entrepreneur 'must be the organizer of masses of men; he must be an organizer of the "confidence" of investors in his business, of the customers for his products, etc.' (1971:5).

    Note how the very real organization of workers in the factory is then extended to refer to the organization of confidence and thence to the promotion of the finished product.

9. 'If political science means science of the State and the State is the entire complex of practical and theoretical activities with which the ruling class not only justifies and maintains its dominance, but manages to win the active consent of those over whom it rules, then it is obvious that all the essential questions of sociology are nothing other than the questions of political science . . .' (1971: 244).

10. I include her, of course, the limitations and partiality of intellectuals. This is taken up in more detail in Chapter 7.

PART TWO

Cultural Differentiations

CHAPTER TWO

The Production of Culture in Local Rebellion[1]

> It has been said that although God cannot alter the past, historians can; it is perhaps because they can be useful to Him in this respect that He tolerates their existence.
>
> — Samuel Butler, *Erewhon*, Chapter 14

In the preceding chapter we have seen how social analysts are agents in society like any others, and, as such, are influenced by the political currents that swirl around them. The fact that analysts are supposed to make a business out of taking a critical stance toward the world they live in, though, impels them to fanciful notions that they, unlike their predecessors, have broken this mould, and now burst forth into the crystal-clear freedom of thought denied their dusty old forebears. The work of people like Alf Lüdtke and Raymond Williams, through its honesty and originality, does have something of this effect, though I referred to this less in terms of freedom of thought and more in terms of the way an engagement with evidence in some sense shot their vision sideways, to escape the lens of dominant images. Antonio Gramsci is in many ways exemplary in this regard; but I ended the chapter suggesting that there were limitations to the way in which we have come to understand political currents. In the next two chapters, I seek to explore the ways in which anthropologists might invigorate and enrich our understanding of *praxis*: collective attempts to grasp the reins of history and change its course.

Introduction

Though we know well that the past casts shadows across the present, we have also drunk deeply of Samuel Butler's cynicism: we are quite aware that our preoccupations of the present, our contentions and our assertions condition the way we understand the past, what we select from the past, how the past 'speaks to us'. Then there's the fact that we're not a homogeneous lot. We differ – in our backgrounds, our present well-being and our future concerns – and, because we are different, we find ourselves disagreeing: it seems obvious to me that 'proper government' should not concern itself with what I do inside my home, amongst my family; it seems equally obvious to you that parents cannot be relied upon to behave properly to their children, and hence any 'proper government' must concern itself with these matters. I, of course, may or may not notice that your notions of 'government' and 'family' have different resonances to mine. Indeed, in some sense it is important that we do not acknowledge too thoroughly the differences we give to keywords such as these in our society. There must be some common discursive ground between us. Just as the local shopkeeper cannot reject my dollar bills, on the grounds that they do not look as he would have them look, being too dirty, too clean or too crumpled, so we must accept certain words as common currency. I think this is all perfectly conventional; it is important to the argument of this chapter that the reader accept these assumptions. In the case to be discussed here it is not crumpled dollar bills or 'proper government' that is the relevant currency, but the notion, 'community'.

The people I lived with in Peru were engaged in a struggle over land that pitted them against the nearby *haciendas* (ranches), the army, the civil guard, and the government in Lima. Though not on the scale of Zapata's followers in Morelos, or Mao's in China, they were rebellious peasants. And amongst themselves they argued: the terms they applied to their traditional past and to the institutions and practices they saw as emergent from that traditional past were a function of their preoccupations of the present. But, even as they shared in this perpetually threatening and often terrifying struggle with others, they felt that there were differences among themselves in background, in well-being and in concerns about the future, and so they argued. Perhaps that is too strong a word: they engaged in dialogue, they conversed. Yet 'argument', 'dialogue' and 'conversation' are not quite the same. Philosophers engage in dialogue about the nature of being. They are paid to do so, and should the dialogue cease, so would their pay. What commitment they have is to maintain the dialogue. At dinner I converse with friends over the virtues of Burgundy over Claret. Since I can rarely afford either, the conversation is largely academic.

There was nothing philosophical or academic about what these people in Peru disagreed over: their livelihoods depended on it. And so, yes: they argued.

Eric Wolf (1982: 6) has remarked on our tendency to endow other cultures with the qualities of internally homogeneous and externally distinctive and bounded objects, despite real heterogeneity within cultures and, at the very least, fuzzy boundaries between them. What this chapter is about is how not just anthropologists and historians, but the participants themselves, are committed both to the importance of the differences among them and simultaneously to the on-going production of an image of themselves as internally homogeneous and externally distinctive; as though, when the curtain rises for the audience of anthropologists and historians and, perhaps more especially politicians, these actors must collude with their audience in this fiction, even as they belie it with their off-stage discord.

Rethinking Convention

If this is so – if rebellious peasants, even so small a group as this collection of no more than 600 families, are shot through with differences among themselves and argue, not just about the use of the oxen today, but about institutions and practices the parameters of which are crucial for each's future well-being, such as 'the family', 'the community' and 'our way of life', and if, partly as a result of their internal discourse and partly as a result of their external struggle each's views of these notions changes, then what sense does this make of the terms of reference we anthropologists and historians in the audience use to describe what we see? Our conceptual apparatus for understanding both 'peasant rebellion' and 'peasant community' may need rethinking.

Convention suggests, for example, that certain strata of peasants are more prone to sustained rebellion than others, or that peasants are attracted to a certain kind of charismatic non-peasant leader, or that they rebel to defend a past rather than create a future. But does any of this make sense if we envisage a collection of rebellious people, fearfully arguing among themselves and, as a result, modifying their position? If at the end of their argument the results are always the same: that this stratum of peasant ends up favouring rebellion and that stratum not, that they will follow behind that kind of leader and not this, and so on, then of course we may as well minimize the role of argumentation and the content of what is argued. But what if it is precisely the intensity of the arguments themselves that determines the relative participation of (and helps to define) one stratum as against another, or goes toward the constuction not just of notions of 'leadership', but also of what is to be fought over and possibly killed for: community, land and culture? Then surely the neat *tableau vivant* retrospectively constructed – possibly by analysts and participants alike – is misleading. It is a retrospective construction imagined for the purposes of 'our basic preoccupations of the present'. And, as such, it may obscure precisely what those preoccupations were in the immediacy of the struggle; pre-occupations that themselves contributed to the reconstitution of historically embedded institutions and practices whose 'proper usage' relies on reference to their place in an (imagined) history of the past.

These embedded institutions and practices that were endlessly being negotiated were pre-eminently embraced under the rubric of 'community'. Since Wolf's seminal article (1955) anthropologists have moved a long way from the reified notion of 'community' and 'a community way of life', by placing peasant communities in historical context and showing how their boundedness and even their apparently internal levelling processes are outcomes of (differing) external economic and political forces of exploitation and domination. Nevertheless, when peasants, confronted by the changing demands of a capitalist world, rebel, we are often tempted to slip back into stereotypical and de-contextualized notions of the peasant community as one of tradition and homogeneous solidarity. Yet what we see in the case that follows is that heightened political struggle intensifies discourse within, bringing to the forefront of people's minds their most vital preoccupations, precisely because it tugs urgently at their sleeves, impelling them to articulate just what those preoccupations should be. Intensified discourse also has a less obvious consequence. In the push and pull of debate, history itself is reconstituted. Nor is this just the relative weight of one institution or another being weighed and rebalanced; the elements of society, apparently so embedded in an unchangeable past history, are actually reconstituted. Moreover, if we advance from the notion of culture as a fixed blueprint by which people act, towards a notion of culture as something produced and reproduced through history, then the evidence to be presented here suggests a further step. Cultural production does not occur with equal intensity from one day to the next. The productivity of culture (to stick, for the moment, with these rather laboured economic concepts) increases at historical moments of heightened resistance and rebellion: increases because the valued components of culture are challenged, threatened from without, and so must be articulated within. And then, through this process, each participant constructs a means for identifying with or against each relevant component of culture.

A disturbance in the countryside means just that. Peasants rebel and things are disturbed: not just in the routine world of the provincial capital, where journalists write articles, policemen reports and lawyers briefs; but among the peasants themselves. Here is the paradox: to explain a disturbance, something 'must have happened'. For something to have happened, there must be a beginning and an end; a subject and an object. And yet for disturbance to remain disturbance, it must resist these closures. From the peasants' point of view, the openness and incompleteness, the dialogic character of disturbance, provides their resistance with a vital element of its ongoing momentum.

This process can be seen sequentially in the local rebellion we are to look at, first in the open-endedness of the early account of rebellion given by the administrator of the remote Hacienda Tucle on 24 April 1964 and then in the more complete account in the local newspaper on the following day:

> With great urgency I write to put you in knowledge of the following: The personnel of this *hacienda*, having already been considerably threatened, have now become aware of a veritable invasion by the community of Huasicancha. These are in the following places: Analanya, a large flock of sheep, cattle and horses. In Picpish they are building huts and there is an alarming quantity of livestock of the community. In the zone of Anchi a large quantity consuming the best *hacienda* pasture – this confirms that by night they passed through the areas of Huachamachay, Arauca Pachca [etc.] with many animals. This movement of the *comuneros* of Huasicancha was still continuing at 1 PM and at Cabildo Pata there is a community authority (Ascensio A.) who is giving orders to all who leave the village telling them where to go and with what flocks, all of them carrying staves and other movables in the direction of the *puna* [highest level of pasture] of the *hacienda*.
>
> The matter must be dealt with urgently in order to avoid confrontations with the *hacienda* staff and the mixing of their animals with ours.

Pedro P. has already lost 10 of his animals, and we shall certainly lose more. I am sending this with the truck driver to make clear to you the gravity of the situation which faces us here at Tucle (ARA).[2]

The disturbance in the highland pastures was first introduced to the townspeople of the provincial capital the next day in a more comprehensive version, however:

Comuneros Break pact: Invasion at Tucle

Approximately a thousand peasants of the community of Huasicancha yesterday morning invaded the lands of the Tucle Livestock Co. in an area covering over 10 kilometres.

Carrying flags, sticks, and banners with the phrase 'Land or Death' on them, the peasants installed themselves – challengers – some 3 kilometres from the *hacienda* buildings. The residence is guarded by 40 employees.

As part of these acts of invasion the *comuneros* trespassed 5,000 head of sheep and 1,500 cattle and have taken over the area, putting up their own shepherds' huts.

Manuel Duarte, the chief administrator of the *hacienda*, said he thought the invaders were being organized by foreign elements with communist inclinations.

The Tucle Livestock Co. is one of the most important of the region. It covers an area of 45,000 hectares and owns 20,000 Corriedale sheep and 2,000 Brown Swiss cattle.

– *El Correo*, Huancayo, 25 April 1964

The headline implies a decisive historical event. But the statement that a pact had been broken between landlord and rural dwellers in the high pastures suggests that this was simply the way in which the Huasicanchinos' centuries-old war of attrition against the *haciendas* was now brought to the forefront of townspeople's awareness. Indeed, for the people of the provincial town, Huancayo, and by extension the people of Lima too, the Huasicanchino land recuperation campaign was a clearly defined historical event: the people of Huasicancha 'invaded' *hacienda* land in 1964, and a struggle followed that reached its conclusion eight years later when the people of Huasicancha took possession of over 100,000 acres of land and the Hacienda Tucle was destroyed. Such is the imperative of closure in retrospective accounts of the past. And today, with a set of preoccupations quite different from what they had then, it is one in which the Huasicanchinos themselves collude.

We do not need to deny these 'facts'; but we can cast them in a different light by trying to reproduce the process by which the heterogeneous preoccupations of the Huasicanchinos during that period gave rise to an intensive, ever-incomplete and ongoing constitution and reconstitution of key components in their culture: in its actual, local setting, their community.

'Back to the Beginning of Time'

During the mid-1960s the Peruvian Andes experienced widespread rural unrest. This was especially so in the central Andes, whence the following evidence is drawn. The term 'peasant land invasions', popularly used in the press, is misleading, however, partly because it does not capture the wide variety of forms these popular initiatives took and partly because it reflects a hegemonic bias that many peasants themselves disputed: the term 'invasion' assumes that the land occupied by the peasantry did not belong to them. What was happening in the Andes was the attempt (by small farmers and rural poor) to realize – that is to say, to make manifest – a quite different interpretation. To this extent it is no corruption of the word or exaggeration of what was happening to say that this was extensive, relatively uncoordinated, rebellion. One especially notorious instance provides the case we are about to discuss here.

Following the events described above, the Huasicanchinos conducted a war of attrition against the neighbouring *haciendas* Tucle and Río de la Virgen that lasted until a victorious settlement was formally recognized in the courts during my fieldwork in 1972–3. Though the ups and downs and ins and outs of this campaign are very much a part of what concerns us here, the greater detail necessary for a respectable historical account must be left for elsewhere (Smith 1989). Here, suffice it to say that, far from the campaign I am about to discuss being something new, the Huasicanchinos' attempts to recover land from neighbouring *haciendas* were long-standing. In the 1880s – during and after the war with Chile – they had expropriated and occupied all the local *haciendas* for a period. Again during the 1930s they pressed their claims specifically against Hacienda Tucle. And in 1947–48 they had undertaken a full-scale campaign against the *hacienda*, one that involved considerable bloodshed and yet led to disappointing results. It was followed by a period of savage repression (the Odria

ochenio), a period from which the people were emerging as the 1960s
arrived. Resistance of one kind or another, then, was more the rule
than the exception. And even during the more intensive eight years
of resistance to be discussed here, moments of apparent victory
and defeat came and went, as did participants in the campaign.
Equally elusive to outsiders was what the Huasicanchinos' goals
were from one moment to the next.

Huasicancha is a high-altitude community, lying to the South and
West of the Mantaro Valley in the central Peruvian Andes. In the
period that concerns us, pastoral farming was complemented by
subsistence cultivation and some artisan and trading activities.
Alongside Huasicancha were a number of vast livestock ranches
(*haciendas*), of which the Hacienda Tucle, owned by Maria Luisa
Chávez and her son Manuel Duarte, was the closest. A number of
Huasicanchino families worked as sheperds for this *hacienda*, while
still others perpetually grazed sheep by illicitly using *hacienda*-
controlled land. All Hacienda Tucle's land, as well as parts of the
other *haciendas* in the area, were claimed by the people of Huasicancha and other nearby communities. By the 1960s out-migration
was such that 40 per cent of the total communal membership[3] of
3,000 people actually resided outside the community, while a further
25 per cent migrated from the village for some part of the year.

The conflict between the Huasicanchino pastoralists and the
surrounding *haciendas* has been so long-standing that it is a state
of affairs taken for granted by all in the community. A common
remark that skips from the lips of man and woman when reflecting
on the matter is, 'It goes back to the beginning of time.' And indeed
it certainly does go back to the beginning of written records.
Hobsbawm (1974) has quite rightly argued that the Huasicanchinos
have been in conflict of one kind or another with landlords over
the centuries. But the force of this conflict took on a cumulative
momentum relatively recently.

From the end of the last century, conflict between the *hacienda*
and the Huasicanchino pastoralists was a result of the irresistible
force of an emerging capitalist livestock ranch coming up against
the immovable block of erstwhile pastoralists becoming involved
in a commodity economy as rural and migrant petty commodity
producers. Driven by competition toward the rationalization of
production, the *hacienda* was perpetually trying to substitute a wage
system for a labour–rent system (in which pastoralists were allowed
access to *hacienda*-controlled pasture in return for labour service)

by enforcing absolute control over territory to the exclusion of local pastoralists. Increasingly during this century it became these same market-induced imperatives for the reproduction of their enterprises that drove the Huasicanchinos to resist. And it was this long history of resistance that, in turn, put Hacienda Tucle in the 'backward' state it found itself in by as late as 1964, when similar livestock companies nearby had at least partially succeeded in becoming capitalist firms.

The competition, which drove the *hacienda*-owners one way, drove the Huasicanchinos against them in another. But for the Huasicanchinos the process was not an even one, and these uneven imperatives provided an ineluctable force underlying the production of culture during the Huasicanchinos' intensive political engagement. So let us turn for a moment to look at the differing forms of the Huasicanchinos' enterprises in the immediate context of the *hacienda* and in the more extended context of the overall Peruvian economy. In the mid-1960s Huasicanchinos were evenly distributed between the highland village and a variety of work centres, among them Huancayo (the provincial capital), Lima and La Oroya (site of the American-owned Cerro de Pasco Company's smelter). In all cases they made their livelihoods through the operation of domestic enterprises whose form varied from one Huasicanchino to another. In Lima, migrants were engaged in multi-occupational enterprises that included ambulant street selling, transportation, market stall operation and a myriad other petty activities. In Huancayo and La Oroya, some owned market stalls or shops, others had skills as electricians, mechanics and builders, while still others had jobs as low-paid employees in government offices. And in the majority of cases the entire household membership produced various combinations of these. Again, in the village itself, though differences in wealth were not great (compared to the Mantaro Valley itself (see Long and Roberts 1978, 1984)), households varied in their commitment to arable as opposed to pastoral production, while still others offset their paucity of either by engaging in weaving, tile-making or petty crafts and trades.

Heterogeneity and Differentiation

What is clear, then, is that the Huasicanchinos were a heterogeneous lot, and that is what matters for what we are about to examine.

While it is important not to lose sight of the role of debate and negotiation in constituting this heterogeneity (as well as being produced by it), once this caveat is accepted, it will be helpful to the reader of what follows to draw up a much-simplified *dramatis personae*. We find among the Huasicanchinos migrants (notably in Lima and Huancayo) and village residents, most of whom have themselves had some experience of migration, and a number of whom still do, seasonally.

Among the migrants we find established older figures who now have quite settled residences in Lima and some in Huancayo. Their visits to Huasicanacha were scarce in 1964, and virtually non-existent by 1972. Other migrants with quite extensive experience in the city were part of what I call 'confederations of households' (Smith 1984), which tied them in to the workings of domestic enterprises in other work centres and the village itself. In the vast majority of cases these migrants had emerged from families with a long history of pastoral farming in the highlands. But beginning to establish themselves in the cities and perpetually attempting to construct such confederations were a new group of migrants, whose backgrounds had been less closely linked to pastoralism directly. Their livelihoods as petty traders, craftsmen and small arable farmers had not given them so secure a network of reciprocal linkages as that of the ex-pastoralists, and so their confederations were often more shaky.

In the community itself we find households firmly tied in to the rural end of the household confederations. Likewise we also find smaller flock-owners who rely more heavily on craft skills and once-off jobs (many of which may require temporary migration) to get by. Like their city counterparts, they strive for interpersonal linkages that will offset their volatile lives, but face constant setbacks. And at the least fortunate end of this group of people are those whose poverty makes them uncomfortably reliant on the occasional work, exchange or straight generosity of other Huasicanchinos. But increasingly during the period to be discussed, we find in Huasic-ancha a few independent farmers whose small number belies their growing influence in Huasicancha's politics and economy. These are farms headed by men returned from work in a local mine, whose proximity to Huasicancha made it possible for them simultaneously to engage in quite remunerative wage labour and operate enter-prises on increasingly commercial lines (for greater detail, see Smith 1989).

Elsewhere I have shown that the heterogeneous domestic enter-prises of the Huasicanchinos, both rural and urban, inclined them toward different developmental logics as they were reproduced through the generations (see Smith 1989). Here we need note just two factors. First, as different sectors of the national and regional economy experienced expansion and contraction over time, so enterprises, inserted differentially into those sectors, developed in different ways. Second, for rural and especially urban enterprises, as ever wider areas of social relations came to be expressed in commodified forms, so the imperatives of commodified relations of production began to take hold (see Marx 1976: Chapter 23; Bernstein 1979; Friedmann 1980; Kahn 1980; Smith 1985; MacEwen Scott 1986). The effects were contradictory. While the Huasic-anchinos' heterogeneity was thereby increased, the volatility of the Peruvian economy as a whole (and even more so, of any one sector within it) had encouraged petty commodity producers to share the desire for a foothold in farming. This was because not only was the future development of any one sector extremely unpredictable (especially so for the poorest and least informed participants in it), but also inflation made accumulation in cash-based enterprises almost impossible. Hence the attraction of retaining a foothold in the farm and, given the ecology of Huasicancha, this meant pre-eminently pastoral farming, with its need for pasture.

It is at this point that the role of praxis plays its part in the production of Huasicanchino culture. Because members of each enterprise were fighting for the maintenance (or expansion) of their 'way of life' (simultaneously a gloss for 'livelihood' and for 'culture'), precisely what the essential elements of that way of life were came to the forefront of attention. Because different enterprises required different elements of that 'way of life' for their reproduction, what was essential and what was less so had to be negotiated. Because these matters were sufficiently important to drive people to con-certed resistance, the commitment to engage in these negotiations was very great. A 'multiplicity of dispersed wills' were confronting external forces that threatened the future of their 'way of life' by denying them access to the land upon which it depended. Against the overwhelming forces that denied the validity of this reality, the contrary assertion of these truths by the Huasicanchinos meant intensive dialogue amongst themselves about what 'ownership' of land meant, how labour might be justly given over to others, or what it meant to identify oneself with (be a 'member' of?) a community, and so on, as well as a multiplicity of relationships subsidiary to these. And such discourse meant the exchange of words whose meanings were both fixed and obvious and at the same time – and because of their very importance – ever-reconstituted and elusive.

'We Talked of Nothing Else. What Else Mattered?'

With the end of the repressive years of the Odria *ochenio* open political debate returned, and in the Mantaro Valley an increasingly commercialized, small, independent farming population began to seek political leverage through a multitude of *federaciones campesinas* (peasant leagues). From 1958 to the national elections of 1962 and again in 1963, migrants from Huasicancha, resident in the valley and in Lima, were influential in channelling much of Huasicancha's campaign for the restitution of land through these *federaciones campesinas*.

Among the migrants who were now well established in Lima and Huancayo there were a few people who had set up small shops or permanent *talleres* (workshops). At the same time, those who did not have some special skill, such as electrician or mechanic, were shifting into investment in market stalls or (second-hand) pick-ups or vans. People such as these saw the *federacion campesina* as a channel through which the land recuperation campaign might be steered, but they saw land recuperation as just one of a number of issues that Huasicanchinos should address to improve their lives. To this end in 1958, one of their number, Elias Tacunan, an electrician, APRA party organizer in the smelting town of La Oroya and now almost a stranger in the village, ran for the position of Personero[4] in Huasicancha, together with similar figures drawn from the migrant Huasicanchinos in Lima and Huancayo.

Organizing a meeting at the small settlement of Vista Alegre, in the highlands near Huasicancha, Tacunan formed the first of his *federaciones campesinas*, the Movimiento Comunal del Centro, based on five municipal districts in the highlands. Although the recovery of 'communal' lands was a major source of enthusiasm for the Movimiento among the highland villagers, Tacunan intended to spread the federation to include the more commercial migrants in the Mantaro Valley. Though it was strategically useful to refer to land claims in terms of customary usufruct, the fact was that these migrants' commercial enterprises relied as much on exclusive forms of property as did the *haciendas* in claiming pastureland. Sensitive to their concerns, therefore, Tacunan stressed the more vague platforms of better conditions in the villages and improved educational facilities, while not clarifying his position with respect to the payment of an indemnity to the *hacendados* (*hacienda* owners) for their expropriated lands.

But village records, two old diaries and informants' accounts lead to the impression that most Huasicanchinos in the village itself, and indeed the bulk of the poorer migrants too, looked upon the activities of the federations with a certain bemusement, as though they were a conversation taking place on the other side of a partition, in an adjoining, crowded and ill-lit room. Suspecting that Tacunan's ambivalence concealed a contractual notion of the exclusive ownership of the pastures, one older Huasicanchino was moved to clarify his own view thus:

> The well-being [*riquesa*] of the *gamonal* (the more traditional term for the *hacienda*-owner) derives not from his vast herds [*rebaños inmensos*], nor from his pastures, which by right belong to the Community of Huasicancha, but from the giving [*dotación*] of labour by our children and our forebears, who have lived for years and years in poverty while serving an unjust patron [*un patrón injusto*] (AC).

The Huasicanchinos' attitude to the Movimiento Comunal was by no means unequivocal or unanimous, then. Many of those still in the village who had been involved in resistance campaigns earlier in the century were lukewarm towards the political initiatives spearheaded by commercial migrants personified by Tacunan.

The migrants' monopoly of the community's positions of authority was an especially visible expression of a process in which Huasicanchino social relations had become increasingly dominated by the dictates of non-farm economic activities beyond the highlands. Changes in the fortunes of the various sectors in which enterprises were inserted had combined with the *hacienda*'s move toward commercial rationalization to undercut the pre-eminence of the community as an institution. For on the one hand the *hacienda*'s dominance in controlling pasture and on the other the tendency of increasingly commodified pastoralist households to pay rent to other villages for pasture combined to pre-empt the community itself from acting as the most significant conduit for access to pasturelands. And the instrumental use made of community office-holding by migrants like Tacunan served less to integrate the highland pastoralists into national and regional political institutions than to draw attention to the distinctiveness of the pastoralists' interests.

There was plenty of debate in the air, therefore – among Huasic-anchino migrants, among villagers and between migrants and villagers – when, from 1960 onwards, spontaneous land occupations and other rural insurgency throughout Peru began to be reported with increasing frequency in the papers. Around the *haciendas* Tucle, Antapongo and Laive there were signs that the daily cat-and-mouse hide-and-seek between *hacienda* foremen and individual herders who trespassed as part of the quotidian struggle for live-lihood was being replaced by open confrontation between the community as a whole and the *haciendas*.

For, in fact, the word 'trespass' is misleading. Huasicanchinos found by the administrator using *hacienda*-controlled pasture without a formal contract were referred to as *pasaderos*. There was an ongoing argument between community authorities and the *hacienda* administrator as to whether *pasaderos* were merely exer-cising their right to graze and, once caught, were prepared to pay a forfeit in labour (the community authorities' view), or whether they were illegal trespassers obliged to do labour service as a punishment (the administrror's view) (ARA, FHT, AC). As the administrator tried to increase the punishment to draconian extremes, in order to discourage repetition of the 'offence', so the dispute grew and the daily round of finding pasture became inherently confrontational. The boundary therefore between the daily business of 'trespassing' and the headline-grabbing 'land invasion' was not a clear one. It reflected a specific tactic for gaining armed support on the part of the *hacendado*, on the one hand, and the increasing incentive of the community authorities to re-establish their position as the conduit through which all Huasicanchinos' access to pasture passed, including that of *pasaderos*.

What we witness now, therefore, is an attempt by various fractions of the peasantry in Huasicancha itself to reassert the community's control of the key areas for the social reproduction of enterprises. The specific form the campaign took – the massive invasion of *hacienda*-controlled land from April 1964 on – must be understood in terms of the community authorities' attempting to maintain leadership over otherwise individually initiated 'trespassing' by Huasicanchinos acting in small groups.

Because leadership was always questioned, it is misleading to see the unfolding campaign in terms of a succession of different leadership factions. Nevertheless, we might pause for a moment here to help the reader through the complexities of what follows with a summary. As we have seen, the campaign began with the well-established migrants from Lima and Huancayo at the helm, with the occasional support of the large flock-owners in Huasicancha. This was followed by a group of small flock-owners from the village supported by the older 'confederated households' in and beyond Huasicancha. Over the period, however, newly established migrants began to make their feelings heard, though never acquiring a vigorous role in directing the campaign. Finally a small group of independent farmers with flocks developed from earnings in the local mines were the figureheads who signed the settlement that concluded the campaign.

Let us return, now, to the early days: through 1962 and 1963 the threat of foot-and-mouth disease made *hacienda* staff especially diligent in preventing the unbathed animals of the villagers from straying on to *hacienda* land. Meanwhile, among those caring for the smaller flocks, pressure to trespass grew: drought made pasture scarcer, encouraging greater movement of flocks; villagers hitherto working at the local mine were returning with cash, which they invested in sheep; and the number of animals owned by migrants and held in village flocks on the basis of reciprocal arrangements between households were now steadily increasing. As a result the number of conflicts occurring between *hacienda* staff and villagers increased (ARA; AC; FHT).

There was a possibility that this would lead to a rift, because the community authorities were the better-off migrants. In the community meetings throughout 1962, these people were urging discretion on the local front while the national political scene clarified itself (AC). And increasingly the community Personero, Elias Tacunan, fudged his position on land redistribution the better to keep his hand free for bargaining with national political figures on behalf of his *federacion campesina*. A rift was postponed, however, because inter-household linkages (between villagers and migrants and between pastoralists and arable farmers) acted as a centripetal force cross-cutting quantitative differences in wealth and qualitative differences in the sources of household incomes (see Smith 1979). Moreover, with confrontations increasing daily between poorer Huasicanchinos relying on 'trespassing' and the *hacienda* personnel, the large flock-owners began to share with the bulk of migrants a renewed preoccupation with 'the community'. For migrants (as much community members as the village residents) community institutions were a means to keep formal control over the direction of events in Huasicancha, where they were now investing some of their resources; for the large flock-owners, emphasis on the community and on that aspect of people's identity that derived from community membership was a means of keeping a handle on the poorer *comuneros*' movement on the scarce pasturelands.

Soon, however, pressure for the removal of Tacunan became manifest. It was initiated by those villagers caring for the smaller flocks, because the areas that were left to them to pasture were most easily accessible to *hacienda* staff. Many of these people had reciprocal ties with Huancayo and Lima migrants, whose animals constituted part of the flocks being pastured 'illegally' on *hacienda* land. As temporary migration and off-farm incomes began to play an increasing role in household reproduction even for the village households, so these ties – expressed through the idiom of shared community identity – were essential to ever larger numbers of Huasicanchinos.[5]

Assembly records for this period are replete with a myriad uses of the term 'community' (*comunidad*), covering a wide range of resonances, from the strictly legal constitution of Huasicancha as a 'Comunidad Indigena' ('Indigenous Community') recognized by the national government and with formal title to local pastures, to the more affectual notion of the community of Huasicanchinos as neighbours with shared interests, to a notion of the Huasicanchino community as the embodiment of certain self-evident (and hence never explicitly stated) principles for living a proper life. Meanwhile, perhaps its most obvious meaning – as a place of common residence – was one accepted not just by residents but by migrants too – who often referred to their (empty and padlocked) houses as a sign of their community-membership.[6]

The point here is not to try to demonstrate an ultra-materialist position by seeking to associate each utterance of the term with groups of people sharing similar 'material' conditions. The possibility that certain Huasicanchinos held consistent notions of 'community' each time they used the term and that these were always marginally different from notions of 'community' held by others, seems unlikely. What is clearly demonstrated in the records is that the term was used so frequently and became such a keyword in the course of the struggle for land's unfolding from one year to the next. In the process of this discourse 'community', as an essential element of identity for Huasicanchinos, became covertly reconstituted; a reconstitution, moreover, that was never completed so long as 'community's' various resonances remained pre-eminently relevant to the social reproduction of the heterogeneous Huasic-anchino enterprises: hence an ongoing discourse within and about the community.

On 11 April 1963 Tacunan was removed from office as Person-ero, accused of stealing money from community funds. This was the first of what became a series of attempts to remove the older migrants, more thoroughly incorporated into urban life. These incorporated migrants had established their domestic enterprises during the lean years in Huasicancha – from an earlier campaign in1936, through the repressive years of the Odria regime in the early 1950s. While their attachment to Huasicancha was emotionally strong, therefore, the reproduction of their enterprises was more thoroughly tied to commitments in their place of migration, than to commitments in the village.

The strongest element carrying out this 'coup' were the migrants and villagers who were tied into reciprocal obligations with one another. There were also those few better-off, relatively indep-endent, flock-owners who had either remained in the village after 1948 or who had returned from migration and were beginning to invest in sheep. And to these were added a group of poorer migrants in Huancayo and Lima who had no strong inter-household links to Huasicancha to speak of, but who relied for occasional favours on the better-off Huasicanchinos.

The new office-holders were small flock-owners who received the support of the older pastoralist families. Reliant as they were on funds raised from the migrants, the new authorities were unable to take a particular direction in the campaign without migrant support. So they decided to petition the president of the republic directly and get the migrants involved in the process (de la Cruz Diary, Huasicancha). And so, duly dressed in ponchos and felt hats sent from the village, Huasicanchino migrants presented themselves to the President as members of the traditional peasantry and delivered a petition linking their claims to their customs and practices, which went back to time immemorial.[7] And on 30 Nov-ember 1963 an agreement was signed with Hacienda Tucle stating that there would be no more trespassing until the government adjudicators had made some decision. The new office-holders now reminded villagers at every meeting that aggression would lose them the support of President Belaunde.

For the moment then, community authorities committed themselves to legitimate channels for the recuperation of land. But things were to change in January 1964, when, after an inspection by the civil judge of Huancayo, the feelings of the community as a whole *vis à vis* the *hacienda* reached boiling point.

Concluding that the judge had been bribed by the *hacendado* prior to the inspection, many villagers had their patience tested to the limit and now dispensed with the cautions of the authorities and began to invade land in small, independent groups, causing the *hacienda* administrator to believe that a full-scale invasion was occurring (ARA). Similar invasions continued throughout February, prompting the community authorities to call a meeting in March that placed them in charge of a land occupation to 'reivindicar nuestros pastos legitimos' ('revindicate our legitimate pastures'). Three authorities who felt unable to support a policy of confrontation were permitted to resign and were replaced by others.[8] On 16 March de la Cruz went to Huancayo, where he appeared before a judge with the community's lawyer to denounce the violent acts of the *hacendado*. In the subsequent six weeks' invasion tactics were discussed, areas of the *puna* allotted to particular groups for invasion, and attempts made to persuade *hacienda* employees to leave their posts. Then on 24 April the invasion was carried out, eliciting the responses of the *hacienda* and the local press we have already seen.

The army was called in, creating a climate of fear in Huasicancha, for by this time so-called 'land invasions' were occurring throughout the central highlands and confrontations with varying degrees of violence were reported in the press almost daily (de la Cruz diary). Many people in the village felt that the time for compromises had passed (ibid.), and when a ministerial inspector was sent once more to survey the landmarks on 7 May, de la Cruz had a violent argument with him and left. Returning from this inspection, he and another community authority were caught by the civil guard, together with three other elected authorities. All were accused of being communist agitators and imprisoned without trial (JT; de la Cruz Diary).

The effect was to throw the Huasicanchinos into yet another period of intense discussion. Soon after the arrests Belaunde announced that no land being occupied by squatters would be considered for land reform. Throughout Peru many peasants therefore withdrew from land. From the point of view of those migrants in Huancayo and Lima who were in touch with national and regional developments this seemed to be a promising development favouring a conciliatory stance, and they wrote to the community authorities urging them to negotiate a compromise with Manuel Duarte, the owner of Hacienda Tucle. (AC). On the other hand the extent of rural mobilization in the central Andes was far greater than anybody had witnessed in this century, and the preoccupation of the army in numerous separate arenas had given the Huasicanchinos actually 'invading' the land more success than they had anticipated. Responding to the migrants' letter in the general assembly, they stressed that Hacienda Tucle was unable to contain their activities. In lieu of the migrants' reference to the contemporary political currency of negotiation and compromise, they evoked the history of Huasicancha's past resistance campaigns, reminding the audience of the period in the 1880s when Huasicanchino *guerrilleros* and their allies had expropriated all the neighbouring *haciendas*.[9] Nevertheless, one speaker was severely chastised when he sought to ridicule the migrants by saying 'Nosotros, Huasicanchinos, no somos profesores; pero si somos guerrilleros.' ('We Huasicanchinos aren't schoolteachers; we're guerrillas.') An older man rejoined, 'No somos profesores, ni guerrilleros. Como todo el mundo sabe, los Huasicanchinos son "Los Zorros".' ('We're neither schoolteachers nor guerrillas. As all the world knows, the Huasicanchinos are "the Foxes".' [referring to the popular nickname in the neighbourhood, for the Huasicanchinos])(AC). So the pressing question of finding a new set of leaders provided the opportunity for further debate along these lines.[10]

Increasingly we hear the voices of those migrants who, originally lacking a significant base in livestock (and hence in the networks associated with livestock rearing) were now beginning to establish themselves outside the village with sufficient consistency for the process to have become institutionalized. And they were joined by a much smaller group who were returning from work in a local mine to become 'independent farmers' in Huasicancha.[11] The fact that livestock were being used as part of the campaign (to 'eat up the *hacienda*' in the words of informants) meant that Huasicanchinos were reluctant to sell animals to raise cash for legal fees, and it was therefore the migrants with access to cash and credit who took most of the responsibility for paying legal fees.

But refusal to pay the *coto* (head tax) was assumed to mean renunciation of *comunero* status and hence of any claim to pasture or to a voice in the community. This meant that so long as there was a significant body of Huasicanchinos determined to continue the campaign, those wishing to gain from the eventual outcome had to keep up their participation. As a result, heated discussion took place to influence the course of events, but threats to withdraw support were never especially effective. Moreover, the village residents were aware of the fact that they had the whip hand, inasmuch as a steadily increasing number of migrants from one year to the next were investing in sheep. In the last analysis, as de la Cruz put it a few years later, 'We had their sheep.'

There were few backsliders, therefore.[12] And the much vaunted solidarity of the Huasicanchinos noted by the Huancayo observers of the time, or the *unión* (unity) recalled by informants reflecting back today on those times, must be seen within this context. Far from the singleness of purpose visible from geographic or historical distance, the heat of discussion over different perceptions of the key elements of what was being fought for gave momentum to the struggle directed outwards, just as the fearful commitment people had to its outcome held them together like warring Siamese twins. Such is the stuff of community: 'What is shared in community is not shared values or common understanding, so much as the fact that members of a community are engaged in the same argument, the same raisonnement, the same Rede, the same discourse, in which alternative strategies, misunderstandings, conflicting goals and values are threshed out' (Sabean 1984: 29–30).

The need to find officials to replace those in prison now provided a forum for further debate. Whilst some – especially migrants engaged in volatile petty commodity production in the cities – relied on the regularity of livestock sales, there were other Huasicanchinos who were not preoccupied by difficulties deriving from unsystematic husbandry such as irregular sales or care during the lambing season. For them this was not a view of farming that prevailed in their enterprises: they observed no special season for lambing. These latter were not therefore seriously hindered in the running of their enterprises by a long-drawn-out war of attrition. And this attitude towards time was shared by the migrant households with whom they had reciprocal arrangments and other villagers and migrants with few or no livestock, whose only possibility of such investment lay in the future.

Among and between these groups debate set in. From the forum of the Sunday meetings in village or migrant club, to urban workplace and village street-corner, to the confines of the household 'patio', discussion was animated. As one informant put it,

> At meetings, did we talk about what to do? Of course we did. But we had already discussed it the day before. And the day before that. We talked of nothing else. What else mattered? After all, we are talking of a moment when it seemed as though everybody ruled in Huasicancha. Hah! And those with office did not rule (*Y ellos con cargos no mandaban*). And so it was. (*Fieldnotes*, Huancayo, February 1973).

'Everybody ruled' and 'those with office did not rule': for with de la Cruz and his colleagues in prison a new set of office-holders were decided upon from among the old-established migrants resident in Lima and two of their village relatives. Their ability to assert their own interests, however, was proscribed by a generally held view that they were now only superficially leaders for the purposes of dealing with outsiders, and that others really 'ruled in the community'. This form of *realpolitik* was sufficiently acknowledged among Huasicanchinos to have a name: *'la cumbre oscura'* ('the summit hidden [by clouds]').

The informant's assessment is born out by a committee meeting called by the Inter-Ministerial Commission in the village itself. Not surprisingly, these new officers invited their figurehead, Elias Tacunan, to attend. The strength of feeling that surfaced in the debate is captured by these outraged notes made by a village resident and inserted into the community records.

> It was set up at the request of Manuel Duarte, who had bribed (*habia comprado*) the two delegates of the Ministries who came to Huasicancha . . . The community received them with a band and then a general assembly was summoned by the guests, in which the two ministerial delegates took over entirely. The authorities of the community were not permitted to speak. Señor Elias Tacunan, who represented FEDECOJ as the general secretary, was however permitted to use his words, which he did entirely in favour of the *gamonal* and for expropriation by the agrarian reform and not by the demand which is being made by the community. From this date Tacunan has lost all prestige as a representative of the community (AC).

It is to be noted that reference to 'the authorities of the community' is not to the newly appointed officers, but rather to the old leaders who had been brought up from the prison in Huancayo especially for the occasion.

The next day the Huancayo newspaper carried the headline, 'Problem Tucle-Huasicancha Still at Page One'. But the *hacienda* administration had been impressed by the evident differences of opinion among the Huasicanchinos, and a few days later another headline appeared in the paper, 'Tucle: We Accept Agrarian Reform', underneath which it was recorded that, aware of the fact that the villagers of Huasicancha only wanted the land in order to rent it out to those who were not residents of the village (the migrants?), the *hacienda* administration would accept a limited amount of expropriation on condition that the beneficiaries were to be found among all neighbouring communities save Huasicancha.

Within a few days the *hacienda* appeared to achieve what it had been seeking. On 4 November, the newspaper carried a large public announcement: 'To Public Opinion: Act of Agreement Between the Community of Huasicancha and the Tucle Livestock Company'. The Commission had arranged an agreement between the *hacendado* and the representatives of Huasicancha, Santos C., Ramon M., Francisco Y., Hermino Z., and Cleto Y. The settlement was remarkably favourable to the *hacienda* and apparently an abject defeat for Huasicancha. But an immediate result was the release of the imprisoned authorities. By January 1965, following a now-familar pattern, the Huasicanchinos removed the officers who had signed this agreement and replaced them with their predecessors. The *comuneros* then rejected the settlement on the grounds that it had been signed by people who had never had the proper credentials from the community.

Throughout 1965 those in the remote area around Tucle and Huasicancha and those in the urban centres were strikingly at variance in the way they read prevailing conditions. In Lima, President Belaunde had declared that the Departments of Junin and Pasco would be the targets of land reform in that year. In the rural locales, however, the government's presence was not represented by these generous intentions but rather by the suspension of individual guarantees and the presence of US-trained 'rangers' in pursuit of the guerrilla fighters calling themselves the 'Tupac Amaru' cell (Bejar 1970).

Union and Selective Tradition

Increased guerrilla activity meant that government sympathy with those especially stubborn peasants who, suspicious of promises, refused to withdraw from land, was now replaced by a campaign of fear. This substitution of a climate of fear for the previous government policy of negotiation effectively drew more sharply the line between 'within', where discourse among participants proceeded apace, and 'without', where dialogue between government representatives and *comuneros* had ceased altogether. The sense of confrontation was now very high, when two apparently unrelated occurrences gave rise to overt resistance. First, the army contingent at the *fundo* was withdrawn; then the Huancayo court delivered a judgement in favour of Tucle in the civil case with Huasicancha. In the wake of these two superficially unrelated events, an apparently mysterious fire occurred at the *hacienda*. The growing hysteria in Huancayo *vis à vis* the peasantry is reflected in the local newspaper headline: 'Red Terror Continues: *Hacienda* Building Burnt Down.'

In fact overall the Huasicanchino campaign is not very well captured by the expression 'red terror'. By late 1967, when de la Cruz was replaced in office by that cohort of Huasicanchinos who had returned from the local mine over the past three years and were now setting up as independent farmers, strategy and tactics were well-established. They were to deplete the basic resources of the *hacienda*: pasture and sheep. Simply by persistently trespassing on to *hacienda* land with livestock, villagers undermined the basis of the *hacienda*'s land-use system. Normally flocks were circulated over extensive areas of pasture to allow one area to recuperate while another was being used. Perpetual trespassing on pasture being left to rest played havoc with this system. Trespassers' flocks were swollen too by rustling; nor was an opportunity ever lost to damage or kill *hacienda* animals when they could not be carried off.

Nevertheless, this long war of attrition in the 1960s plus the century-old history of Huasicanchinos' resistance to the Chileans and subsequent insurgency through the 1880s (see Manrique 1981; Smith 1989) combined to give them a reputation in the central sierra as *guerrilleros* (lit. warriors).[13] The Huasicanchinos themselves were not unaffected by such a potent appellation. In Huasicancha, however, the term is used with great caution. For what distinguishes them – both in their own eyes and in the eyes of their neighbours

– is the effectiveness of their fight: not the fight itself. Unsurprisingly, informants are not at all unaware that many peasants are prone to resistance: to picking a fight. It would be hard to live in the central sierras with any other view. Yet, important though their reputation as *guerrilleros* might be to them, it is above all the effectiveness of actions that selects those actions from experience to be reconstituted in memory, letting the rest fall away, and hence producing a specific notion of resistance.

Tactics made army surveillance very difficult, as it did too the patrols by the *hacienda caporales* [armed foremen], who were familiar with the hazardous mountain terrain. Small groups of invaders entered the *hacienda* land at widely dispersed points with their livestock. *Hacienda* staff, called upon to patrol over 30,000 hectares of mountainous terrain, could not travel in sufficient numbers to take immediate action once invaders had been spotted. Forced back to base for reinforcements, more often than not they returned to find the invaders gone.

The civil guard and army were still less successful. The fact that rural unrest was widespread in central sierras meant that no large contingent could be kept in the area for any length of time. Instead a varying number of men (depending on the perceived state of affairs in the area) were quartered either at the *hacienda* buildings or in a location where they could keep an eye on the Huasicanchino bridgehead, whence invasions occurred. But the job was boring and morale low, exposing their Achilles' heel:

> On at least one occasion – it's hard to tell: it may have happened a lot more than once – a group of men arrived at the guard post near Huaculpuquio well stocked with *aguardiente* (cane alcohol). After some friendly banter and some joshing between themselves and the soldiers a bottle appeared and was passed round. Unhappy at how the soldier's suspicions restrained their jollity, one or two men left the group, returning some time later with three or four young women and a couple of musical instruments. All with good effect. The following morning their *cabo* (corporal) found his men all but incapacitated, while villagers had long since driven their flocks past the post into the high pasture. [The wonders of *aguardiente*. It seems one never gets a head for it.] – *Fieldnotes*, Huasicancha May 1972.

Then, when the frustration and impotence of being confined to the observation post drove more adventurous small contingents of soldiers to journey away from the *hacienda* in pursuit of trespassers, as likely as not they were led deep into the high mountains and there abandoned by trespassers turned decoys.

In effect it was a war of attrition, in which one side was continually diverted from getting on with its business while the other side was pursuing its familiar daily struggle for livelihood: pasturing livestock whenever and wherever possible. As a result a gradual decline in the morale of both the *hacienda* administration and the civil guard set in from the latter part of 1966.

The relative conditions of the two disputing sides by the end of the following year are nicely captured by a subtle change that was taking place in the role of the Personero: while he continued to control the invasion campaign by designating people to 'enter' the *hacienda* in specific places, this no longer meant so much a cat-and-mouse game with the *hacienda caporales*, as the actual allotment of *estancias* [high-altitude shepherd's huts with animal corrals] and surrounding pasture to specific families, who began to settle for that area and protect it not only from *hacienda* personnel but also from fellow villagers. This reinstatement of the authorities of the community for the distribution of means of production cannot be over-estimated, and the fact that these positions were now energetically sought – and successfully gained – by the new independent farmers who were systematically accumulating flocks had the effect of subtly reconstituting the various resonances of 'community'.

Meanwhile, for the owners of Hacienda Tucle the climate was changing. While there remained government sympathy toward reasonably efficient public stock companies like the Ganadero del Centro, which ran the neighbouring Hacienda Laive, nationally famous for its cheese, this was not so for *haciendas* like Tucle. Hobsbawm (1974:141) has suggested that 'Tucle, as its neighbouring estates were frequently forced to note, was somewhat deficient in diplomacy, legal acumen and good management . . .'. And this was undoubtedly true, though it cannot be isolated from a context in which this *hacienda* for over a century had been forced to deal with perpetual peasant resistance. I have shown elsewhere how, time and again, the ability of Hacienda Tucle to institute rational management practices was pre-empted by peasant resistance both of newsworthy moment and in a myriad daily forms (Smith 1989). We have seen too what little success the administration had on the few occasions when it favoured diplomacy over less subtle means. In the case of legal acumen too, we should note the kind of opposition Tucle had in the Huasicanchinos. For the sake of the

territorial survey made by the civil judge, children had been carefully trained in the misnaming of landmarks. On another occasion,
determined to have the army removed from a spot where it could
observe their use of one squatter site as a bridgehead for deep
incursions into *hacienda* land, the Huasicanchinos acquired a
number of army uniforms, dressed themselves as soldiers and, with
the help of a migrant who was an ambulant photographer in
Huancayo, managed to produce photographs for the Huancayo
district judge of 'soldiers' molesting village women. (The army were
instructed to withdraw from the area.)

So it was that by the time the military government of Juan Velasco
replaced President Belaunde at the end of the 1960s, the positions
of the two sides were reversing: as Hacienda Tucle became increasingly decrepit and incapable of carrying out the changes necessary
to make it into a capitalist enterprise, the leadership of the Huasicanchino campaign was falling into the hands of independent
farmers, the rationality of whose enterprises was ever more capital-
istic.

Much of the Huasicanchinos' reconstruction of their experience
of struggle has the ongoing effect of constituting 'the rebellious
peasant' that they are so very conscious of being seen as by 'outsiders'. Yet it is at the moment when the Huasicanchinos' accounts
refer to the effectiveness of their dealings with opposition that the
narrative imperative toward plot and closure is resisted. This is not
just because, in their eyes, the story is as yet unfinished. It is also
because what is being accounted for is not a global history of well-
marshalled forces and decisive battles in a distant past, nor socio-
economic trends of longue durée, but the effectiveness of piecemeal
victories when a major loss is turned into a minor gain, or the tight
band of urgency is loosened for a week or a month, through sleight
of hand or slip of tongue. So what identity the Huasicanchino feels
as a rebellious peasant is not captured so much in the notion
guerrillero (as we saw earlier in an interchange in the general
assembly), as in the *apodo* (nickname) 'Los Zorros' ('The Foxes'),[14]
and many are the stories in which a person *vivo* and with *astucia* is
juxtaposed against others *con ánimo* and with *educación* (the words
lose much in translation: a quick or sharp person possessed
with cunning juxtaposed against those with formal training and
those with just guts: *ánimo* in its sense of valour (see Smith 1975;
1977)).

Conclusion

A relatively successful rebellion by a peasant community in the face of a large ranch pressing forward toward capitalist rationalization would appear to be a perfect case for imagining an idealized peasant culture characterized by its uniformly shared implicit critique of capitalist culture (see, for example, Taussig 1980), or accepting the notion of community in terms of a homogeneous body of people deriving their solidarity from their uniformly shared perception of the world in terms of custom and tradition. In fact, of course, we now have a well-established body of literature on the peasantry that addresses both the importance of socio-economic differentiation among them and the way in which different kinds of peasant communities have arisen through history as a result of their resistance and incorporation into modern nation-states. The evidence here adds a somewhat different angle to this literature.

In the opening of this chapter I noted Eric Wolf's observation that anthropologists tend to endow other cultures with unwarranted homogeneity. Yet more recently a number of writers have described the phenomenology of various peasant people's culture (Marcus and Cushman 1982; Kearney 1996), remarking on the dialogical open-endedness I have stressed here. Their emphasis on the notion 'discourse', however, has led them either to limit the dialogical element to discourse alone, or to expanding the notion of discourse to embrace virtually all forms of social interaction. Far from their understanding discourse to be about struggle, in the example I have presented, they would see the struggle to be over – and only over – discourse itself. Yet such a conclusion can only be patronizing of the people studied, making them appear like dogs fighting over a useless scrap of bone.

Nothing could be further from the case here. Huasicanchino discourse can only be understood in the extent to which it was not an academic discussion about the immaculate conception or the allusions in T. S. Eliot's verse, but about what the participants saw to be the most immediate elements of their livelihoods: the community, the extent of reciprocated aid, ways of possessing land, and so on. I have tried here to begin an enquiry into the way in which the constitution of the meaning of an institution is constructed through intensive negotiation during and within usage – a negotiation inseparably embedded in the praxis of daily life, itself embedded in very real material constraints and imperatives.

The construction of meaning cannot therefore be understood merely by the analysis of discourse alone, even if the term is expanded to include social intercourse more generally.

But I am suggesting something more. I am suggesting that it is not just the known importance of certain institutions and practices to social reproduction that so thoroughly commits people to negotiating over the meanings of these institutions. It occurs also when, during political struggle, negotiation takes place in the face of present threats to that ongoing reproduction. Because of the intensity of discourse during resistance, experience of these times has the power to engrave lasting images into the channels of participants' minds. One only has to talk to people about past moments of collective rebellion and resistance to discover the heightened imagery engendered at those moments of intensive cultural production.

But because so many phenomenological studies of the production of peasant culture remove it from the far broader sociological forces of which it is part, disparaging the plough to focus on the pulpit, dismissing the sword to idolize the word, they are more than a little coy about the political agenda implied by their writings. Yet it would certainly not be through verbal statements that Huasicanchinos would expect to have revealed to them the realities of the state. Ninety-nine times out of a hundred a speech given in Huancayo by a junior minister, a general or a campaigning politician, would have to be sifted through very carefully indeed to find anything of immediate relevance to Huasicanchinos. Nor would Huasicanchinos assume that the state took their verbal expressions seriously. And this reality reaches back into the recordable past. It is within this context that political consciousness must be assessed. In effect it is this that defines the space within which people, whose entire lives are spent in such a situation, put together a social world. It is a space in which hegemonic definitions of the world are simultaneously loaded with the symbols and actuality of terror, which derive from massive power differentials, and yet at the same time are articulated in fragmented and discontinuous form. Under such circumstances the role of local dialogue in negotiating the interpretation of these fragments in order to assess their immediate or long-term relevance to the peasantry becomes an important dimension in the formation of political consciousness. Without such a dimension, 'consciousness' loses any significant creative dynamism.

Aware of the limitations of such a one-dimensional view of consciousness, social and cultural anthropologists have preferred the notion of culture, but they have not thereby found greater precision. Studies of culture tend to be bereft of the critical features of class relations, which cannot be neglected in any contemporary social formation. The failure to integrate cultural studies within class analysis has meant that anthropologists have found great difficulty in relating the local cultural distinctiveness of a group being studied within a larger social formation to the particular class configuration of that social formation. As a result we are deprived of the possibility of seeing cultural production specifically in terms of simultaneous interdependence and opposition at the level of the social formation (not just at the level of the local fieldsite).

This locating of the production of culture within the context of larger societal forces, both for integration and for autonomy, can be seen by condensing the evidence presented above. Local init- iatives in the countryside gave rise to policy responses on the part of the State. Specifically, the Huasicanchinos' immediate and daily grievances, stemming from relationships with Hacienda Tucle in the early 1960s, were met by official statements that a thorough- going land reform was about to go into effect. This gave rise to intense discussion among Huasicanchinos, during which a wide range of possible interpretations of the prevailing situation were exercised. Eventually the Huasicanchinos made what might be called a very forceful political statement: they occupied stretches of disputed land. Promises of reform if they removed themselves then gave rise to further interpretations of reality, various manifest- ations of which we saw in the case material. Eventually, however, they chose to stick with their own 'land reform' in preference to promises of a state-run one at some time in the indefinite future. This led to arrests, to imprisonment, to violence and very real fear on their part: feelings no doubt as emotionally pregnant as a circumcision, a face-scarring or other manifestations of 'cultural specificity'. And these were feelings quite familiar to Huasic- anchinos, as no doubt they are for peasants the world over.

Most of the Huasicanchinos' political expression, then, should not be seen outside the context of these conditions. Their political action and what specific identity they derive from engagement in that action arise precisely from these conditions. Whichever way you look at it, therefore – whether as a political analyst seeking out the coefficients of political mobilization, or as an anthropologist

concerned with the production of culture – the very specificity of
this situation matters. The production and reproduction of culture,
moreover, in this light is an intensely political affair.

I have tried to get at this particular process by showing how
insertion into different sectors of the economy reproduced and even
increased the pre-existing heterogeneity of Huasicanchino enterprises; enterprises, moreover, absorbed increasingly into the bottom
end of a highly volatile commodity economy, and hence drawn
together by a common need for the security deriving from access
to pasture. While at one level it was taken for granted that customs
and practices served agreed-upon goals, at another the heterogeneity of enterprises meant that there was in fact a plasticity in
meaning. So one reason why Huasicanchino political expression
took the form it did was that key institutions remained in place
while transformations in their meaning and practice occurred, at
first as a result of articulation with more dominant systems and
then as a function of internal heterogeneity. It is tempting to
propose that shifts from one meaning – for example, of 'community' – to another correlated perfectly with the sway held by one or
another group when it came to prominence in the leadership of
the campaign. No such correlation exists, and this for at least two
reasons: one, 'leadership' was never hegemonic; and two, meanings
arose not just from the material interests of one or another group,
but from engagement in the debate itself.

Contentiousness has a momentum of its own. With a momentum
all its own, for people with a history like that of the Huasicanchinos,
contentiousness becomes inseparable from the daily coin of
common discourse (for France, see Tilly 1986). As a result, for such
people it becomes inseparable from the production of culture. The
Huasicanchinos were not, *de facto*, a homogeneous mass sharing
common interests. And so, although the historical act of the land
recuperation campaign required performance by 'collective man'
(Gramsci 1971: 348), this acting in unity not only presupposed 'the
attainment of a cultural-social unity through which a multiplicity
of dispersed wills, with heterogeneous aims, are welded together
with a single aim' (ibid.), it required a continuous process of the
intense negotiation of meanings. A process, moreover, in which
the attainment of a cultural unity was never complete, but always
unfinished business throughout the intense periods of resistance.
Among the Huasicanchinos themselves, this meant the intense
constitution and reconstitution of key institutions. In the process,

the words used to refer to them therefore undergo 'changes which are masked by a nominal continuity so that words which seem to have been there for centuries, with continuous general meanings, have come in fact to express radically different or radically variable, yet sometimes hardly noticed, meanings and implications of meaning' (Williams 1988: 17).

What I am proposing is that words referring to key relationships have a rich set of resonances. When (heterogeneous) people get together to resist or rebel, they become energetically committed to negotiating over those resonances. In this sense contentiousness (to return to Tilly's useful word) is both an internal and an external matter. It is this kind of engagement, moreover, which gave to the Huasicanchino resistance a momentum of its own – dare I say, beyond the perceived interests of the group and beyond interests emergent from the long- or short-term economic goals of one or another participant? Until eventually we arrive right up against the existential issues about identity and existence that are the constitutive components of culture itself.

But stressing the importance of this kind of political praxis in the production of culture does not mean that political engagement can be artificially separated from the daily imperatives of social relations of production. In the case of Huasicancha, political mobilization has brought into play existing institutions to serve the purposes of the political struggle, as the land recuperation campaign demonstrates. The institution of 'the community', for example, as well as a myriad subordinate institutions contained within that notion, were essential for both the daily reproduction of Huasicanchino enterprises and for political resistance. The same goes for reciprocal ties between households, and a variety of other relationships. The use of such institutions, in times of political struggle, itself modified the institutions; but it also gave a political dimension to the preservation of those institutions in subsequent periods of quiescence. Community institutions not only served a daily livelihood function: they also became inseparable from the political identity and survival of the participants. Then the campaign was articulated through this ongoing interaction at the level of the expressive meaning of institutions bound up with the 'community'. As a result, political engagement had the effect of modifying the idiom of community and at the same time investing it with contemporary relevance and vitality. Participants had not only negotiated among themselves over the essential meaning and value of key institutions; they had simultaneously asserted them-selves against outsiders intent upon denying their meaning and value by blowing them into oblivion.

One question remains. How are we to fit this kind of everyday and essentially local contentiousness into the bigger stuff of rebellion and revolution? James Scott's (1985, 1986) name is most commonly associated with the expression 'everyday forms of resist-ance'; but Scott feels that the glamour of revolution has misled social analysts, encouraging them to downplay or misread practices that may never get as far as open rebellion, let alone revolution. He is less concerned, then, with understanding the ways in which local resistance might be more broadly organized than he is with suggest-ing simply that daily resistance matters and is too often overlooked. We will turn to Scott's work in more detail in the next chapter, but the evidence we now have might suggest that we should be very wary of singling out for study 'everyday forms of resistance' while turning off our broader historical interest in collective rebellion. By no means all peasant groups have the kind of contentious history of the Huasicanchinos; indeed, theirs is the exception, and we need a fine analytic pen to distinguish between *their* everyday resistance and similar gestures that have quite different political results.

Eric Hobsbawm, for example, referring specifically to the Huasic-anchinos, has pointed out that, '[a] movement which only claims to "recuperate" communal lands illegally alienated may be as revol-utionary in practice as it is legalist in theory. Nor is the line between legalist and revolutionary an easy one to draw' (Hobsbawm 1973: 12–13). Yet both Hobsbawm and Wolf see the kind of rebellion I am talking about as 'self-limiting and, hence, anachronistic' (Wolf 1987: 373). The very elements that give them what potency they possess militate against broader alliances. But, while the structural constraints built in to local forms of resistance are undeniable, this should not obscure the role experience in concerted resistance itself plays in the historical accumulation of a people's consciousness. We turn to these issues in the next chapter; but the point is that, seen in this light, the local focus of political activity and the particularistic character of cultural identity itself need not be a hindrance to the development of class consciousness, but may be an essential contributing factor.[15]

This is not to say that the *experience* so powerfully evident here and so isomorphic with the anthropologist's ethnographic horizons need therefore become the only touchstone for subaltern praxis.

Rather, as I argue at various points throughout this book, our methodological attention needs to shift modes in quite complex ways to grasp different levels of social reality. This is an issue taken up by David Harvey (1995) in his interpretation of Raymond Williams's work, where he addresses precisely the issue of the relationship between the militant particularism of local content-iousness and a broader political programme.

In a manner that recalls what has been discussed here, Williams talks of the 'striking diversity of beliefs' in which the local people he has known in Wales have expressed their autonomy '. . . an ingrained and indestructible yet also changing embodiment of the possibilities of common life' (!989: 322). And Harvey then draws out this point:

> The embeddedness that Williams here wants to celebrate is the ability of human beings, as *social* beings, to perpetuate and nurture in their daily lives and cultural practices the *possibility* of that sense of value that *seeks a commonality in social life even in the face of striking heterogeneity of beliefs*. But the maintenance of such a sense of value depends crucially upon a certain kind of interpersonal relating *that typically occurs in particular places* (1995: 80, i*talics mine*).

Harvey goes on to argue that the move from the kinds of solidarities that can thereby arise in locally knowable communities to the conceptions required for a broader purchase requires a move toward abstraction and critique that may require a qualitatively entirely different kind of intellectual stance.

Notes

1. A very slightly different version of this chapter (Smith 1991a) was originally published in O'Brien and Roseberry, 1991. I am especially grateful to Bill Roseberry, Jay O'Brien, Jane Schneider and Gadi Algazi for their advice and help.
2. ARA refers to the archives of the Agrarian Reform of the Ministry of Agriculture; AC refers to Huasicancha's community archives; FHT to documents found at the *fundo* of Hacienda Tucle; and JT to documents in the Juzgado de Tierra, Huancayo.
3. Membership in the community had legally recognized status. All household members whose head was a *comunero(a)* were themselves members of the community. In 1972 there were only eight households

without community membership. This contrasts sharply with the settlements in the nearby Mantaro Valley (see Long and Roberts 1978, 1984).

4. The Personero was the senior authority in the officially recognized Comunidad Indigena.

5. Elsewhere (Smith 1984) I have discussed the particular characteristics of these reciprocal linkages, referring to them as 'confederations of households'.

6. The interests migrants had in retaining a foothold in the community and the interest residents had in allowing them to do so is best understood in terms of the complex intertwining of their enterprises most visible in the 'confederations of enterprises' (see Note 5) and the dispersal of migrants' animals throughout the flocks of village residents. Government attempts to discourage citywards migration by insisting that full-time residence be a pre-requisite for community membership was interpreted by villagers as an attempt to 'chop the head off the chicken' rather than as a means for reducing local demand on land.

7. The fact is that Huasicanchinos, some of them electricians and junior government clerks, presented themselves to the President in this traditional gear. I am not concerned to interpret how the President might have read this or how the migrants intended him to read it, but simply to stress that such acts inevitably affect the ongoing re-constitution of tradition. The complexity of the issue can be illustrated by the last term – 'time immemorial', – which appears to be a clear reference to tradition but which in Peru at the time had a clear legal resonance, since all land claims using the term 'time immemorial' referred to the registration of Community properties that began in 1919.

8. This 'minor incident' – entirely absent from oral accounts – is significant for our understanding of 'solidarity'. A number of migrants from Huasicancha, now permanent residents of the jungle colony of Satipo, date their departure from this period.

9. Although General Caceres, who led the resistance against Chile, initiated this campaign by referring to it as 'una guerra en pequeña o de guerrillas' (Caceres 1973), the highland fighters were in fact more generally known as *montoneras* rather than *guerrilleros*.

10. The arrest of the elected authorities caught the Huasicanchinos by surprise, and made them extraordinarily suspicious of any outsiders arriving from the direction of Huancayo. All adult males were afraid of being taken for 'undesirable elements', and thus hid in nearby caves and other retreats when outsiders approached. This explains the headline that appeared in Huancayo's newspaper at this time: 'Incomprehensible Community of Huasicancha: Led by Women' (*sic*).

11. I use the term 'independent farmers' because these enterprises contrasted with others among Huasicanchinos in which reciprocal linkages were quite were quite extensive (see Smith 1984, 1989).

12. But see Note 8.

13. There is of course no harm in glossing the Spanish word 'guerrillero' with the English word 'guerrilla' (as I have done earlier). But from the word's entry into English during the Peninsular Wars, it has connoted a rather special kind of fighter. This is present too in its Peruvian usage, but I wish here to draw attention to its proximity in Spanish to the word 'war' (*guerra*) and to the notion that such a person's life is perpetually embedded in that practice and its associated behaviours (as for 'warriors').

14. 'How is the fox? Above all he is alone. He comes. He does his work. And he disappears. Then he is cunning (*tiene astucia*) and he is quick (*vivo*).'

     'And the vixen?'('*Y ¿la hembra?*')

     '. . . worse.' ('. . . *mas mala*').

     Fieldnotes, Huasicancha,. August 1972.

15. The evidence presented in this very microscopic study of a local rebellion has implications too for what Wolf (1969) and Hobsbawm (1973) have to say about the role of leadership, and the role of tradition, in peasant rebellion. This evidence doesn't so much contradict their conclusions – for example, about the role of outside leadership. Rather it casts these observations in a different light. For example, referring to the role of tradition for a (middle) peasant faced with a commercializing society, Wolf (1987: 371) remarks '[H]is is a balancing act.' And much of what we have seen here has to do with negotiating a balancing act, the effect of which is a continuous, dynamic and ever-incomplete constitution and reconstitution of that package of concepts embraced by the notion 'tradition'.

CHAPTER THREE

Secret Agents, Hidden Meanings: Domination and Resistance Re-examined

> Our account will have to deal with [the older] modes of analysis, their insights and their silences. But it is too easy to turn such an argument into a simplistic and self-congratulatory opposition. . . . They were benighted; we know better. We need to pay attention to the arguments themselves, what they were about, how the questions were structured in certain ways, how they allowed certain problems to be discussed and others to be avoided. We can then examine more recent reconsiderations and criticisms in a less presentist light (Roseberry 1993: 320).

Introduction

In an article entitled 'Beyond the agrarian question in Latin America' (1993) William Roseberry refers to various *generations* of scholars, asking how each formulated questions, delimited problems and so on (cf. Abrams 1982: 227ff.). In this chapter I seek a similar shaping of the terrain, but this time around the issue of domination and (rural) resistance, trying also to place my own discussion of these themes (in *Livelihood and resistance* (1989)) amongst the foothills of these various approaches.

Roseberry suggests that in any approach to a social issue we might ask 'What could and could not be talked about?' (1993: 321). What was left out, what could not be seen, or was considered unimportant? Like many people who entered graduate anthropology at the end of the 1960s, I was struck by the gap between the interests of those *academic* social sciences that purported to study the 'Third World' and the kinds of things that seemed to me to be historically important in those parts of the world. Whereas over the past decade ordinary people had been or still were involved in socialist or anticolonial struggles in Cuba, Algeria, Congo, Mozambique, Guinea-Bissau, Angola, Vietnam and so on, I felt that the established generation of anthropologists, sociologists, and people interested in development were pre-eminently concerned with consensus, the way deprived people *adapted* and became socially *integrated*. As I saw it they had spent insufficient time asking how, given their meagre resources, such people might turn the direction of history to their advantage. Though in many places revolution was very much on the agenda and often seemed the only way to achieve any positive change at all, my own particular interest lay in the ways in which relatively powerless people might turn the paths of 'development' in directions of their own choosing. My interest in collective mobilization had particularly to do with finding ways of discovering what the participants themselves thought to be important in this regard. Identifying what *they* saw to be the problems to be addressed seemed to me to be the specifically *anthropological* dimension to the question of rural mobilization.

Then as I turned to rural mobilization, I encountered a small group of left intellectuals who were indeed less interested in adaptation and integration than resistance and rebellion. Yet Roseberry locates very precisely the discomforts I felt with this literature when he notes that an older generation of scholars tended to see peasants as reactors to oppression rather than as protagonists and initiators. 'It was in this movement, in the very manner in which the class analysis was conceived, that we came to understand so poorly 'the manifest ways whereby peasants have continuously engaged their political worlds' (Stern 1987: 9)' (Roseberry, 1993: 336) Indeed, what Roseberry says of 'universal Marxism' (1993: 341) was what I felt about liberal scholarship on 'development' – not only did both of them belittle the particularities of specific historical experiences, both shared in the view that peasants and their politics were locked in a world that sought to hold back the currents of history: words like primordial, traditional, primitive and archaic were common currency. In my research proposal I therefore duly took to task writers who saw the goals – and hence the success or failure of one or another 'peasant movement' – only in their own (as I saw it, ethnocentric) terms. Further, it seemed to me too that, by claiming to know what peasants' political goals should be, we appeared to be saying that we also knew *how* they should mobilize, so I also felt a special need to ask how peasants went about mobilizing.

So I felt that the kind of work anthropologists might do in local ethnographies could put a hole in the side of these over-armed galleons, but clearly these issues and questions arose from certain assumptions I had: about how the world worked; about priorities – what I thought to be important and requiring study and what less so; what I thought it appropriate for me to do (as a leftist, as an anthropologist, as a white male foreigner in Peru and a non-local, non-peasant in the central Andes) and so on. They reflected what I saw my intervention in particular intellectual and political questions to be, as well as how I situated myself *vis à vis* an older generation. In short, we see here at least some of the myopia I suffered.

But just as this selective process occurred in the past, so it occurs today. The intellectual images and political forces at the end of the century have highlighted a quite different set of social phenomena from those that faced an earlier generation. So what is different about the intellectual and political currents that *they* face, compared with those I have just described? And what can and cannot be talked about within *their* terms of reference? One principal characteristic of this work is its broad cross-disciplinary self-reflection. Shifts in processes of capitalist reproduction have produced important reflections on the extent to which both economic and social institutions have become so 'flexible' as to be indistinguishable from one another – churches becoming banks, banks becoming houses of worship; shifts from a Taylorist preoccupation with factory regimes to much more general techniques for the regulation of a wider arena of space, giving rise to neo-modernist concerns with 'good' or 'bad' regions (see Chapter 5); hitherto narrowly legal questions of citizenship running over from issues of narrow liberal 'freedoms' into issues of self-expression, thence to issues of social identity, thence to culture (see Chapter 6). As a result recent scholars have sought to advance over an older generation by attempting not so much to cross disciplinary barriers as to dissolve them, especially in the two areas that were my original driving interest – political movements and development (Ferguson 1990; Sachs 1992; Crush 1995; Escobar1995; Peet and Watts 1996).

We see this especially where work on domination and resistance has sought solutions in social philosophies that focus on the relationship between individual and collectivity in terms of *the characteristics of people's subjectivity* and how this might be appropriately studied. Intellectual images of the world as shifting, flexible, plastic, possibly as chaos, suggest that, as the concerns of social movements have become so diffuse, their targets and goals so moving, so the interest component of the movement – how the movement serves the interests of particular social actors: women, peasants, and so on – becomes less sociologically important than the way participation gives rise to personal expression and self-reflection – provides the possibilities to express and hence constitute one's identity – *as a woman, as a peasant.* Social movements then should be understood *first and foremost* in terms of the way they form social subjects (Pizzorno 1978; Melucci 1980, 1989, 1996; Cohen 1985; Slater 1985; Escobar and Alvarez 1992; Morris and Mueller 1992). It is this emphasis that makes it appropriate to refer to such studies as 'expressivist'.[1] If we were to ask of such expressivists what they saw to be the problems of older approaches, one answer would be that for an older generation social revolution was a master concept; its promise shaped the way they formulated problems. The forging of a national revolutionary bloc effectively positioned subaltern political actors along a spectrum of potential allies and enemies (if not part of the solution, then definitely a problem). From the expressivist perspective, moreover, the vital role of proletarians and peasants in this imposed history appears to be arbitrarily assigned.

By contrast the expressivist refusal of any *a priori* assumptions about either the participants or the political goals of a movement powerfully shapes the way they formulate the problematic of domination and resistance. As subjects become plastic and goals keep shifting, so interests and strategies must perforce themselves provide only distorting insights for understanding political movements. Strategies can no longer be understood as prior to the way strategizers are culturally constituted. Yet, once purposes and goals become so open-ended, speculations about strategies and interests become profoundly problematic, so that an interest in the *forming* of social subjects through their collective *expression* becomes not just a priority – it is the only recourse available for the 'understanding' of a movement.

Moreover, this sense contemporary theorists have that all that is solid melts into air – their stress on the mobility of capital and of people, which leads to the reshaping of socio-economic institutions and large cohorts of politically and economically *dis*placed persons, shapes older questions in new ways. Once the slipperiness of this mobility is taken into account, issues addressed in earlier work – about the limitations of localized resistance (especially in respect to rural peoples) and sectoral fragmentation (especially in respect to urban workers and small-scale entrepreneur/workers), are now addressed differently. Students of domination and resistance find themselves having to rethink both the locus of power and the way power manifests itself in such a world. It is hardly surprising, then, that recent writers accuse their forebears of the hypostatization of power. Landlords and capitalists had it and used it to influence the direction of the state; peasants and workers did not, and as a result were dominated and exploited. Seeing the social world in these terms an older generation sought to elucidate the structured relationships between the one and the other. Seen from an express-ivist point of view all too often dominators' and subalterns' conduct was then read off in terms of *instrumental action* to achieve *preconceived goals*. These are important concerns; yet we need to take Roseberry's caution at the outset of this chapter quite seriously: intellectuals' preoccupation with originality and thence a new 'fix' encourages a highly selective version of history.

Thus, as I have argued earlier, the issue of *structured* relationships may be misplaced. Crucial to at least the more sophisticated of the older views was not so much the image of society as a structure, but rather an understanding of society in historical terms that produced an image of social *reproduction* and social *transformation* (see Smith 1979b). It is with *this* metaphor that we can grasp rather better why an older generation, seeing social actors caught in particular *relationships* and hence a certain logic of reproduction, wished to understand the physics of each particular: not just the agrarian question or peasant rebellions then, but the web of forces and counterforces of which they were part. And classes *are* relation-ships before they are groups to be identified through sociological statistics. 'Class' was not just the focus of attention because Mao or Ho Chi Minh employed the term, but because it was *crucially* tied up with the way collectivities of people were inserted into relations of production and reproduction. It is not so much, then, that landlords and capitalists have disappeared, but rather that, through this world of mobility and political obscurity, the complexities of power have become more problematic. Let me try therefore to strip off some of the dust and grime that has accumulated on some older *oeuvres* to see if we can thereby see their freshness and originality, not all of which need be lost to us as we face the problems and difficulties of our contemporary political world.

'Peasants' and Collective Resistance

Roseberry's discussion, of course, deals with a different literature to the one that concerns me, though in one important respect the literature overlaps, for the agrarian question in Latin America has very often been a question about the peasantry. Yet why, as resistance and rebellion became of interest to anthropologists, was it nearly always talked about in terms of peasants?

An obvious answer is that people who might reasonably be described as 'peasants' were so numerically predominant in the countries where anthropologists tended to study – from China, to India to 'Latin' America. This was the point made by one of the most outspoken and best-known of the radical anthropologists of the 1960s, Kathleen Gough (1967). At that time this talk of 'peasants' was itself by no means universally accepted by anthropologists. It reflected the impact of political economy in anthropology, which stressed the need to understand all people *from the beginning* as being part of wider social, economic and political fields. The term 'peasant' reflected this characteristic as other terms, especially bands and tribes did not, and alongside Kroeber's (1948 [1923]) and Redfield's (1940) more culturalist understanding of peasants living in part-societies and part-cultures came Polanyi's (1968) discussion of complex forms of *social* exchange and Firth's (1958) discussion of the interface in peasant societies between 'social organization' and 'market relations', making peasants characteristically both linked to markets and yet engaged in large areas of livelihood unmediated by such relationships. Meanwhile Wolf and Mintz were undertaking careful studies of rural people whose collective forms emerged from changing historical struggles across fields of power within different states (Wolf and Mintz 1957; Mintz 1973; Wolf 1955, 1956). In 1972 the English translation of the important Polish sociologist Boguslov Galeski (1972) appeared, followed a year later by the first issue of the *Journal of Peasant Studies*, with seminal articles by Hobsbawm, Shanin, Alavi, and Mintz. The influence of the idea of class was extremely broad and undogmatic. It mostly meant that these people wished to refer simultaneously to an element of autonomy *and* an element of dependence; likewise they saw this relationship between peasants and the wider society as something that had to be understood *historically*.[2] These particular uses of the notion 'peasant' were in fact remarkably *un*structuralist, and were roundly criticized for their failure in this regard (see Ennew, Hirst and Tribe 1977).

If you were an anthropologist whose first interest was 'popular movements', 'resistance to authority' and so on, you might well have found yourself already living with these kinds of people when these questions arose. On the other hand, if you were an anthropologist whose original interest had been less politically motivated and you were simply interested in a particular group of people in, say southern India or Central America, political currents in those places in the 1960s might well have encouraged you to shift from an understanding of these people in terms of their cultural distinct-iveness and varying degrees of integration into 'modern' society to an understanding of their political *potentiality* – what for them might be politically possible.[3]

But, as Chapter 1 makes clear, for many on the left peasants as political actors came late on the scene, and the issue became one of strategy. Faced with a recalcitrant situation and/or opponent, members of the proletariat or 'working class' (key figures in the politics of engaged social enquiry partly for the reasons discussed in Chapter 1) have historically chosen the collective strategy of withdrawing their labour from the factory (or occupying it). In short, they strike. In so far as this had been a fairly successful collective strategy, it seemed reasonable to ask what might be the peasant equivalent? Withdrawing labour was not always an altern-ative, though occupation often was (Hobsbawm 1974; Martinez-Alier 1977). In any event it was this kind of question that drove enquiries into peasant forms of collective resistance and rebellion. It is as misleading to assert that writers such as Hobsbawm (1959), Wolf (1969) or Worsley (1970 [1957]) were concerned with peasant politics only in so far as it related to revolutions, as it would be to say the same thing of writers in the urban context who devoted their attention to the way in which minor industrial skirmishes could turn into strikes, and one-site strikes escalate from limited local demands to a wider set of participants and a broader set of *social* issues: health, safety, decision-making, working hours and so on. Domination and resistance then, for anthropologists, was largely a question of the forms of dominating *peasants* and their forms of resistance.

How do Roseberry's guidelines help us to reflect on the para-meters of such studies? First, what was or was not asked in studies such as Hobsbawm's (1959, 1969, 1973, 1974) or Wolf's (1969)?[4]

We might begin by asking not what they left out, but what the put in. First, they concerned themselves with *the kind of movements* that peasants got involved in. This is especially clear in Hobsbawm's book, *Primitive rebels* (1959), which is organized along these lines – from the more spontaneous, smaller-scale (in terms of goals and size) and less needing of organizational resources, to their opposites. He was concerned too with the kind of people who might become leaders, and what kinds of alliances might be open to various kinds of movements. Second, they concerned themselves with *the kind of peasants* who got involved in movements – as well, of course, as the two combined: what kinds of peasants got involved in what kinds of movements. What kinds of people might become leaders, or bridges between movements, and so on?

Hidden in this question is the issue of *how* we might talk about 'What kind of peasant?' In answering this question these studies tended to be broadly 'objectivist': that is to say the question was answered in terms of rather objective criteria. These objective criteria were expressed *in terms of relationships*. We have to be careful to avoid stopping at the short-hand designations used by writers – Lenin's (1974) rich peasants, or Wolf's middle peasants – and thereby not noticing the fact that in the texts themselves these are always situated in terms of specific social relationships in the overall social formation. Wolf, for example, had already alerted us to this in his earlier book *Peasants* (1966), in which he characterized in some detail the features of these kinds of relationship, as he had also described them in *Sons of the shaking earth* (1959).

By 'objectivist' I also mean that, in Roseberry's words, 'theirs was a question posed *about* the peasantry, not necessarily *of* or *by* the peasantry'. Yet I think we should recognize that this was less an oversight on their part, than an extension of their understanding of what they saw their intervention in particular intellectual and political questions to be. I'm not sure, for example, that they would arrogate to themselves the solution of writing peasant histories 'from below'. It does not follow that, because they didn't do 'interpretative anthropology', they were not ultimately interested in issues of subjectivity (see for example Hobsbawm 1971). Rather, the issue is where they placed subjectivity in the order of things. Wolf, for example, doesn't just make a set of correlations between peasants on the periphery of state control and their involvement in rebellion; he speculates as to why this might be so. Hobsbawm doesn't just talk about the role of what he calls 'social banditry' in forms of

political resistance among peasants, he links it to Robin Hood stories
that abound among peasant groups (see also Smith 1977).

Can these be construed as attempts to understand 'the manifest
ways whereby peasants have continuously engaged their political
worlds' (Stern 1987:9), or attempts to get at the kinds of questions
peasants themselves might want to address? – Well, yes and no. –
On the minus side, clearly this is a limited interest in peasant
subjectivity, reluctant to go much beyond speculating about hypo-
thetical peasant interests: the reasons why certain kinds of peasants
might do x or y, for example. On the other hand it has to be said
that there is something comfortingly fuzzy and disturbingly elusive
about 'the manifest ways whereby peasants have continuously
engaged their political worlds'. So, if we are to question the way in
which 'objectivist' accounts wish to categorize 'kinds of peasants' –
based on the sets of relationships required for their social reproduction – surely we should be equally hard-nosed and ask for greater
precision about the levels of social reality being referred to by
'engaging a political world'.

And if this sounds a little unfair – an overly scientist kind of
critique from the side of 'objectivism' – then it helps make the
point that different priorities prevail, generating different *kinds* of
questions. We see this especially clearly when we explore the relative
weight given to grand generalizing statements with universal
ambition and 'a historical materialism that sees the analysis of
specific historical conjunctures as a necessary starting point for
political and economic analysis' (ibid.: 341), because though people
such as Hobsbawm and Wolf do lie in the second camp – their
starting-point, as a social historian and as an ethnographically-
inspired anthropologist, is with specific conjunctures – nevertheless
this should not obscure their comparative ambitions. Both *Primitive
rebels* and *Peasant wars* have little meaning except in their broader-
than-local ambition. True, at the time they were written, the idea
that a socialist project could address problems faced by the rural
poor, though much debated, was not regarded as arrogant, utopian
or simply not worth thinking about. It is hard to believe that this is
a project that should now be abandoned; rather than burying the
idea, we need to interrogate it, the better to empower it.

For attitudes such as these did have limitations, and I shall
turn in a moment to people whose work has been motivated by a
desire to supersede them. But in doing so, it would be a mistake to
think that people like Wolf, Hobsbawm, Worsley and Gough were

unaware of more 'subjectivist' approaches to domination and resistance. Theirs was a conscious sense of political urgency no less pressing than our own today, and they chose their own priorities accordingly. Much in evidence were studies more concerned with the mind, though seldom tied to a rigorous understanding of specific social formations. Those who were especially interested in 'the peasant view of the world' were less likely to be university academics than party cadres or development fieldworkers, while those who were university academics, especially Marxist 'critical theorists', were more interested in the way domination (and certain forms of resistance) influenced the formation of subjectivities in the West than they were interested in peasants and rebellion (see, for example, Marcuse 1964, 1969). The first current reminds us that evoking folk priorities in rural areas in the 1960s and 1970s was far less influenced by a rigorous and historically informed Marxism than by highly selective readings of Mao, Che and Cabral. 'Speak bitterness' sessions and similar exercises to encourage the less articulate and less powerful villagers to come forward in public meetings were seen to produce a fuller range of participation as a necessary preliminary that would aid in the subsequent acceptance of policy applications, be they 'revolutionary socialist' or 'liberal developmental'. It was this that popularized the work of Paolo Freire and Ivan Illich, and its expressivist dimension is neatly reflected in the terms then used to describe it in South America: *concienciación* and *capacitación*. We come still closer to present concerns when we note that, in a subsequent development, all this became married to interest in appropriate technologies popularized in the West, but by no means discovered, by Schumacher's (1974) *Small is beautiful*.

It is only therefore through a highly selective reading either of 'Marxism' or of anthropologists' interests in peasants that we could conclude that nobody was formulating problems and questions so as to 'learn from the locals'.[5] What *is* noteworthy about these earlier interests in *expression* is first, that *their* priorities led them to sever the study or encouragement of local expression from careful analysis of prevailing social relationships and material conditions, and second that there seemed to be a sense in which the enthusiasm, expression and performance seemed almost to require the idea of a radical break with the past, and a kind of historical innocence. That German and French ethnologists, for example, just a century earlier had been employed by the state to use very similar methods for recording local folklore for the purpose of making laws and generating state-istics would have come as something of a surprise to them (Linke 1990). It would be a shame to repeat the mistake.

Questions By and For the Peasantry

It was not these more subjective-oriented writings on peasants and resistance that have been influential in anthropology, however, but the more objectivist studies. I will discuss here two especially influential attempts to address some of the limitations in these studies, arguing that each of them has done so by use of two key images: the first, the notion of agency or its less active variant, autonomy, and the second, an image of society in terms of what can be seen and what is obscure.

The first of these attempts was James Scott's (1985, 1986; see also 1976). His use of the notion of 'everyday forms of resistance' was to provide a corrective to studies of resistance and rebellion that had tended to focus only on peasants' participation in major social and political upheavals. Peasant involvement in such historically visible movements as Andalusian anarchism or the Mexican or Chinese revolution obscured other forms – smaller, more localized, of which *the* most 'local' would be everyday, even individual, expressions of resistance. The effect, it was said, was to give us too sharp a distinction: peasants were either politically active in so far as they swept across the landscape like wind across the wheat; or they remained docile and obedient in their huts and fields.

The second response, that of Subaltern Studies in India, took very seriously Roseberry's question about what could and could not be talked about in pre-existing intellectual paradigms, and answered by attempting to find means for uncovering the subaltern subjectivities that had never been placed at centre-stage in an earlier historiography. This, then, was not a response directed so much at people like Barrington Moore, Hobsbawm or Wolf, but rather at the conservatism of colonial and post-colonial historiography. Yet the tack it took did constitute a highly productive rethinking of popular resistance. Subaltern studies (Guha 1981–7), was closely analogous in its sentiments and goals to left criticism across a broader map, within historiography. It shared with the early *Annalistes* in France (Braudel 1958) and the later Popular History Group in Britain (Samuel 1981), a desire to encourage an eclectic set of approaches not just confined to historians, but extending throughout the social sciences,[6] and it shared with Hobsbawm and the New Left historians a desire to counter the hegemony of elitist history. Nevertheless, because the group wished to write the history of and on behalf of those who had been excluded from the elitist historiography of India – a history of the politics of the people – their work was especially concerned up with popular *resistance*, and hence has become a significant position superseding earlier studies of resistance.

James Scott took the central image for his *Moral economy* book from Tawney's suggestion that a peasant could be fruitfully seen in terms of 'a man standing permanently up to the neck in water, so that even a ripple is sufficient to drown him' (Scott 1976: 1). Scott suggested in this early study that the relationship between share-croppers and traditional landlords could be understood in these terms. So too could the peasant eruptions that arose from time to time. For peasants and traditional landlords shared in a moral economy, he proposed, one in which the landlord maximized his exploitation of the peasantry in the good years, and was then relied upon to reach into his storehouses in an act of paternal generosity to help out in the bad.

One effect of increasing commercialization in Southeast Asian countries was that many local landlords began to invest in urban commercial ventures, and even to move into the cities. In the years of good harvest, peasant rents could be drawn off for investment in these ventures. But what happened in the bad years? – A conflict arose in what constituted moral behaviour. For the peasants, the patron should be on hand to bail them out. For the landlord, this was hopelessly old-fashioned and inefficient. How could he simply withdraw investments in his new ventures, at the whim of nature's dealings with the crops? Indeed, we might even think here of two competing cycles: the good and bad years of harvest and the ups and downs of Southeast Asian capitalism, a not unimpressive roller-coaster. In any event, here was the mix that would make for resistance. In his second book, Scott developed the idea of more persistent, humdrum, but eventually very telling, forms of daily, weekly, yearly resistance: not just a shift from the great mobilizations of history to the local peasant outbreak, but from outbreaks that warranted a newspaper item, to those that slipped unnoticed past the chroniclers: desertion from a conscript army, dropping a wooden clog into a machine, absconding with bits and pieces from the workshop, and so on.

There are reasons why it is not easy to be so precise about Subaltern Studies, for we are not just turning from one author to a number of authors; we are also turning to a group that wish to 'let all the flowers bloom and we don't mind even the weeds' (Guha 1988: 43). Even so, while it may be unhelpful to encapsulate a body of writing that was heterogeneous from the outset and has moved in diverse directions since,[7] we can get at a couple of underlying principles. The first is that, besides the arena of elite and middle-class politics in India that have been written about by conventional historians using the idioms of Western historiography, these writers insisted that there existed (and exists?) another domain – 'This was an *autonomous* domain' (ibid.: 40) – that had its own idioms and its own momentum, and should be understood in those terms. We are reminded strongly here of a very similar imagery in Thompson's and Williams's understanding of 'working-class culture' discussed in Chapter 1. A major assertion of the subaltern studies group, though, is that these movements played a significant part in producing contemporary Indian society. These weren't just peripheral and quaint currents that could be tapped into at will, by superior nationalist and anti-colonialist elites when they needed some selective traditions. And the failure to recognize this is not *just* a problem of an elitist historiography, it is also wrapped up in a much more profound *'historical failure of the nation to come to its own'* (ibid.).[8] This relatively autonomous arena had certain distinctive characteristics.

> Popular mobilization in the colonial period was realized in its most comprehensive form in peasant uprisings . . . the figure of mobilization derived directly from the paradigm of peasant insurgency.
>
> The ideology operative in this domain, taken as a whole, reflected the diversity of its social composition with the outlook of its leading elements dominating that of the others in any particular time and within any particular event. However, in spite of such diversity one of its invariant features was a notion of resistance to elite domination (ibid. 43).

So the first feature to be noted for the subaltern studies way of approaching peasant resistance is that it has to be understood in terms appropriate to the relatively *separate sphere* of peasant life that reproduced itself parallel to the world of the colonial classes. But what made this sphere so essentially different from that of the

Indian bourgeoisie? The experience of exploitation and of inferiority in power relationships. So the second feature of subaltern studies is the understanding that, in the process of social reproduction, the two spheres cannot be hermetically sealed off from one another. Their studies, while respecting the *différence* of subordinated people, nevertheless refuse to extract that subjectivity from the wider fields that produced it; and these fields are understood in terms of social relations of production, studied for their historical and regional specificities.

These two kinds of studies, then, those of James Scott and the various people who have used his notion of 'everyday forms of resistance' (see, for example, Kerkvliet and Scott 1986), and those of the Subaltern Studies group (see Guha 1981–7) advance on 'objectivist' approaches by employing two key elements, autonomous agency and historical obscurity, though they deal with each quite differently.

With Scott we find a sense of agency that is inseparable from his sense of individual choice, while for subaltern studies writers we find less individual agency, more an understanding of society in terms of spheres of relatively autonomous social relationships and appended cultural constructions. Both advocate a kind of social phenomenology for the understanding of the world, but the phenomena they extract for interpretation are quite different: the one *an acting agent*, the other *a socio-cultural sphere with an important degree of autonomy*.

Agency, which refers in part (but only in part) to the ability to act freely, is not in this sense far removed from autonomy. (Though it carries with it also the sense of historical praxis: not just freedom, but the ability to impose one's will on the historical process.) Yet the picture of society that attracts Scott to the notion of agency is one peopled by *strategizing individuals*, weaving self-gain into social resistance; while the picture of society that calls on the idea of autonomy in Subaltern Studies refers to *whole movements of people* and the cultural constructions that go along with them. Thompson famously (1978a) employed 'agency' to attack French marxists' (and their British disciples') use of structural determination (see especially Althusser and Balibar 1970). Yet agency did not then emerge unshackled from the very real constraints of the pervasively class-infused society of late-eighteenth-century England. The *making* of working-class culture was a struggle over spaces of collective autonomy in which agency could take effect. Even though I don't have the stylistic faculties of an E. P. Thompson, surely the image of society being drawn here is clear, and draws our attention not to Scott but to the Subaltern Studies historians.

True, for Scott the primary colour is agency – he sees his advance on older approaches to be associated with his particular pheno-menology (1976) – but it is a phenomenology that is profoundly interest-based, extrapolating from notions of (individually grounded) choices and strategies. We can see this in the way a political act is explained to us. Take the all-but-submerged peasant, who despite his discomfort and (one can't help noticing) relative disadvantage and powerlessness, up to his neck in water, manages to *act*. Ultimately, it is because this individual peasant makes choices, weighs odds, sorts out goals and so on, that we begin to understand his resort to rebellion/resistance. We do not have to disagree with Scott, or to belittle the importance of his contribution to our understanding of peasants, to recognize this particular form of explanation.

Moreover, this is important, because it says something about the way Scott seems to understand how social subjects are formed through the crucible of history, an understanding that seems to me to be profoundly at odds with Thompson's (and, as we shall see, with the Subaltern Studies group). Throughout Scott's work protagonists produce tactics in a field of freedom, *prior to* the political acts themselves, and though the accumulation of these everyday acts subsequently contributes to the way they engage further in tactics, the history of political engagement is not itself profoundly written into our understanding of the forming of social subjects.

Take for example, the case of pilfering. Scott works through a number of what I would call 'rationalistic' or 'games theoretic' arguments in an attempt to find a means for assessing whether pilfering is merely an act of egoistic self-interest, or whether it is a conscious act of resistance – a 'Got you there, mate!' gesture. Rightly of course, Scott recognizes that no answer can be found without entering, through one door or another, into the subjective inter-pretations of the actor. The door he chooses is the one that imputes certain possible strategies to the actors. But we need to know quite a lot about the strictures of social relations of production through history, before we can say much about the situation the actor faces (let alone the subjectivity he or she brings to it). Maxine Berg *et al.* (1983), for example, talk of the institution of 'long pay' in small-scale manufacturing in Britain in the eighteenth century. Here, in lieu of cash or its equivalent, straitened small owners gave their workers 'an interest' in the business, to be collected at some unspecified time in the future. Owners could of course shorten or lengthen the pay, i.e.: they could reduce the workers' interest in the business by paying them some of what we would call their arrears. Workers, on the other hand, were prone to 'actualize' their interests in the business – by taking some of its produce home. Pilfering? Resistance? The point is not whether or not we can answer these questions, but rather the kind of historical processes within which we can begin to see them.[9]

For it may be that, with more insight into these historical processes, we are able to distinguish *resistance* (Scott) from *misrecognition* (Bourdieu and Passeron). In Chapter 1, we saw Lüdtke referring to factory indiscipline neither in terms of resistance nor accommodation, but rather in terms of *eigensinn*, a stubborn assertion of personal autonomy, while Burawoy (1985), talking of what appear to be forms of everyday resistance through the go-slow shopfloor tactics of workers in mass-production factories argues strongly, and in my view convincingly, that in so far as such tactics act to reproduce a sense of 'Got you there, mate' while allowing the work process to continue relatively uninterrupted, they actually *reinforce* the system of regulation. A similar point is made by Willis (1977), in his study of the 'resistance' of working-class 'lads' in school. Increasingly in the literature everyday forms of resistance are found everywhere. Rarely are they situated within careful analyses of historical processes of social reproduction, and often authors such as Willis or Burawoy are mistakenly cited as supporting evidence. Yet the findings of these authors oblige us to examine much more thoroughly the political effects of everyday forms of resistance. It could be that factory and school settings are very different environments for the working out of everyday forms of resistance than Scott's peasant villages – far more like the kinds of 'Got you there, mate' conduct found in the institutions that Goffman refers to in *Asylums* (1977). But, if so, the differences need to be explored more thoroughly: what makes 'Got you there, mate' conduct *effective as resistance* in a peasant village, but only evidence of misrecognition of how power works in the case of more strictly institutional settings? (Bourdieu and J.-C. Passeron 1977: xiii).

Dipankar Gupta goes so far as to suggest that the 'misrecognition' is of a quite different kind, going in entirely the opposite direction.

Beginning a chapter on 'Routine repression: weapons of the strong' with an epigram from Lord Cornwallis – 'Every native Hindustan, I verily believe is corrupt' – Gupta (1997a: 115) suggests that Scott has been taken in by dominant groups' insistence that petty theft demonstrates underlying insubordination, and their resulting tendency to exaggerate the extent of such misdemeanours.

> Scott is . . . forced to concede that the actual instances of theft are very few and accounts of them are vastly exaggerated (1985: 256). There are only three motor-cycle thefts in twelve years (ibid. 266), and . . . even if one were to go by the accounts of the rich, the total amount of paddy stolen is only about one-hundredth of the paddy harvested (ibid. 268). This immediately gives us the idea of the utterly low incidence of theft in the villages and how disproportionately the rich exaggerate these crimes . . . And yet Scott succumbs to these exaggerated versions which is why he can dignify such petty thefts as subaltern forms of resistance that make 'shambles' of official policy (ibid. 35)

Agency then, becomes only agency in the liberal sense of the word, not in the sense of historical praxis. Let me turn now to the second body of writing. Subaltern studies scholars are especially interested in identifying the specificity of historical processes, which they wish to study within the *autonomous arena* of popular politics. While their language comes closer to that of Gramsci, the spirit of their work is very close indeed to Thompson's: though the arena they wish to study is vastly larger, more complex, and heterogeneous than was Thompson's. Here the second feature that I have identified as an advance on older studies becomes important. What is obscure and what is manifest? Of course the argument of the 'everyday forms school' has been that we have too often focused on what is manifest – the big rebellions that get into the newspapers and history books – and that this obscures more mundane forms of resistance. The left, if anything, is more to be castigated here than the elite historians, who never much cared for peasant revolutionaries in the first place. But the subaltern studies group find the process of obscuring coming from an entirely different direction: elites who either denied the importance of mass mobilizations, or entirely misread them. 'They have come together in an effort to recover the experience, the distinctive cultures, traditions, identities and active historical practice of subaltern groups in a wide variety of settings . . . which have been lost or hidden by the action of elite historiography' (O'Hanlon 1988: 195).

How does one bring to light what has been obscured? The remedy is different in each case. We have already indicated how Scott's answer would go: what has been obscured are the smaller resistances to domination and, in these early two books, the issue of scale becomes crucial. It is by focusing on smaller units and daily concerns that we begin to see how this kind of resistance occurs. But what of the Subaltern Group? To begin with, 'the subaltern' have not been obscured because of their 'silenced voices' – their failure to articulate or act. Rather their history has not been written because of elite historians' failure to recognize and interpret the idioms they use to express themselves. Rather than peasant expression being seen in such dismissive terms as atavistic communalism, or custom-bound tribalism, they might more sensitively be seen in terms of the highly dynamic social relations and institutions that arise in the context of their exploitation and subordination.

So this is one dimension of the obscure and the manifest for the subalternists. A second is that as one reads the various contributions to the unfolding collections of essays, it is hard to avoid the sense that the whole complex process of social reproduction itself, at its various levels (which might be termed, for example, the social, the political, the cultural and so on) needs unearthing. Making it manifest is part of the ground-clearing operation that many subaltern studies writers (but not all) use as a preliminary to their focus on the level of *collective expression*. Once again, one is reminded here of Thompson's example in *The making of the English working class*, in which 'culture' and 'agency' arise always out of a thorough characterization of prevailing social relationships and institutions, understood historically. This is not to suggest that the wide variety of approaches represented by the Subaltern Studies group can be understood as 'following from' Thompson, but rather to stress the continuities in the two.

Yet anthropologists are left with an uneasy sense that we have been here before: that 'autonomy' comes too close to 'cultural coherence' and that subalternist historians' admirable eclecticism *vis-à-vis* the social sciences has led them to read literature on ethnicity and stratification that has long been under criticism from within the social sciences themselves. Not only were the dialogics among colonized subalterns uneven, often internally incoherent, and disputatious; they also inevitably reproduced the echoes and shadows of colonial domination (Sarkar 1998). This in turn raises an awkward 'culturogenesis' question: whence comes subaltern alterity? Dipankar Gupta has suggested that many subalternists, especially Guha himself, have been prone to a kind of Hegelian idealism, in which the question can be answered 'in terms of what culture allows and not in terms of what the structure forecloses' (1985: 10). By restoring agency to subordinated groups (against elite historiography's image of passivity or atavism), the subaltern group run the risk of needing to discover their autonomy in some *cultural space*, as though the social, political and economic dependence inherent in class relations might somehow leave the 'estate' of culture (in the village or religious community?) relatively untouched. When 'culture' is thus elevated it can thereby be blamed too; the failure of movements can be seen to reside in their cultural shortcomings, a conclusion oddly similar to older modernization theories *vis-à-vis* 'development'.

As I have said, the subaltern studies group started out as a heterogeneous bunch, far from being, or wanting to be taken as, 'a school of thought', and over time, even amidst their heterogeneity, they have, overall, shifted their views – mostly away from older remnants of (liberal) progressivism, and away from measures of peasant resistance against the litmus of 'class consciousness'. Release from these kinds of evolutionism leaves the door open for a much richer understanding of the multiple ways in which collective subjectivities take on their form, through insertions into systems of power and appropriation on the one hand, and into circuits of social reproduction having (a greater or lesser degree of) autonomy from those systems and hence alterity and potential resistance.

Local Conjunctures

If we use Roseberry's set of questions as a framework it becomes apparent that 'the manifest ways whereby peasants have contin-uously engaged their political worlds' is now understood in a more catholic way, to include a wider understanding of their actions in terms of *resistance*. But this is not just a question of range, but of vision. The kind of social phenomena these authors 'see', the kinds of metaphors and devices they use, generate quite different images of the social world – both from those of Hobsbawm and Wolf and also within their own group. I have suggested that this comes sharply into focus when we note the different ways in which Scott and his followers have tried to shift from 'questions posed *about* the peasantry' towards those put *by* the peasantry, and the ways in which the Subaltern Studies historians have made such a shift.

Referring to Scott, Roseberry addresses a different dimension of what can and cannot be talked about within his particular approach, noting that Scott's work seems 'sociologically and historically empty' (Roseberry 1993: 359). As we have seen, Roseberry calls instead for 'a historical materialism that sees the analysis of *specific historical conjunctures* as a necessary starting point for political and economic analysis' (ibid.), and he cites two examples of this kind of approach, Jeffrey Gould's *To lead as equals* (1990) and my *Livelihood and resistance: peasants and the politics of land in Peru* (1989). The question is, however: how did the priorities in that 1989 study configure what could or could not be talked about? What did *it* shunt off to the margins?

Livelihood and resistance, as the title suggests, was an attempt to explore the relationship between different kinds of livelihood[10] and different forms of resistance – to make economic anthropology more thoroughly political and to insist that an anthropology that focused on political expression embed that expression in the awful imperatives of making a living. I was temperamentally attracted to the *cultural* element of the student 'revolutions' of that time, a sentiment that showed impatience with the dry economism and sheer practicality of the postwar generation (the Second World War, of course), the men in grey-flannel suits, but I was aware of the lure of this way of thinking to one like myself and the 'economics' I saw as a corrective. When I went to the field the shirt I wore had Che emblazoned on it and the hat I wore (literally!) 'A Mao Cap', but the tools I carried in my pocket were shaped by Hobsbawm, Barrington Moore and Wolf. Eric Hobsbawm was the person who suggested the fieldsite and, as I have said, Eric Wolf's *Peasant Wars* encapsulated my own political priorities, bucking a professional bias in anthropology, as I saw it, to avoid forthright engagement with the radical political currents that swept through 'the Third World'.

I wanted to try to understand social relations through the interaction of *structure, experience* and *practice*. Each of these translated into a set of questions for ethnography. *Structure* I saw as the ties that bind people (to use Gerald Sider's (1984) evocative expression) in the pursuit of a livelihood: the conditions that unfold as sets of social relationships work themselves out. *This* was the particular way I wanted to 'see' social relationships – *in these terms*; an

intentional exercise and one that I felt ran against the common-
sense fieldwork experience. I will try to make this clearer. The
supervisor of my MA thesis, for example, would have had no
difficulty with the expression, 'the conditions that unfold as sets
of social relationships work themselves out', but he would have seen
them much more in the way that James Scott sees social relationships. The *conditions* that would have concerned him, would have
been closely tied to the way in which actors make strategic decisions
(Bailey 1969). I was quite aware of this dimension. Indeed, I think
it is hard for most people who have done fieldwork in small-scale
face-to-face communities *not* to be so aware. But I felt that by
prioritizing the strategies of individuals I might overlook the more
obscure ways in which the social relationships they were thrown
into to reproduce their livelihoods operated. *This* was the hidden
transcript that I tried to unearth.

But I didn't see structure and people's *experience* as two separate
compartments; rather, I thought they would be problematically
connected – connected, that is, in rather difficult and often contradictory ways, but connected nonetheless. My sense of structure then,
coloured my sense of experience. And experience itself I rather
pragmatically tried to understand in terms of the more general
historical experience that people in the community could draw on,
and then a slightly different, more immediate and daily sense of
experience, felt differently by various people within the community.
Practice, too, I tended to understand in a similar double sense –
both dialogical and concerted: the manoeuvrings and conversations
among people, as well as their collective practices of resistance and
rebellion. How the latter contained and drew upon the former, and
how the former produced and shaped the latter, were questions
that exercised me continuously as the fieldwork progressed. Indeed,
precisely the way in which each of the elements was unthinkable in
any useful sense without resort to the others, was what produced
the endless connundrum of the research.

I will try to draw a picture with these elements. It will perforce
be a wallet-sized snapshot cut from the larger scene reproduced in
Livelihood and resistance. An example of the kind of thing I had in
mind as I thought about the conditionality of structured relationships would be the interaction between emerging *petty commodity
producers* in the village and the *social relationships necessary for
the reproduction of 'the community'* – community, moreover, that
was absolutely essential for the successful practice of concerted

resistance. I will take the example of the the way households substituted cash fines for the contribution of actual labour to the teams working on communal land (the *faenas*).

Herders, agriculturalists, *hacienda*-shepherds, traders, migrant shop-owners and street-sellers, to name but a few, the Huasic-anchino household enterprises were kaleidoscopic in their variety. Most households were multi-occupational, making them the sites of negotiation over the often contradictory requirements of different kinds of livings, and this was intensified by the propensity of households to become tied into clusters of other household enterprises to form, over time, 'confederations of households'. Nevertheless, amidst all this variety and complexity there were a few household-enterprises in Huasicancha who, either because of their past family ties or because of specific advantages accrued through migration, were able to use capital in a relatively systematic way to increase the productivity of their own household labour or the labour of anybody they chose to 'hire' through the various institutionalized systems available to Huasicanchinos. The purchase of a rotor-tiller, for example, would allow family members to plough their fields faster, and then to use the extra time to engage in other productive activities, or perhaps, instead, to acquire more land than could be worked by a household of the same size not owning such a machine.

Acquiring the machine in the first place may have required that this particular household retain cash or its equivalent when family, friends and neighbours – especially those in allied confederate households – would be clamouring for 'help'. Then, once bought, the machine itself would be the object of similar demands. But there were various 'ideological' devices these kinds of households – petty commodity producers – could use, prior and subsequent to buying the rotor-tiller, which allowed them to dam up the river of obligation long enough to produce this small reservoir of productive advantage *vis-à-vis* their fellow community members. The ideological strategies, I argue, were of course more or less understood as such: the obfus-cations they involved were remarked on both by petty commodity producers and by other villagers, either in argumentative fashion or in humorous or sarcastic asides. But what made these strategies necessary, not just the first time, but on a continuing and accum-ulating basis, as the process of capitalist reproduction took hold, was not, I believe, transparent to any of the actors. There was a rationality, a logic, to the system of social reproduction here that was not the experienced rationality of the strategizing actors.

This can be illustrated if we look at the way in which petty commodity producers first haphazardly and then systematically avoided sending family members to communal work *faenas* and were prepared to pay ever greater fines in lieu of their labour. This is because a particular kind of rationality occurs almost behind the backs of the actors as the productivity of the increasingly capitalized petty-commodity farm begins to outstrip the productivity of labour on the communal land (i.e.: the *faena*). As this gap widens, the cash paid in a fine can be greater than the value of the communal labour withheld, and still yet not as great as the value of labour thereby retained for work on the family farm.[11] What is 'structural' about this rationality is that it has an effect of unintended consequences; its logic manifests itself without actors recognizing the process at hand.

This becomes clear when we see petty commodity producers shedding not just their *faena* obligations but many other of their community linkages precisely as the outcome of this logic. As petty commodity producers these entrepreneurs are dependent on the market and on their competiveness therein (Friedmann 1980). Yet once they have gone forth into that dark night of open competition, they encounter capitalist enterprises engaged in expanded reproduction.[12] Since their initial advantage *vis-à-vis* these enterprises derived precisely from the cheap non-commodified labour available to them through the community – which they have now shed – they effectively find themselves perpetually on a cusp: threatened with ruin if they 'take off' entirely into the market, and with the sapping of their productive advantage if they return to full communal participation. In the book, I try to show that one effect of this was to make such people, often reluctantly, leaders of the resistance campaign. At an ideological level they were clearly smart operators, possibly just the kinds of crooks who could outsmart the crooks we're fighting; at a structural level, expansion, through re-possession, of the pasture postponed the day of reckoning inherent in the contradiction between the reproductive logic of their own enterprises and the reproductive logic of the community as a whole.

Even so, fitting households with precision into one or another of these categories would have been a rather taxonomic and unfruitful exercise. This was not a society *just* of structures, and I was not trying to derive class membership from structural positions.

For one thing, few if any households exhibited in pure form the systemic logic I am talking about. Then too, overlaying my characterization of social relations as I found them unfolding in the present, was the issue of *experience*. In the book I took experience in terms of a larger-scale experience and a smaller-scale one. On a larger scale, the strong magnetic pull of 'community' that I have just referred to was a product of the way history had unfolded in the area, especially since the Pacific War in the 1880s. An important site for the recruitment of resistance fighters against the Chileans, Huasicancha had become the core of a movement that expropriated all the neighbouring *haciendas*. It had taken over a decade for the government to re-establish a semblance of control over the area, and this period of 'alterity' was an important component in understanding the force of 'community'.

But at a smaller scale, kin groups and clusters of households had quite distinct historical experiences; one particularly striking feature was the way in which migration became an institutionalized practice. Through the ups and downs of local people's control over pasture for their animals, many herding families had begun to use inter-household linkages as stepping stones in a gradual migration process. From highland *estancia* to mining centre, to market town, to national capital, different kinds of household-enterprises began to take shape. But those with herds were not the only Huasicanchinos to experience the institutionalization of migration. For others, there were no such well-established stepping-stones on the path of migration. Life histories were replete with instances of chance, but also of stories about being cunning and astute (*vivo, astuto*). Once again, I am simplifying what I think was a very complex phenomenon. And once again, it would be a mistake to rush quickly to the security of categorizing household A and household B along the lines of experience. For one thing, these more personal and immediate experiences cast the 'community history' in quite different perspectives – painting it with the fine brush of cunning here, the broader brush of networks and connectedness there – cunning and connectedness, moreover, that in turn provided the ideological backdrop for the success or failure of household enterprises along the structural dimension I have discussed earlier.

For another thing, this would be to assume that people did not talk and share experiences with one another! And this became increasingly the focus of my attention: the practice of dialogical political discourses.[13] As a student of various forms of resistance, from strikes to cargo cults, I had come to expect an important role for 'solidarity' and 'unity'; and indeed the Huasicanchinos themselves were fond of explaining past successes, in contrast to the disappointments experienced among other local people, in terms of their *unión* (G. Smith 1976). Yet I committed the common mistake of tying solidarity in the face of external threats to homogeneity within. Raymond Williams (1977) has pointed out the tension between people's experiencing of the present and the writer's own tendency to see culture in terms of retrospective figurations of that presentness. Nowhere is this more distorting than in studies of collective resistance, since, with very few exceptions, resistance is not studied as it happens, but as it is recorded. Here I was fortunate. In the first year of my fieldwork the Huasicanchinos' resistance campaign was still on the go, and what at first struck me as a disturbing degree of discord I gradually began to see as a dynamic feature of what we might rather fancifully call the Huasicanchinos' ongoing intercommunicative practice (see Chapter 2).

But here *practice* dovetails with *experience*, because engagement with present crises – internal and external negotiations and confrontations, internal discussion and debate, clarifications and new positionings – were inextricably bound up with accounts of past experiences. In fact the very *practice* of this accounting was the best indicator of the heterogeneity that the *content* of the accounts tended to gloss over. Gathered together in street, or in highland *estancia* [shepherd's hut], people would recount a common experience – an area of *hacienda* land invaded, for example. Continually agreeing over the facticity of the events, they would point to different sets of landmarks, stress the key role of one figure, but change the name almost randomly, refer to different elements of oppositional forces, and thus end with a mutual sense that they had properly encapsulated what had happened!

Thus we saw in Chapter 2 how, two years after finishing *Livelihood and resistance*, I drew these conclusions:

> The Huasicanchinos were not *de facto* a homogeneous mass sharing common interests. And so, although the historical act of the land-recuperation campaign required performance by 'collective man' (Gramsci 1971: 348), this acting in unity . . . required a *continuous process* of the intense negotiation of meanings – a process, moreover, in which the attainment of a cultural unity was never complete but was always unfinished business throughout the intense periods of resistance . . .

What I am proposing is that words referring to key relationships have a rich set of resonances. When (heterogeneous) people get together to resist or rebel, they become energetically committed to negotiating over these resonances. In this sense contentiousness ... is both an internal and external matter. It is this kind of engagement, moreover, that gave to the Huasicanchino resistance a momentum of its own – dare I say, beyond the perceived interests of the group and beyond interests emergent from the long- and short-term economic goals of one or another participant, until eventually we arrive right up against the existential issues about identity and existence which are the constitutive components of culture itself.

While I believe that what I did in that study was retain the spirit of the work of such writers as Hobsbawm and Wolf, while trying to push a little further into the area of how peasants themselves engage with their political worlds, there are three observations about that study that I now see to be especially important.

One is the attraction of working with resistance at the level of individuals and small groups; and yet also the way in which work at this level actually limits the kinds of questions we are inclined to ask. If the structural dimensions of social reality that surface in large-scale, universalistic social studies give rise to a kind of obscuring of the complex conjunctural dimensions of social reality and immediate ethnographic experience, then it is also true that the scale of the kind of work I did among the Huasicanchinos (in village, *estancia*, mine, market-town and capital-city) risks giving artificial force to the dimensions of practice and experience to the exclusion of dimensions far less available to immediate awareness – both theirs and mine; indeed precisely the objective issues addressed by Hobsbawm and Wolf. So here my plea is that we resist the temptation to render too quickly individual and small-group short- and longer-term perceptions and manoeuvres in terms of *tactics* and hence, agency. That is to say, a wilful propensity – taken *a priori* as an *ability* by us analysts – to dispute hegemony intelligently, creatively and (from the resistance point of view) productively, rather than myopically, albeit disrespectfully, and possibly even quite ignorantly and hence with counter-productive results. Minimally, it would be more fruitful to put this kind of thinking on hold – by using concepts and language that do not anticipate the conclusions we hope for.

Secondly, we have to put on hold too the equal attraction of seeing people as coldly contained persons facing situations like technicians at a lab bench, so that our explanations are based on an idea of already-completed individual and group subjectivities. This is Williams's concern once more: the tendency to render the tentativeness of the present too quickly in terms of retrospective accounts. We need a kind of practice-oriented version of the hermeneutic circle – something that allows us to replicate the way people go into an experience as one kind of social subject and come out of it as another and then 'experience' it again through retrospection.

Both these issues lead us toward a focal plane that is neither too short – too small in scale – nor too long. There is nothing wrong with the literary device of a well-wrought vignette or the colourful rendering of interplay between lively actors, nor is there anything wrong with evoking the grand melodies of the vast chorus; but neither of these should monopolize the other to such an extent that the dialectical interplay between different kinds of social phenomena is lost. It is obvious, I'm sure, that I am thinking here of the work on everyday forms of resistance; but I am not sure that, at the other end of the spectrum, subaltern studies, possibly constrained by the availability of historical sources, does not err in the opposite way – toward unison over discord in the subaltern voice (Sarkar 1997).

A third problem has to do with my (and others') use of the notion 'resistance'.[14] On reflection I don't think livelihood and resistance is an especially useful pairing. This is not because I have shifted my views about the importance of different forms of livelihood in influencing people's political activity – and vice versa. Rather it is because the elements of the pair – livelihood and resistance – in the real world collapse into one another in important ways. We see this immediately when we ask working people how they are making out in their livelihoods – 'Keepin' up the fight', they may respond; French farmers might even say, *On résiste*. One does not have to be one of the highly resistance-conscious Huasicanchinos to recognize what such expressions allude to: that in attending to the daily business of livelihood one also has to attend to the protection of the conditions that make that livelihood possible. If we, as anthropologists, are cautious about the misapplication of such apparently neat terms as 'economy' and 'religion', then perhaps we should show an equal sensitivity across the widely different institutional settings of 'work' and 'politics'. There have been historical circumstances in which the making of a living and the politics of resistance have been compartmentalized, for example through wage-work in the factory and membership in the union; there are others where they cannot be so separated. And if this is so, then we need to know what other possible separations and integrations, compartmentalizations and overlappings, are possible, and how they effectively reconstitute the way people experience practice – the *practice* of work, the *practice* of politics, the *practice* of intimacy or the *practice* of distance.

Yet clearly my unease is not widely shared. The term 'resistance' has attained ever more common currency. And it is here that my second problem with the notion 'resistance' arises. In fact, despite its apparent political punch (in contrast to older and colder sociological terms) I don't think 'resistance' is a very precise way of describing political conduct. Hence I cannot agree with Ortner that 'even at its most ambiguous, [it] is a reasonable category, if only because it highlights the presence and play of power in most forms of relationship and activity' (1995: 175). I am concerned that its usage encourages ambiguity and hence short-circuits important questions. Once we acknowledge the many and insidious forms power takes, for example, infinitely elastic uses of the idea of resistance do nothing to clarify the nature of its exercise, its sources, mystifications and effects.

There is one especially persistent ambiguity that results in great analytic and hence political confusion. There is one dimension of resistance (to a force) that inheres in certain sets of relationships *as such*, and another dimension of resistance having to do with the expression of willed agency, yet writers are persistently ambiguous about which sense they are using . They thereby miss the opportunity of exploring how the two inter-relate. The statement 'peasants in place X have long resisted commodified labour relations', for example, is ambiguous in this way. Chayanovian (1966) views of the peasantry, to give one instance, would suggest that there are structural features in the reproduction of the peasant household that make incremental uses of commodified labour very hard to absorb without so modifying those features that households cannot reproduce themselves with their essential characteristics intact. Do some of the more wilful features of peasant 'resistance' to capitalism derive some element of their form and expression from this other kind of 'resistance'?[15] Certainly, use of the term here does *not* help us to understand the different dimensions power can take in different social settings: it obscures them. It is because of this confusion between two different dimensions of resistance that critics often mistakenly accuse 'structuralists' of endowing abstract structures with apparent agency.

The three approaches – 'everyday forms of resistance', subaltern studies and my own – have in common that they attempt to advance on their predecessors by replacing questions *about* the peasantry with questions *of* and *by* them; yet they all stop at the threshold of an interpretative methodology. This was not a problem for those whose explanations of peasant resistance did not rely significantly on participants' subjective views of the world. But it certainly is for those who follow them. Scott's phenomenology of this subjective world assumes a certain kind of social subject, one who makes choices based on his or her 'interests' so as to achieve 'realistic' goals. O'Hanlon suggests that the Subaltern Studies group were limited by the residue of their own perceptions of 'political consciousness' from really facing up to the issue of a sustained method for getting at subaltern subjectivities (O'Hanlon 1988). My own study seems to work as far as it goes, but doesn't seem to go very far in this direction. The tentative and partial way in which people seem to re-experience their (past) experiences, I see as being 'resolved' in the toing and froing of their intersubjective exchanges, made the more intense by their practical engagement in collective struggle directed outwards. Yet this seems to catch the game half-played. What confronts most politically interested anthropologists is *latent* political actors, for whom tentative and personal experiences do not cross-germinate in the kind of intense hothouse I found in Huasicancha, and who may operate in an arena where the sites of power and the agents of domination are by no means so clearly situated and immobile. Contemporary authors feel the need to extend our methodologies to address the issues of what appears to them to be a more fluid economic and political world.[16]

From Deeds to Words

Reflecting a shift both in the way people (individually and collectively) are engaging power in today's world and also I think a crisis for social analysts seeking a place and purpose post-Gorbachev, we see a shift in the baseline from which to start a study of resistance *away from* the material conditions of livelihood. As I suggested at the outset, we are moving along the road from a question of how we might explain social and political movements, to the question of how social movements can help us understand the way people express themselves and in so doing shape their own agency; a question of the interplay between social participation and the forming of individual and collective identities. I have referred to this as the 'expressivist turn'.

But on the road to the expressivist turn we meet a James Scott, who has flipped the coin of everyday resistance to reveal on the opposite side to *acts,* a hidden transcript of *words,* and before discussing the turn to full-blooded expressivism we need to address this half-turn. If we stick with Scott's dramaturgical metaphors, we might say: a small turn in front of the curtains, while the scenery is being thoroughly shifted for the more ambitious act that follows it.

To the strong distinction Scott makes in *Weapons of the weak* (1985) between the power of physical force and the power of persuasion, he now adds an equally strong distinction: this time between deeds and words, between practice and ideology, between actions and thought. I have already tried to draw our attention to a subsidiary question to Roseberry's 'What questions does a certain approach ask, and what questions does it prevent us from asking?' – that is: how does the social analyst imagine what is manifest to view in the social world, as against what is obscured, or is not available to immediate appearance? This question becomes the central issue of *Domination and the arts of resistance* (1990), contained in its subtitle: *hidden transcripts.* Scott explores the *interaction* between public transcripts of domination and resistance and the hidden transcripts – not just of resistance, but also the hidden transcripts used by the dominators in order to suggest ways in which manoeuvring disguise and deception can coalesce into a public, mass manifestation of alterity, rejection, and possible renewal.

For Scott, so eye-catching is the 'official version', the 'public transcript', that it dazzles us, constricting our pupils, so that when we try to look into the darkened recesses to find the mite that has fallen into a corner beneath the bed, we see only spots floating across our vision.

> The 'official transcript' as a social fact presents enormous difficulties for the conduct of historical and contemporary research on subordinate groups. Short of actual rebellion, the great bulk of public events, and hence the great bulk of the archives, is consecrated to the official transcript. And on those occasions when subordinate groups do put

in an appearance, their presence, motives, and behaviour are mediated
by the interpretation of dominant elites (1990: 86).

Note the similarity here with Guha's discomfort with elite historians.
But Scott turns in a slightly different direction, asking why hegemony has retained such an appeal for social scientists and historians,
when the evidence would suggest that, if anything, far from acting
as though in thrall to the dominant ideas of the dominant class,
subaltern peoples are quite prone both to think for themselves and
even to act 'against all odds' as it were. If anything, suggests Scott,
it is not submission and something called 'false consciousness' that
should draw the attention of our analytic enquiry, but their opposite:
the residue of agency exemplified by these kinds of behaviour; a
kind of turning of Gramsci on his head.

For surely, what is surprising is that, given all the powers of
ideological persuasion at the disposal of elites, subordinate groups
do indeed manage to retain spaces in the social fabric where they
can voice and exchange among themselves their own alternative
version.

> In Gramsci's original formulation, which has guided most subsequent
> neo-Marxist work on ideology, hegemony works primarily at the level
> of thought as distinct from the level of action. The anomaly, which the
> revolutionary party and its intelligentsia will hopefully resolve, is that
> the working class under capitalism is involved in concrete struggles
> with revolutionary implications but, because it is in the thrall of
> hegemonic social thought, is unable to draw revolutionary conclusions
> from its actions. It is this dominated consciousness that, Gramsci claims,
> has prevented the working class from drawing radical consequences
> inherent in much of its action (ibid.: 90).

Scott then quotes a passage from Gramsci in which the practical
activity of the mass of people is contrasted with their lack of a
theoretical 'consciousness'.

This is surely a puzzle. Scott's Gramsci, like Scott himself, makes
a radical distinction between thought and action, and then suggests
that while subordinated people may *act* with some agency, some
independence, they are constrained *at the level of consciousness* from
turning such acts into revolutionary praxis. It would surely be more
accurate, suggests Scott, 'to consider subordinate classes *less* constrained at the level of thought and ideology, since they can in
secluded settings speak comparatively safely, and *more* constrained

at the level of political action and struggle, where the daily exercise
of power sharply limits the options available to them' (ibid.: 91).

How could Gramsci have been so silly? Surely his *Prison Notebooks*
alone are evidence of his relative freedom of thought, in the context
of restrictions on his actions? Scott often prefaces his use of
hegemony with the term 'ideological', yet in the formulation quoted
here, it would seem that the prefix is superfluous. Hegemony seems
to be analogous to a form of social control exercised through brain-
washing. Institutions of education, mass media and so on, render
the masses soporific. And on this rendering, we are left with the
choice that either these people buy all this, or in some way they
don't: the difference as it were between respect (those who do)
and mere deference (those who don't). Using this rather restricted
understanding of hegemony allows Scott to suggest that while
subaltern people by this reckoning should be trapped in the web
of hegemony, in fact he finds that they operate in a realm of
freedom using faculties of reason unconstrained by such ideological
domination. It follows that notions of hegemony are misguided.
They are attractive because scholars are distracted by more accessible transcripts and, through their own arrogance, thus treat
subalterns as what Harold Garfinkle in another context called
'sociological dopes'.

If we are to have a jousting match about hegemony we should do
so on Gramsci's terms, not on Scott's. Scott seems to be arguing
that either you accept that people's ideas are formed in a rather
passive way as a result of the exercise of power through cultural
means – hegemony; or you don't. If you don't, then you must have
nothing to do with hegemony. Yet the way in which Gramsci writes
about history and practice, his forceful criticism of positivist
sociology, and his persistent use of dialectics (see Chapter 7) make
it hard to believe that he would accept the radical distinction
between ideas and actions that Scott wishes to insist on.

Nor do we have to do a Talmudic reading of Gramsci to refute
Scott's position. We need only note that Gramsci was interested in
engaging with a very pressing political issue, which, as he
understood it, could only be resolved by a careful reading of history
(in his case Italian history) – something of surprisingly little interest
to Scott. In this history quite specifically *bourgeois* hegemonic
processes can be identified. Not, be it noted, the way hegemony
operates as an opiate of the people from Babylon to Bangkok. Not,
be it noted, a *theory* of hegemony; but, more modestly, the rise of

bourgeois hegemonic processes in Italy. Fundamental to this kind of hegemonic process was a series of ideological and institutional separations, an issue taken up before him by Marx (Sayer 1979, 1987) and Weber (Habermas 1984; see also Mitchell 1990). Though a narrow reading of hegemony – as ideological domination at the level of thought alone – focuses our attention on educational institutions and the mass media, it seems perverse in this day and age to leave it at that. There were also the whole battery of organizational and institutional resources associated with capitalist production and circulation, among these the large-scale factory and the market – both of which concerned Gramsci. The way we understand the effect of these kinds of social relations as they reproduce themselves over time is a matter of specific historical investigation. But it is hard to imagine that they have no role to play in the production and reproduction of social subjectivities. You may want to call this hegemony, you may want to call it something more easily pronounceable: what's in a name? But you can't write it off by confining all that is obscured from social scientific and historical enquiry to hidden *transcripts*.

In forcing us to turn our gaze to micro-processes of dispute and struggle James Scott has done a great service to those of us who try to understand better domination and resistance. He has done us a service too in the precision of his intellectual armoury. What Scott has done as a non-anthropologist is to raise the importance of local and perceptive enquiry; ironically, to the interpretative anthropologist this must surely call for a greater cultural sensitivity than Scott's interest-driven explanation suggests, while to the anthropological political economist the short shrift given to history and the absence of a wider range of material and social conditions have the effect of exaggerating the centrality of hidden transcripts for our understanding of domination and resistance.

Expressive Resistance

As I have suggested in the earlier discussion of expressivist approaches to the study of domination and resistance, the interest in social processes by which actors become formed as effective social subjects encourages them to understand collective movements by prioritizing their subjective and expressive elements over functionalist, structuralist or rationalist criteria. The effect is to take up the cultural brush with which we paint pictures of our social world, reaching ever less frequently for more sociological tools. Their own pronouncements notwithstanding, the Zapatistas, for example, are seen to be a 'postmodern' movement because they position themselves *ironically* toward orthodox Mexican society. People have been killed, humiliated, imprisoned, it seems, all in the cause of irony. In its strongest version, seeing all political action in terms of culture and cultural expression runs this risk – of translating *realpolitik* into nothing more than putting a different interpretation on the world than the one held by those in power.

Writers vary in the extent to which they justify their strongly culturalist emphasis by arguing that it is a *reflection* of the self-professed discourse of the movements they study. Some analysts see their particular ordering of priorities as an intellectual task that balances earlier intellectual absences, irrespective of the character of the movements they study. Others couch the authenticity of their own accounts in the claim that they *mirror* the self-perceptions of protagonists. Escobar (1996: 63), for example, asserts that: 'Theory must start with people's self-understanding, with giving an account of people as agents whose practices are shaped by their self-understanding. It is only by getting as clear a picture as possible of this self-understanding that we can hope to identify what should be relevant for theory in the first place.' Charles Hale (1997: 569), on the other hand, is critical of this conflation of the analyst's perspective and that of the people she or he is studying. He is critical too of many writers' tendency to exaggerate the divide 'between postmodern theoretical innnovation and materialist reassertion' (ibid.: 570), and wishes to draw on the best practices of both: 'I do argue that past theoretical polarities – between materialist and discursive analysis, between emphasis on social totality and particularity – have declining utility as organizing principles . . .'. And he looks to Latin America and finds there a multiplicity in forms of collective expression.

There is no question that overly drawn differences between approaches and insistence on overly radical breaks in history – the old and the new, the modern and the postmodern, etc. – are unhelpful. Thus in Chapter 1 I have argued that materialist approaches need to be far more aware of the dialectic between actors' own constructions of the world and their praxis, and in this chapter I have tried to show how we might recognize the value of older approaches while rechecking the value of our own. But it can only lead to theoretical misunderstandings to describe the division as one between 'materialists' and 'discursivists' and then argue that this division can be easily bridged, and a synthesis found, by simply joining the two together; for to do so is to dovetail understandings of the world that *begin* with a historical realist epistemology that *demands* resort to characteristic conditions of social reproduction, with those that *begin* their understanding of the world by taking it as socially or culturally constructed. The starting-points for the two positions – both their separate heritages and the different objectives with which they formulate their priorities and begin their studies – cannot be so easily occluded.

The distinction is not one between an interest in materialism (often glossed as synonymous with 'economic determinism') on the one hand, and discourse (often glossed as 'culture') on the other, as any reading of Thompson, Williams or Hall makes clear. Instead, we have on the one side a persistent refusal to disregard or play down the way the requirements of the reproduction of capital pervade – albeit in a myriad different forms and appearances – every recess of the social world, so that all forms of politics, identity or not, confront the question of their relationship to the future of capitalism. Hence the need to integrate this kind of enquiry with the pressing need to interrogate the political agendas – global, national and local – that are required to ensure capitalism's future.

On the other side is an intellectual vision of society in terms of space, such that deprivation can be written as exclusion and a 'third way' is discovered in interstices of the social fabric where oppositional politics are displaced by the pursuit of autonomous political spaces. We need to ask again, with Roseberry, what can or cannot be talked about in such approaches. Once we are inclined to talk of multiple inequalities and to treat all social forces as though they had equal historical weight, it becomes very difficult to confront the pivotal way in which capitalist reproduction provides the linchpin for inequalities and gives leverage to social forces.

This can be nicely illustrated by interrogating the way in which Charles Hale (1997: 568) suggests what makes politics '*identity* politics' in his perceptive review of this material: 'The phrase "identity politics" will refer to collective sensibilities and actions that come from a particular location within society, in direct defiance of universal categories that tend to subsume, erase, or suppress this particularity. "Location", in this sense, implies a distinctive social memory, consciousness, and practice, as well as place within the social structure.'[17] It is immediately striking that this would make identity politics of much earlier movements in history. Certainly, 'collective sensibilities and actions that come from a particular location within society' seems a very nice way to describe class consciousness and actions, and the geographical identification that lay at the heart of so many collective struggles, from the British miners' strikes throughout this century to the Chinese peasants discussed by Eric Wolf (1969), would seem clear examples of defiance against universal categories that tend to suppress particularities. The power to make categories universal, apparently above history and just 'natural', is a function of hegemony, and is unlikely to be abandoned as a political project of the powerful, however much intellectuals may seek to render other groups as seeking a more enlightened political agenda of difference and discourse.

Indeed, an especially crippling false dichotomy is the one that effectively cuts off terms like 'the everyday' and 'the local' from the historical and the universal, so that the only form of joining things together is in some rainbow coalition of fragmented identities. For the reality is that it is hard to read a Zapatista statement without finding a reference to neo-liberalism or to NAFTA. After the signing of NAFTA and the subsequent financial crisis, the Mexican state has been facing a kind of Versailles syndrome in which the centre becomes a black hole, and the conditions are set for reconstituting hegemonic interpretations of reality. Under these conditions subaltern movements play an especially acute discursive role in 'reappropriating nationalism', as Lynn Stephen nicely puts it (1997b: 93). In these volatile conditions, she argues, the stumbling block for negotiations between the government and the various indigenous and peasant groups involved has to do with fundamentally different views of the national state and of membership therein. On the one hand are notions having to do with *the autonomy of practically directed, self-constituting collective subjects*, on the other are notions of an undifferentiated *mestizo* nation made up of *individuals* not constituted through their practically directed action, but rather by being *recognized* – called into being – by the liberal state. As Stephen puts it, 'The contradictions of a multi-cultural collective project versus the stratifying individualizing one of late 20th-century global capitalism set the terrain within [which] movements for indigenous autonomy must act' (1997a: 34).

Stephen's treatment of domination and resistance in contemporary Mexico are grounded both in a historical understanding of
capitalism and in a sensitive interpretation of the way movements
of opposition have created the conditions for new realities. In
Austin's terms Mexican peasant and indigenous movements are not
so much *constative utterances* – 'We are here, we're staying so accept
us' as they are *performative utterances* – 'As we do these things, we
become these people.' Or it would be better to say, with Austin,
that, even as constative utterances of everyday livelihood, by fighting
for the conditions of their survival people make them performative,
and the reformulating of the state, the absences and corruptions
of the centre, make this possible. Stephen then, does offer us the
kind of political economy that is responsive to the challenges of
more expressive approaches, but she does so without abandoning
the historical realism that makes her analysis critical and not just
evocative.

Conclusion

I have referred to earlier approaches to domination and resistance
as 'objectivist' and to studies of 'new social movements' as 'expressivist'. In between I have talked of James Scott's interest, first, in
daily acts of resistance, and later in hidden transcripts. This kind
of labelling can be misleading. I have suggested that there *was* in
earlier studies an interest in the role structured social relationships
played in peasant resistance, just as in Scott's work the instrumental
conduct of individuals and small groups *is* an important part of
his explanations, and in expressivist studies, the cultural formation
of subjects becomes a central concern. Yet all these approaches
contain elements highlighted by the others, though the way they
imagine these is different.
    This is partly revealed through the metaphors they use to give
us a picture of society. In Chapter 1, for example, I suggested that
we could learn something useful about the basis of many arguments
between social analysts by noting a distinction between approaches
which stress an image of society in terms of *production* and
reproduction, and those which use terms such as 'marginality'
'exclusion' and 'participation' to render society in more spatial
terms. The way you imagine society, the images you use to evoke
its reality, have an effect on what you see to be worth studying.

Thus, as I suggested earlier, Hobsbawm's and Wolf's discussions of peasant consciousness should be understood in terms of their particular understanding of the historical process. This example illustrates the fact that analysts' images of society affect the stress they place on its various elements. Scott's stress on strategizing arises from the way he sees the relationship between action and social structure; expressivists' stress on the social construction of reality serves to highlight cultural features of domination and resistance . . . and so on. These imagined pictures draw our attention, in the mess of social phenomena, to certain shapes and patterns – to certain forms (of domination and resistance): an interest in small-group strategizing may highlight *local* features of rebellion and compliance, in a way that more structural interests would not. And an interest in collective resistance in terms of expression may bring more sharply into focus movements' intersubjective characteristics *trans-locally*.

This brings us back to what I have described as a sub-category of Roseberry's question about what can or cannot be asked within a certain frame of enquiry, i.e.: what does an author see to be openly manifest to social enquiry and what requires more penetrating, or *critical* attention? For example, James Scott makes this issue quite explicit – at least along one dimension of social reality: there are public transcripts and there are those more hidden and hence requiring more percipient endeavour. Yet, as resisters make strategic decisions about how they might resist, they take into account certain conditions, what goals would be realistic, the anticipated room for manoeuvre of the dominators, and so on. These are dimensions that, if not actually hidden, are 'off-stage'. Now, we can acknowledge, with Scott, that particular choices are made under given conditions; but, *contra* Scott, we must recognize that those conditions are not only the *present* conditions; nor is their invisibility *just* a function of people's acts of hiding. The forces off-stage that condition their actions are also *historical*.

Along one dimension, this might be seen as the advance express-ivist approaches make on the work of Scott. Unlike Scott they try to understand the processes by which subjectivities – collective and individual – are formed. In the mess of social phenomena that confronts us, they begin to give shape to the way collective solidarities and self-conscious movements of assertion generate social subjectivities – from urban squatters' growing sense of social citizenship to gays' recognition of the social constructions of sexuality. To do so they explore historical processes, giving special attention to the way personal narratives, through discourse (among 'us' and with 'others') account for the characteristics of movements. Here understanding has less to do with extrapolating people's 'interests', putative or otherwise, to explain why they do what they do; rather understanding is more closely associated with people's narration of their experiences (Somers and Gibson 1994). The way we constitute ourselves as particular kinds of people – like a certain cluster of other people, unlike another cluster – in other words, our identity, has greatly to do with the way we give an account of our lives and shape the narrative to our ongoing world, so as to situate ourselves within it.

Yet this *is* only one dimension of the issue. Their stress on politics as cultural practice has the effect of producing precisely the kind of image of hegemony Scott condemns; the formation of social subjects runs the risk of appearing to be far *too much* a cultural and ideological project; far too disconnected from a rigorous understanding of the concrete abstractions – profoundly historical, only obscurely experiential – that produce the particular forms of power that give rise to certain forms of collectivity *and prevent the formation of others* (this latter should surely take up our attention). For example, I noted at the outset of this chapter the high mobility of capital and people and the plasticity of hitherto rigid institutional structures (from states that have lost their monopoly over internal forms of violence, to flexible corporate structures). These may indeed be *experienced* as political and economic 'crisis'; but we need to understand how such crises have been ideologically dissociated from particular (neo-liberal) political projects. It is hard to imagine a study of Stalin's collectivization that did not tie his justification for targeting the kulaks as victims to his political project for the greater good of Soviet socialism. We should be equally concerned with the way capitalist constructions, conscious or otherwise, effect-ively target victims and inoculate social subjects against collective agency.

I am convinced then, with expressivists, that collective expression interacts dialectically with the subjectivities of individual partic-ipants: culture *is* produced in the hothouse of rebellion (as the previous chapter suggests). Yet this is not really all that original an insight. Thompson wrote a history of the emergence of English working-class culture along just these lines. But cultural studies will always be limited in the questions they ask if their priorities lead them persistently to sidestep *characterizing the principles by which capitalist relations of production are reproduced* at any one time, in any one place (and over time; through space). What's more this, in turn silences, obscures – casts back into the patternless mess of social phenomena – certain kinds of potential and latent resistance. This is so because the kind of militant particularism that gave, for example, the Huasicanchinos their collective identity, *works through selectivity*. As Scott I think perceives, there is a sense in which *historical praxis can work only by denying and obscuring the structural forces that underpin it.* 'The shift from one conceptual world, from one level of abstraction to another, can threaten that sense of value and common purpose that grounds the militant particularism achieved in particular places' (Harvey 1995: 84). The level of abstraction so alien to militant particularism is of course the one practised by such as Hobsbawm and Wolf – one that requires a strict characterization of the way in which sets of social relationships achieve their reproduction through history. Moreover, one should not over-stress these writers' commitment to the power of concrete abstractions over agency. If writers such as they thought collective struggle had no role to play in the historical process, it is hard to explain why they have devoted so much of their lives to the study of resistance and rebellion.

Nevertheless, the political conditions have changed. Among other things they have led to the radical fragmentation of collective forms of resistance for the protection of livelihood. This is what I mean when I say that we have to be able to understand not just 'new social movements' that encourage us to enquire into the role they play in the forming of social subjects; we need also to be able to understand the way the destruction, the absence, of collective movements effectively stunts social subjectivity (here in Marx's sense of historical praxis). This seems to require anthropological work that can go beyond the scale of a struggle like that of the Huasic-anchinos, and yet still ask the kinds of questions that would allow us to understand the historical interaction between the principles of capitalist reproduction, the way experience works intersubject-ively to generate self-awareness, and the link between (utopian) goals and practical action.

Notes

1. The term is borrowed from Taylor 1989: Ch. 21 and 413–18.
2. Two important collections of the period were Rodolfo Stavenhagen's (1970) *Agrarian problems and peasant movements in Latin America*, and Teodor Shanin's (1987 [1971]) *Peasants and peasant societies*. Both played an important role in left anthropology in the period.
3. We should also note that, alongside the work of people interested in peasants' *collective* political behaviour, at this time – the late 1960s and early 1970s – there was a body of literature on peasants' 'local-level politics'. This was a literature that tended to focus on the politics of individual strategizing and factionalism. The title of Bailey's *(1969) Stratagems and spoils* captures well the spirit of these works, and Barth's study of the Swat Pathan (1965) was likewise about factions, leaders and followers. It is significant that this literature has become so well obscured in the US that Ortner's (1984) article on 'Theory in anthropology since the sixties' passes over it entirely, and James Scott takes no inspiration from it. This is especially revealing, since both Bailey and to a lesser extent Barth turned increasingly in the direction that Scott has taken – towards linguistic metaphors as a means of getting at the subjective dimension of everyday politics. See Bailey, *Gifts and Poison* (1973); *Debate and Compromise* (1975).
4. It is hard to over-emphasize the influence of Hobsbawm's *Primitive Rebels* for rural historians and radical anthropologists through the 1960s. Together with *Captain Swing*, it employed evocative historical ethnography and widely drawn comparisons to make its case. Coming a decade later, Wolf's *Peasant Wars* (1969) likewise had extraordinary shock value, partly because, as I have said, anthropologists had generally not shown an especially systematic interest in popular mobil-ization, except in the exoticized form of 'cargo cults' (but cf.: Worsley's 1970 treatment here), and partly because its bold comparative project answered many of the concerns of young anthropologists of that period. I therefore take these two writers as pivotal figures for Anglo-phone scholarship in this discussion. The third 'key text' of the period was Barrington Moore's *Social origins of dictatorship and democracy* (1966). Needless to say, however, in any particular country where peasant mobilization has figured strongly in recent times other major works have had powerful significance and affected subsequent scholarship.
5. Two important studies of specific local cases that came out in English and had a very powerful impact on radical anthropologists were William Hinton's (1964) *Fanshen* and John Womack's (1969) *Zapata and the Mexican Revolution* – the one a vivid account of the effects of revolutionary change on a rural village, the other a detailed social

history. These two books – the one just preceding Wolf's, the other just following it, form an important backdrop to any account of 'peasants and resistance'.

6. Compare 'Our enterprise is an act of faith, in the exemplary virtue of honest work, conscientious and solid' (Bloch and Lefebvre 1929: 2 [quoted in L. Tilly 1983: 6]) with 'We have no doubt that many other historiographical points of view and practices are likely to converge close to where we stand. Our purpose in making our own views known is to promote such a convergence. We claim no more than to try and indicate an orientation and hope to demonstrate in practice that this is feasible' (Guha 1988 [1981]: 43).

7. Here I stick to Guha's programmatic statements.

8. The connection Guha makes between subaltern expression and the need of the nation to come to its own, has been taken up by numerous anthropologists outside the Anglophone world. See for example DaMatta 1994 (for Brazil), Lebovics 1992 (for France), and Narotzky, n.d. (for Catalonia). There is, of course, a very extensive literature for Quebec.

9. The point I want to stress here is not just the importance of studying the complexity of locally specific, historically embedded, social relationships and practices, but the way in which over time these become so institutionalized that we impute 'strategy' and 'interest' at great peril. Something analogous to 'long pay' was practised by herd-owners in Huasicancha (Smith 1989). It is practised too in the 'informal economy' of the Pais Valenciano, where I am at present conducting fieldwork.

10. These included herding livestock and working arable plots with non-commodified labour; working for *haciendas* under a variety of kinds of labour-regimes; running petty commodity enterprises in city and country; and so on.

11. In purely economic terms the mobility of factors between petty commodity producer (PCP) household and communal *faena* derives from the fact that there is advantage to both parties. The community receives a cash fine from the PCP household that is greater in value than the labour input of a worker on the *faena*, but the PCP household pays a fine that is less than the value of labour retained by keeping the worker at home, because the productivity of labour within the PCP household is greater than the average productivity of labour in the community as a whole.

12. This argument is a simplified version of Chapter 6 in *Livelihood and resistance*. The important distinction between simple and expanded reproduction is there explained at some length. See also Smith 1985.

13. As Sherry Ortner (1995: 180) remarks,

If we are to recognize that resistors are doing more than simply opposing domination, more than simply producing a virtually mechanical re-action, then we must go the whole way. They have their *own* politics – not just between chiefs and commoners or landlords and peasants, but within all the local categories of friction and tension ... (1995:176–7) ... an understanding of political authenticity of the people's own forms of inequality and asymmetry, is not incompatible with an understanding of resistance but is in fact indispensable to such an understanding.

14. Although for obvious reasons I call this chapter 'rethinking domination and resistance', I deal more fully with domination in Chapter 7.

15. Reference to 'structure' here may be misinterpreted. The process by which social relations are reproduced – in this case within what Chayanov (1966) called 'peasant economy' – is not an abstract *deus ex machina* but involves quite identifiable practices and relationships of work, social intercourse, and the broad array of daily, yearly and generational cultural practices, in short what I have been calling 'livelihood'. The fact that these practices can also have a resistance effect simply reasserts the problems I have with the distinction between the two terms.

16. I put the issue in this way because whether economic and political fluidity is a profound and significant characteristic of capitalism and modern power, or whether it simply appears so, needs to be demonstrated, not taken as a point of departure, as it is for many studies, which then address themselves entirely to matters of 'culture'.

17. As I have noted earlier, there is a problem with conflating memory and 'place within the social structure' under the one term 'location'. It is heuristically more fruitful to keep the two conceptually distinct so as to explore potential tensions and correspondences between them.

PART THREE

Modernity and New Socio-Economic Forms

Knowing Their Place: Regional Economies and the Social Construction of Place in Western Europe

> There is no doubt whatever that the people of England work harder, mentally and physically, than the people of any other country on the face of the earth, whether we take the town or the country population, the same plodding industry is apparent, and the respites enjoyed by either in the shape of holidays are few and far between. ... It is due to their untiring industry and to the natural advantages of the country of which we are justly proud, that England holds the foremost rank among the nations of the earth.
>
> — *Mechanics Magazine* III, p. 280, 27 April 1860
> [Quoted in Samuel 1977: 6]

> What are we to do with a discipline that loudly rejects received ideas of 'the local', even while ever more firmly insisting on a method that takes it for granted?
>
> — Gupta and Ferguson 1997: 4

Introduction

'Untiring industry and the natural advantages of the country': here lie two of the most elemental common-sense views of the pertinence of place for human well-being – the cultural: the propensity to work hard of the inhabitants; and the natural: the god-given advantages of geographical bounty. These are indeed somewhat time-worn explanations for a people's specificity within anthropology – though, as we shall see, not as obsolete as all that in other disciplines; but where should we go, as Gupta and Ferguson ask, after we reject such received ideas of 'the local'? Ethnographies may have become more sophisticated in the way they relate the places where fieldwork is conducted to larger fields; there may even have been important works reflecting on the value of seeing congeries of these places in terms of cultural 'regions' – yet it is still true that doing ethnography in a place remains the norm for anthropologists. Thus, introducing a book on Ireland, Silverman and Gulliver (1992: 21) note, 'Locality has been a key concern in contemporary anthropological analysis. Whereas an earlier anthropology focused mainly on "a people", "a culture", or "a society", most anthropologists today are concerned with "a place".' And Sherry Ortner (1995: 175) describes ethnography as the 'kind of understanding [that] has been closely linked to field work, in which the whole self physically and in every other way enters the space of the world the researcher seeks to understand'. But, with the restructuring of capitalist social relations of production, 'the space of the world the researcher seeks to understand' has changed, giving *place* a different resonance in the everyday world of people making a living. Here I explore attempts to theorize place for the particular case of people whose livelihoods embed them in characteristically *regional* economies.

What are the challenges to our ethnographic methods of these kinds of *places*? The unfolding dynasty that has sprung from the marriage of social geography with economic sociology makes the claim that the restructuring of capitalism has given rise to quite particular links between the social reproduction of daily life and the constitution and reconstitution of place. The particularity of a place arises not only from its natural characteristics and its peculiar history, but also from magnetic currents of force and counter-force that arise through the present-day strategies and constraints of capitalists and policy-makers. How does this particular perspective on the social constitution of place impact on an older anthropological 'method that [took] it for granted'? To provide a sense of the distinctions involved, I take as my point of departure the rather striking difference I felt in the sense of place as I shifted my own ethnographic work from highland Peru to Western Europe.

The initial work on Peru was an attempt, quite common among anthropologists at that time, to resist the easy fieldwork temptation of doing a predominantly local study. Through various metaphors and images I tried to evoke the interface between the local setting and the (historically changing) wider fields of force in which it was found.[1] Yet I was sufficiently initiated into the customs and rituals of ethnography for it to take a few weeks before I realized that it was not in fact a place called 'Huasicancha' that needed to be situated in broader fields of force, but the *huasicanchinos* – the people themselves. This was not the result of deep thought. It gradually dawned on me as I processed the fact that 50 per cent of *huasicanchinos* lived in the provincial capital, the mining towns and the national capital. Yet we all agreed – I as the anthropologist and the people I lived with – that *huasicanchinos* they were – in village, highland *estancia*, or Lima *barriada*.

Then, in the 1980s, I embarked on my fieldwork in the Bajo Segura, to the extreme south of the *país valenciano*, that is, Southern Alicante, in Spain. Because complex social relationships associated with the politics of land had preoccupied me in Peru, I decided to take a look at landownership here too. It seemed likely that the shifts in tenure from the large properties before the Civil War to the medium and small ones of the present would reveal something about social relations and, ultimately, local politics. But it was a very complicated procedure, and I ended up recording the land-tenure history of a large block of irrigated land that had entered this century as one large *finca* and was now a hodge-podge of holdings with almost infinite varieties of tenure arrangements. It became a fascinating puzzle, like a Borges story leading me ever further into a labyrinth. Yet, interested though they were in this land, and bemusedly in me and my survey, local people often pointed out that making their living took them well beyond this one local landscape. As they saw it, they perpetually had to divide up their interests 'between one thing and another' (see Chapter 5).

A casual remark such as this was unheard of in Huasicancha, though external landownership was not absent.[2] No doubt part of the difference lies in the fact that, though agriculture was intensive and reasonably profitable in the Bajo Segura, most households were multi-occupational, people receiving homework and employed in factories over an area encompassing some twenty or so municipalities, as well as some of them migrating to the richer countries of Europe. As is increasingly the case, many informants were more cosmopolitan than the anthropologist studying them.

The point of these examples is to illustrate how I became aware of the different ways in which people come together around the sense of place. Because 'placeness' was a pretty muddy business among *huasicanchinos*, sticking to their boots wherever they went, I didn't find myself spending much time questioning it. When the

people studied do a lot of talking about *their* local place and seem
to thread their everyday lives unreflectively through it, as they did
in Huasicancha, it becomes easy to take the way that social constitution of place came into being for granted. But what of the
opposite predicament – where people have by no means lost their
sense of place, but that sense keeps shifting and changing its shape,
explaining much and then little, being a value and then a curse,
noisily imposing a collective name, then silently turning a collective
cold shoulder – when 'the identity of places has weakened, become
more hybrid in composition', as Richard Sennett puts it (1995: 13)?
Here the 'naturalness' of people's identification with their locale
is far less obvious, far less taken for granted – by either them or
me. The location of income sources, the viability of the environment, the use made of local networks, these all serve to make the
concerns of people's everyday livelihoods revolve around questions
of the region or locale. But this region or locale is a far more elusive
trope than it was in central Peru. In their book on *Social Memory*
Fentress and Wickham (1992) remark on 'the constantly recurring
importance of local geography as a structure of remembrance' for
rural people whose everyday routine acts to socialize geographical
space – 'both space and time thus locking together to construct
community identity'. Yet the material conditions of late capitalism
are radically re-moulding the geographical landscape. True, the
region in which they live does provide the organizational setting
for their daily lives; but this sense of locality carries an element of
the instrumentally created 'place', a less extreme version of what
Marc Augé calls 'non-places'. In a sense the changed dispersal of
light on the social world that I found in the two settings is one that
reflects a societal shift. In this sense my experience is similar to
Marc Augé's (1995). In his book, *Non-Places,* Augé contrasts the
setting of his West African fieldwork, where association with place
was 'a principle of meaning for the people who lived in it, and also
a principle of intelligibility for the person who observes it' (1995:
52) with something like its opposite, the airport lounges and traffic
jams where many of us spend a large part of our days. Though less
extreme, my experience has a similar ring to it.

The shift from the Peruvian setting, where 'placeness' appears
to fit nicely with the conventions of ethnography, to the European
one, where the fit is sufficiently awkward to warrant attention, has
made me uncomfortable with the way in which the methodologies
of fieldwork and people's own sense of place fit rather too neatly

together to be properly interrogated. The *problem* of placeness in the contemporary European setting risks getting lost in the conventional design of anthropological ethnography. This is because, though a byproduct of capitalist production and reproduction has always been the constitution, destruction and reconstitution of places, in its present form these formations and reshapings of place and space have become increasingly self-conscious and instrumental.

This leads me to a reading of the geography and economic sociology literature on place and region; but it is a cynically anthropological reading. Either explicitly or as a kind of unspoken but continually alluded-to *leitmotif*, culture recurs throughout the literature on regions.[3] Yet the term itself remains fuzzy. Indeed, because the idea of 'culture' is generally taken to be fairly obvious, and hence apparently needs no further scrutiny, analysts and policymakers as well as the local people themselves tend to use the notion in widely different ways; so in the course of examining this literature I want to ask what role the idea of culture plays, both in theory and in practice.

Regions as Units of Analysis

What new can be learned about the way regions take their form, by turning to the growing literature on 'the regions' in western Europe? Put another way, what makes this recent literature different from the long-standing anthropological interest in locales?[4] Anthropologists, tending to work in units that can be studied practically within the space of one or two years, have nonetheless frequently been drawn to regional studies, as their fieldwork became enmeshed in the complexities of modern states. While Julian Steward produced a group of students whose work was deeply informed by fields of power wider than the fieldsite, for example, Skinner's work in China sought a wider field through the workings of markets, a heritage taken up by Carol Smith in her early work (C. Smith 1976). Nonetheless, it took some time before these rather programmatic agendas began to take account of different *historical processes* in the formation of regions. This was noted both by Mintz and by Wolf (1978) as they thought back on the Puerto Rico project and much of their later work was devoted to this problem, while students of Skinner from Carol Smith (1984) to Claudio Lomnitz (1992) have made historical periodization a hallmark of their more recent work.

In Europe, conventionally anthropologists have tended to use the notion of region to refer, not to a sub-national unit, but rather to the broader sweep of the idea of a culture region. In its best-known exemplification, that of 'the Mediterranean Region', the notion has been controversial, not just in terms of its existence or not, but also as to whether or not anthropologists should concern themselves with cultural areas at all (Braudel 1949; Pitt-Rivers 1963; Davis 1977). Yet, even where debates such as this are not explicitly engaged, a sense that cultural attributes, from honour, to humour, to expressions of sexuality, can be attached to regions such as Andalusia or southern Greece is retained (Gilmore 1987; Brandes 1980; Pitt-Rivers 1963).

Oddly, there is a tension in these kinds of extrapolations. The care taken by people such as Arensberg (Arensberg and Kimball 1940) and Pitt-Rivers (1957) both to resist using their findings at community-level as microcosms of something larger and also to set the communities they studied within the setting of a quite specific larger society, seems to work against the use of their ethno-graphies for constructing cultural regions. By the 1970s the issue of the interface between the local setting and broader socio-economic structures began to attain far more historical precision, under the influence of a turn toward 'political economy' both within anthropology and in cognate disciplines (especially Wallerstein's influential *The Modern World System* (1974)). Silverman's (1975) study of the regional history of *civiltà* and of the local system of *mezzadria* is exemplary of a regionally sensitive ethnography, while the influence of political economy and historical geography can be seen in the work of Jane and Peter Schneider (1976) and Cole and Wolf (1974). More recently ethnographic monographs have themselves been thoroughly embedded in detailed, careful and original historical interpretations of the role of the state and economy in the texture of local life (Herzfeld 1985; Rosenberg 1988; Holmes 1989; Blim 1990; Rogers 1991; Terradas 1995 [1979]).

Anthropologists, then, have been interested in regions *per se*, and they have turned to other disciplines to provide them with the more global forces conditioning their fieldsites. What puts a different spin on things now is that writers in other disciplines have them-selves begun to concern themselves not just with centre and periphery or interlocking modes of production, but with regions *as themselves relevant units of analysis*. In a sense this means that their work produces a body of useful middle-range theory, compared with world systems theory. While this brings such studies close to issues long faced by anthropologists, what makes them (fruitfully) distinct, is that they have arrived at a focus on locality from precisely the opposite direction. Traditionally, anthropologists have begun with the fieldsite and looked outwards; the new regionalists have begun with 'restructuring capitalism' and been forced to regional specificity. Both are concerned with relationships between the one and the other, but from different perspectives.

Indeed, in my own case, many of the characteristics I have found in the Bajo Segura – dispersed industry, multi-occupational households, homework, informal economic 'contracts' and so on – are precisely the phenomena that fascinate socio-economic studies of the European regions, especially and most provocatively, studies that were catalysed by the example of Emilia Romagna, a phenomenon now known as the 'Third Italy' (Bagnasco 1977). Superficially, the area is not dissimilar to the Italian case. There is a long history of prosperous agriculture and alongside it small manufacturing, which, as in Italy, is concentrated by product: Crevillente is associated with rugs, Callosa with fishnets and rope, Alcoy with blankets, Elda and Elche with shoes, and so on.

To this well-established pattern of pockets of product-specific manufacturing centres interspersed amid prosperous commercial agriculture, with its complex patchwork of clustered interpersonal networks and intricate inter-household economic ties, came the demands of the new international division of labour, first affecting local shoe production, and subsequently reverberating out to a whole series of other activities. If asked 'Why here?' many, man or woman, entrepreneur or home-worker, mayor or academic, will reply, almost as though it were a refrain, 'The Valencianos in the south are hard workers. *Aunque no somos muy cultos, somos muy trabajadores* [We might not be terribly cultivated, but we're real workers].' And, referring to a taken-for-granted distinction between greater Catalonia and Spanish-speaking Spain, '*Aunque no hablamos valenciano, somos mas valenciano que los que sí se hablan* [Even though we don't speak Valenciano, we're more valenciano than those that do].'[5] To anybody who has spoken to entrepreneurs, workers or academics in Emilia Romagna, this has a very familiar ring to it, and it is repeated in similar allusions in the area of La Brianza, to the north of Milan, where I am presently working.

Something is happening then, if not uniformly throughout Europe, certainly in very many regions.[6] Whatever this phenomenon may

be, and it is certainly much in dispute, it has been seen as a challenge
to the social sciences. As with all paradigmatic shifts (and many of
the advocates would see it as nothing less), this one has generated
a large body of literature in which very little is not controversial, so
it becomes difficult either to cover the ground adequately or to
reproduce the sense of tentativeness and spirit of eclecticism in
the literature. I therefore take one article which is one of the most
perceptive and comprehensive examples of what I call *socio-economic
approaches*, as the means for exploring the issues: Charles Sabel's
'Flexible specialization and the re-emergence of regional economies'
(1989). I then highlight the specificities of this way of explaining
contemporary regions by setting it alongside another article: David
Harvey's 'The geopolitics of capitalism' (1985),[7] which begins from
a different epistemological starting-point.

Though clearly influenced by one another – Harvey trying to
keep abreast of the latest developments in flexibility by eyeing the
socio-economists' latest work; socio-economists making a passing
gesture toward Harvey's work to produce the left-hand version of
their models – the two approaches come from rather different
epistemological traditions The socio-economic approach has tended
to take the empirical study of paradigmatic regions, such as the
Third Italy, Baden-Württemberg or Silicon Valley, to fine-tune a
conceptual apparatus for understanding 'regional economies' in
contemporary capitalism. As a result the baseline model can be
had with many added features. (In what follows I therefore add
observations by other socio-economists to Sabel's piece.)[8] Harvey,
at least in his earlier work, has tended to be interested in the
sociogenesis of spatial configurations, rather than any one configuration or region.[9]

Socio-economic Approaches to Regions

Sabel opens his article by establishing a pedigree. 'Even as late as
the 1920's, Alfred Marshall, a founder of neo-classical economics,
was fascinated by the regional character of much industrial production. He spoke of Sheffield and South-East Lancashire, for
example, as "industrial districts" to emphasise that the matrix of
production there was the area, not the firm' (1989:17). As we shall
see, much of what socio-economists see to be the challenge of
'the regions' derives from this pedigree. Though Marshall never

elaborated on his original observations, in using the term 'industrial district' he set the stage for two extrapolations. The first, as Sabel observes, was to take the area or region, rather than the firm, as a unit of study for neo-classical economics. Put another way: to study the region *as though it were a firm*. And the second was to acknowledge that there was some element about industrial districts that could not be explained within the conceptual frame of neo-classical economics.[10]

Sabel then goes on to link economic crisis and volatile markets to 'flexible forms of organization which permitted rapid shifts in output'. These in turn lead to 'the reconsolidation of the region as an integrated unit of production' (ibid.: 18). So in this formulation the coherence of exemplary regions is a product of capitalist crisis. While there has always been a historical connection between the economy and the waxing and waning of regions within a country, 'the relation between the economy and its territory is changing' (ibid.: 20). Something new is happening.

And these changes are by no means restricted to the realm of firms, markets and workplaces. Relations between the state and the economy, mediated by the organizations connecting the two, are undergoing often radical reorientation. Sabel suggests that local institutions, from municipal governments to trade and labour organizations, are taking on entirely new functions and strategies, municipalities directing attention less to issues of collective consumption, and more towards generating favourable economic conditions for capital, and trade unions cooperating 'often under duress' in reorganized industrial arrangements.

He then combs through the evidence from exemplary regions, to provide the basis for a model that might be more broadly applied.[11]

> The first conspicuous case was the Third Italy, identified – in contrast to the impoverished South and the old industrial triangle of Genoa, Turin and Milan – by Bagnasco. It is a string of industrial districts stretching from the Venetian provinces in the North through Bologna and Florence to Ancona in the South, and producing everything from knitted goods (Carpi), to special machines (Parma, Bologna), ceramic tiles (Sassuolo), textiles (Como, Prato) agricultural implements (Reggio Emilia), hydraulic devices (Modena), shoes, white goods, plastic tableware and electronic musical instruments (Ancona). But the example of the Third Italy is conquering the first two, as the organizational practices of the industrial districts spread to Turin (factory automation)

and the Canavese (software and computer equipment) in Piedmont, the Milanese provinces (furniture, machine tools) in Lombardy and Bari in the South (ibid.: 22).

Bagnasco coined the phrase 'the Third Italy' to contrast the peculiar character of what he called its 'social market', to the mass production factories of Italy's old North and the generalized poverty of the South.[12] A market that had a strong *social* component to it demonstrated that the competitive efficiency of the region came neither from the open competition between firms that conventional economics might have expected, nor from a similar struggle between capitalists and workers. It came instead from some kind of historically established balance between competition and cooperation. A balance made possible, perhaps, through the mediation of local culture, understood here as values, goals and interests.

As increasing attention was paid to the Third Italy in the years that followed, what analysts found was a network of small firms dispersed through small and medium-sized towns, often with some specific product associated with a town, as Sabel describes above. A number of different classifications were used to capture the character of the Third Italy (see, for example, Brusco's (1982) vs. Fuá and Zacchia's (1983)); but broadly there were to be found small firms with a number of different but complementary characteristics: firms in which family labour ensured high-quality work and long hours, perhaps producing a finished product; others similarly structured, but producing an item needed by another firm; still others receiving 'put-out' work; and still others providing only a service or coordinating function. Further labour costs were reduced by sending out low-skilled work, perhaps even away from the district. Such firms were closely integrated through networking, discussed production and marketing problems, and shared solutions. Networking then, became a major source of learning, a feature that was further extended by the fact that there was considerable mobility of people through different jobs within the region. Firms were often run by entrepreneurs who themselves had unionized labour experience, so that – so it is argued – where non-family labour was employed a cooperative spirit existed between owners and workers, 50 per cent of whom were unionized (Becattini 1992). And then, when family labour *was* used, 'much of what first seemed like child labour proved to be the carefully monitored initiation of children in their parents' work-day world' (Sabel 1989: 24).

What conclusions can be drawn from examples such as these? Sabel cautions us against drawing general conclusions from specific examples (ibid.: 23; 29), but nonetheless goes on to suggest that, evidentiary problems aside, 'an industrial system, novel for this century and able to hold its own against the world's most powerful enterprises' can be identified. Explicit, though loose and only partially formalized, alliances between businesses are matched by capital–labour relations that, however hard fought, tend to be constructive in terms of the redisposition of resources (flexible tools and workers) in the next round, and local non-economic institutions come into play to regulate internal competition (ibid.: 25-9).

Sabel then turns away from regions towards a discussion of the reorganization of multinational firms. What he shows is that, as firms shift away from hierarchies and markets towards networks, their organizational features begin to resemble precisely the features we have just described for the Third Italy. Conventionally, a hierarchically organized capitalist firm, faced with the production of a component, can be seen to make a decision between internal costs and transactional costs: whether to make the component through mobilizing its own organizational resources, or whether to have it made through market transactions (Williamson and Ouchi 1981). Ordinarily, 'informalization' of the economy can be seen as a tendency to favour the latter over the former strategy, i.e. to favour (sub)contracting (Castells and Portes, 1989).

Against this 'Fordist' model, Sabel suggests another, in which 'workers and subcontractors are treated . . . as (junior) partners in production with some capacity to reshape the product or the production process. . . . The operating units [within the firm], meanwhile, come to resemble autonomous small- or medium-sized firms' (1989: 32-3). This network model within the firm's organization then extends to these units' relations with subcontractors. Contractors, finding themselves working for a number of large firms in as many industries, begin to develop inter-industry production networks, exchanging information such that 'network production is best viewed as a learning system' (ibid.: 35).

It is not hard to see how such a 'social economy' provides awkward challenges to a discipline whose dominant discourse refers to an actor's satisfaction of needs and desires through the instrumental use of scarce resources. For here we have the rationality of one firm thoroughly penetrated by the rationality of another.[13] Sabel talks of Moebius-strip organizations and a 'blur[ring of] the

boundary between firms and between the economy and society',
(1991) which results in the formation of 'regional economies'
(1989). It is hardly surprising then that we find writers such a
Granovetter (1985) returning to Polanyi and talking about the social
embeddedness of the economy, and the need to theorize 'the social'
within an albeit modified neo-classical frame of reference.

But if economic science is to become more sociological, we should
also note a move in the opposite direction. By creating an elision
between region and the re-modelled multinational firm there is a
dangerous shift from the rationality of the firm as an instrumental
actor, to *the rationality of a region as an instrumental actor.* Hence the
substitution of the study of (successful) regions for the older interest
in successful firms. The criteria for discussing adaptations,
traditions and cultures become those of success, success defined
moreover in the same terms as that of shares on the New York
Stock Exchange. Pollert (1988) argues for example that, even among
self-professed writers of the left, the well-being of workers and local
residents has been replaced by a discourse that talks entirely of the
well-being of firms. Good regions, attractive regions, regions with
a future are not places that would attract (over-worked) people –
just enlightened, flexible firms.

It is just possible, of course, that this is not a problem confined
to academic economists. In the fourth part of his piece, Sabel turns
attention to the ways in which industrialists, bankers and development officials (note: no unions or residents' associations are
mentioned here) can begin to coordinate various government
programmes and agencies that were originally addressed to quite
separate problems, so as to coordinate the entire package toward
'regional success'. This is a kind of streamlined modernity, a naked
economic instrumentalism with respect to all institutions and
players in the social arena. Sabel gives an especially vivid example
which should provoke us into very careful if cynical study of the
pragmatic (as opposed to normative (see Bailey 1969)) functions
of social institutions in a region:

> [I]n West Germany, [a] district hospital, which depends on a strong
> local economy to keep firms' medical insurance payments within
> acceptable limits and hence its own finances in balance, could well
> become a nerve centre of economic planning. Because the hospitals'
> governing boards are composed of leading local industrialists and
> politicians whose own fate reflects the institutions', these committees

provide a natural forum for discussion of the problems of co-ordination (Sabel 1989: 44).

Things change, then, and yet there is something that always remains the same about a region, some elusive element of regional continuity, and Sabel now turns to this. For most analysts it comes down to social solidarity. Contemporary actors can reinforce trust and cooperation through their actions, so the argument goes, but they cannot generate such values where they do not already have a healthy earlier growth (Putnam 1993). So the question arises: to what element of past society should we look for this key?

Sabel rehearses the argument that finds the key in material social relations and long-instituted practices. Thus Bagnasco and later others such as Becattini find the origins of key values in pre-existing land tenure patterns and artisanal by-employments. The argument goes:

> Land holdings were so small that proprietors had to supplement agricultural income with income from artisanal work . . . or industrial employment (in, say, the urban construction industry during the agricultural off season). . . . *Mezzadria*, or sharecropping, combined with handicraft production exported via trade routes first opened by the Rennaissance city states, were typical of the Third Italy. . . . The . . . results were the formation of entrepreneurial families which survived by shifting resources quickly from activity to activity, and the creation of local institutions such as banks and small merchant houses which helped the families to move rapidly into national and international markets when the opportunity arose (Sabel 1989: 46).[14]

Sabel rejects the argument that suggests that a certain set of pre-existing social relations of and in production can be the basis for contemporary social solidarity. It cannot account for counter-examples, he suggests, nor can it explain in itself the continuity of these essential sentiments from then to now. The fact is, he observes, trust and cooperation are necessary in some measure in *any* coordinated production process, so that the question becomes precisely how their meaning as local traditions is interpreted in the present (ibid.: 49). Earlier, Sabel has insisted on asking questions that convey well the kind of chicken-and-egg problem that socio-economists have when they try to identify designated areas as coherent 'regional economies':

But should these regional economies be considered a negotiated alliance of fundamentally distinct groups, or integral communities with a fluid but discernable [sic] division of labour? If the latter, does the community operate according to a single logic . . . or does [it] depend on the fusion of more fundamental distinct principles . . .? Each conceptualization suggests different potential fault lines in the industrial districts – class against class, individuals or factions against the whole, families against one another or against merchants – and different principles for remediating conflict. All are plausible, none wholly persuasive (ibid.: 29).

So for Sabel the question comes down less to what happened in the past than to what rabbit is produced out of the hat of the past. He has called this section of his essay 'the politics of memory', and he now suggests that conflicts supposedly resolved in the past may simply be the product of a regional politics in which the past is redefined as traditionally harmonious (ibid.: 47). Clearly this is a far more sophisticated understanding of culture than that of most of the socio-economists, but Sabel appears to use ideologies of 'family', ethnicity and 'local pride' as causal factors. Yet if these ideologies are presented without the institutions and relationships that bring them to the level of practices the effect is to give great causal priority to culture, a local culture moreover that seems to have no important historical basis. Resort to culture of this kind runs the risk of becoming a substitute for more demanding historical enquiry. As Meric Gertler argues, it is 'important to examine the process by which cultures are actively produced and reproduced by social practices and institutions over time' (1995: 6). And he uses his own work in Canada and Germany to show that, time and again, when either informants or – more culpably – analysts use cultural explanations for certain locally distinct practices, 'culture' is being used as a kind of gloss for the history of national and regional social institutions and state regulations, which ultimately provide far stronger causal criteria for regional patternings.

In summary, then, I began by noting that the Marshallian (neo-classical) pedigree was not incidental for socio-economic discussions of the regions, but (as the term 'socio-economics' itself implies) has been carried forward in attempts to expand the realm of economic explanation. We have noted too that Sabel ties the growing interest in 'the regions' to the idea that we are now witnessing a new form of capitalism ('flexibility'). One effect of these new forms is that business institutions begin to spread into social institutions that had hitherto retained a certain distance and distinctiveness from them. The region becomes an industrial system that can hold its own against powerful enterprises, and powerful enterprises respond by blending into regional systems. Then, as the region takes over from the firm, so the regulatory functions hitherto contained within the firm's hierarchical organization have to be performed through a dispersed set of social institutions and culturally-sedimented practices.

Dispersed sets of interpersonal ties between commercially-oriented agriculturalists and artisans provide the historical precondition for contemporary *networks*. 'Networks' have entered the socio-economics vocabulary as a peculiar and distinct set of social practices (having neither the characteristics of formal institutions ['hierarchies'] nor of egotistical market relations). Though dealt with differently by various groups within the socio-economics discourse, networks always contain an unavoidable *cultural* dimension. Sabel, for example, sees the principal feature of networks to be their capacity as learning systems, passing information in multiple directions and with great situational adaptability. Law (1986) and others refer quite specifically to the role of 'organizational cultures' either as outgrowths from network relationships, or as their pre-condition.

Reading this literature as an anthropologist I find that certain observations seem acute, as though, starting from a different base-camp, these writers have formulated problems and issues somewhat differently from anthropologists looking at places through the lens of fieldwork, and as a result, we can learn from them. I have a strong sense, for example, that the more elusive feelings people have about the Bajo Segura might fruitfully be filtered through some of these perceptions, while I have an equally strong sense that most of what they have to say would not be especially useful in the context of Huasicancha. On the other hand, reading this literature as an anthropologist I also find, amidst the acute insights, a number of conclusions that give me a sense of *déjà vu*. The rather gross understanding of commercial sharecropping as an explanation of contemporary social mores would be one example; the chicken-and-egg discussion Sabel gives us about *community* as either a 'negotiated alliance of fundamentally distinct groups' or operating 'according to a single logic' would be a second. Indeed, while Sabel's work is rich in example and sensitive in interpretation, providing much for an anthropological agenda, it is, ultimately and despite the occasional disclaimer, empirically derived. There is nothing wrong with empiricism, which it has become fashionable to berate; but empirical evidence is only as good as the theoretical frame through which the data is processed; and yet the way in which socio-economists seek to explore the features of one region to provide the solution for another can give the impression of being theoretically, possibly even politically, neutral. Yet the resolute functionalism of virtually every explanation can be translated into policy initiatives that become a kind of neo-modernist insistence on what is 'good' or 'bad' for the common weal.

It is important to emphasize this point. Their way of thinking may be post-industrial, certainly post-Fordist, but absolutely not post-modern: contemporary analyses seeking to understand and enhance regional economies are, without exception super-modernist in the way they imagine the social world (see Chapter 1). Prone to painting a rather monolithic view of history, Zygmunt Bauman (1992: 53), in his discussions of modernity, for example, nevertheless captures well what I mean by this characterization:

> The new, modern order took off as a desperate search for structure in a world suddenly denuded of structure. Utopias that served as beacons for the long march to the rule of reason visualized a world without margins, leftovers, the unaccounted for – without dissidents and rebels; a world in which . . . everyone will have a job to do and everyone will be keen to do the job he has to: the *I will* and *I must* will merge . . . No wonder utopias chose architecture and urban planning as both the vehicle and the master-metaphor of the perfect world that would know of no misfits and hence of no disorder.

Of course this earlier modernism set reason *against* culture, while regional studies tend to rely on the term. Yet the role occupied by the notion 'culture' in studies of supposedly *social* markets and knowledge-transmitting networked firms is both essential to their understanding of regional success and at the same time confused and problematic. (Marshall referred to industrial *atmosphere*.) In so far as these are social markets, so it follows that the arena of purely 'economic' decision-making is profoundly penetrated, contorted and elided by local cultural dispositions. This should mean that the utilitarian undergirding of neo-classical economic reasoning be-comes profoundly modified as the economy is understood to be embedded. In practice though, as I have just said, this is a tough cat to drown, so that these principles of explanation remain, and 'culture' becomes 'a "dustbin category" for anything we can't explain', as Sayer and Walker have noted (Sayer and Walker 1992: 177–8). There may be no epistemological inconsistency in throwing culture into the recipe in one place or another; but it does become problematic as soon as it is used as an essential element of an explanation.

So one reason that 'culture' enters the discourse of these kinds of regional studies has to do with the tension between their theoretical tools and the new kind of *social* economy they claim to have discovered and seek to advocate. Another is that actors in exemplary regions have become adept at championing the value of 'local culture'. This is one reason why 'culture' becomes so visible at just the moment when regional economies too get a high profile – it attracts investors. But we need to be rather more penetrating about what specific features of culture have this effect. This has to do with the fact that the practice of dispersing work into factories-without-walls requires forms of face-to-face surveillance and social regulation that call up time-tested forms of 'proper behaviour'. The specific characteristics of local culture become a medium of social regulation and rather selective and particular local cultural under-standings and practices take on an almost frenetic and instrumental afterlife.

Culture, then, a term once confined mostly to anthropologists and art critics, has come into much wider currency. Yet both the use of the notion 'culture' on the part of analysts and this latter kind of usage effectively reconstitute what culture is doing in society, and hence what we mean when we use the term.

Harvey on Spatial Coherence

The way in which they focus on how social processes give shape to *place*, then, makes socio-economic studies of regions useful for anthropologists working in late-capitalist social formations, but we need to be aware of the extra baggage we bring with us when we attempt to import their epistemological frame into our own explan-ations. The figure of David Harvey is both emblematic and inciteful here, for Harvey's name is often adduced by social economists to authenticate their left credentials, and he has also become the non-anthropologist of choice for anthropologists wanting to make a quick reference (Harvey 1989) to the special features of contemporary capitalism. Yet Harvey's entire epistemological edifice is distinct from the customized neo-classical economism that informs the kinds of analyses I have just been discussing. We can therefore clarify especially clearly the specifics of that approach by comparing it to Harvey's, yet to do so we need to recognize that Harvey's work is not about the newly emergent regional economies of Europe. Instead, the pieces I discuss here represent an attempt to understand the way in which the processes of capitalist production and circulation give rise to social relationships that, through history, become sedimented in physical places, giving them their distinctive shape and character.

He begins, therefore, with what he takes to be a fairly uncontroversial position: 'We can I think all agree that the reproduction of daily life depends upon the production of commodities produced through a system of circulation of capital that has profit-seeking as its direct and socially accepted goal' (Harvey 1985: 128). Yet for such circulation to occur, a physical and social infrastructure must be in place: everything from roads, built environments and telecommunications systems, to legal, educational and financial institutions. This of course has a special importance for the relationship between advantaged and disadvantaged regions, and I shall return to it in a moment.[15]

But before doing so, we should review some of Harvey's itemized points about this system of social relations, for they will have implications for what I have to say later. Moreover, as the principles for beginning enquiry, they differ strikingly from Marshall's (neoclassical) point of departure. Harvey starts with the observation that the basis for continued capital circulation lies in *the production of real values*. To obtain profits through unequal exchange (for example, between regions) is simply to displace this process from one locale to another (cf. Emmanuel 1972). He then goes on to talk about *exploitation*, not in its pejorative sense but rather in technical terms. Labour creates more in production than its gets for the sale of its labour power; exploitation is measured by this ratio (Harvey 1985: 130). This means that the circulation of capital has two inevitable consequences. First, exploitation can be increased (in its technical sense) through the increase in overall productivity: for example, through making more efficient machines. Second, this overall process of circulation is predicated on a class relation, and hence implies opposition and struggle. This is not simply the quantitative issue of how much capitalists have to pay to procure the rights to labour, it is also the qualitative one of what those rights comprise: the conditions and intensity of work, the way in which skills and the like might be perpetuated. (Hence it has a crucial cultural dimension.)

Harvey then goes on to show how the competition between one capital (or firm) and another, together with the capital–labour relationship, encourages capital as a whole toward greater technical dynamism and hence increased rates of circulation, which eventually lead to an overaccumulation crisis (in any one region). Here we encounter capital being devalued (inflation, default on debts, and so on) and labour too (unemployment, diminished life chances, and so forth). Crises of this kind can be at least temporarily resolved, however, through a 'spatial fix': i.e. displacements into other geographical areas. This ability of capital and labour to move quickly from place to place, i.e. to overcome space, *depends on the creation of fixed, essentially immobile social and physical infrastructures.* 'A part of the circulation of capital slows down in order to promote accelerating turnover times for the remainder' (ibid.: 136). We have here then, the beginnings of an understanding of the way in which certain kinds of social relationship generate sediments of environmental reality in particular places, and how that environmental reality facilitates (or restricts) regional development.

These are features that are of great importance for understanding the character of a region: its towns and roads, its countryside and schools. Indeed, we are beginning to get a sense of gravitational and magnetic currents that might circulate through and around these physical areas and social institutions, giving to them a certain distinctive character, such as a prominent city with its theatres and shopping areas. But the coagulation of capital into these fixed places requires intervention above and beyond 'natural' market forces. As the turnover time for returns to investment gets ever shorter, so it becomes harder to entice capital to invest in fixed infrastructure, with its slower pay-off period. Here local state institutions or regional banks become crucial. (As they have been in Baden-Württemberg and Emilia Romagna respectively). The one may offer subsidies, while the other may float bonds offering rates of return higher than returns to capital in the present round of circulation. Needless to say, in either case some kind of regional self-consciousness and political will are pre-requisites for interventions of this kind.

Here lies the kind of contradiction built into the production of place for the overcoming of space: the embedding of a region, with all its social and physical attributes, serves to increase the mobility of circulating capital; but then the freeing up of circulating capital as a result, threatens to undermine this very spatial coherence. As Harvey puts it, 'There are processes at work . . . that define *regional spaces* within which production and consumption, supply and demand, . . . class struggle and accumulation, culture and life style, hang together as some kind of structured coherence within a totality of productive forces and social relations' (ibid.: 147, *italics in original*); and there is also a process at work that undermines this coherence, as local capitals try to move out in order to find a 'spatial fix' through exploiting geographical unevenness in rates of profit.[16]

What I want to stress here are *two* interlocking processes of differentiation: on the one hand class differentiations arising from the exploitation relationship between capital and labour and on the other uneven regional differentiations, arising – not entirely, but to a significant degree – from the way in which the need to circulate more freely and rapidly through space encourages capital to invest in the fixed elements of place. Moreover, just as processes of differentiation are inter-related, so too are the counter-processes that break down those divisions between classes and dissolve regional distinctions: the tension between regional persistence and global tendencies toward dissolution comes up against the other tension, that between classes within a region.

The effect of these 'space wars' *on a particular region* is to throw up quite specific issues for the character of the relationships between classes. As a result of the 'need to make a certain portion of capital immobile in order to give the remainder freedom to move', 'the basis is laid for the rise of a territorially based alliance between various factions of capital, the local state and even whole classes, in defence of social reproduction processes . . . within a particular territory' (Harvey 1982: 420). The history of these tensions in class interests and the struggles that result from them are then written on to the physical and social landscape in the form of interest-specific social institutions and physical infrastructures. By *interest-specific* I mean that institutions don't just arise through history to meet various regional requirements; they arise out of the conflicts and compromises between interest groups. Certain institutions, from chambers of commerce to union locals, may arise specifically to articulate the interests of one or another such group, and these in turn become elements of the regional reality that one group may be prepared to sacrifice and another to fight to preserve.

Meanwhile, along another fault line 'space wars' can give rise to struggles *between regions*, producing movements in defence of territorially based interests. Generalized economic crises, which, as we have seen, can result in devaluations of fixed capital and local labour, can lead to bitter struggles 'over which locale is to bear the brunt of the devaluation that must surely come' (ibid.).[17] Harvey, then, would tend to see the changing function of state institutions at national and local level as the result of the pattern of these kinds of class and regional contradictions, tensions and possible alliances.

Yet the nature of these class relationships has indeed changed with new forms of industrial organization. In more recent work, Harvey therefore notes that at the local level social institutions do begin to take on changing functions with recent shifts toward flexible accumulation. 'Organized sub-contracting , for example, opens up opportunities for small business formation, and in some instances permits older systems of domestic, artisanal, familial (patriarchal), and paternalistic ('god-father', 'guv'nor', or even mafia-like) labour systems to revive and flourish as centrepieces rather than as appendages of the production system' (Harvey 1989: 152). There is a danger here that the concentration of a multiplicity of very complex and locally specific forms of production relations and labour regulation[18] may become glossed over (and thereby obscured) by use of what are now familiar catch-phrases, 'familial', 'patriarchal' 'paternalistic' and so on; a danger too that these may be seen as 'older systems' – systems (systems?) dredged up from the past, rather than actively sustained and reproduced in the present – letting the present off the hook, as it were, by passing the blame back to a darker, more grinding past. Then the, in my view undeniable, fact that these forms of labour regulation (which Marx referred to as the formal subsumption of labour) require resort to elements of local culture, can too easily be read off as though 'culture' is 'custom' and 'custom', 'tradition'. This question of the uneasy slippage between 'culture' and history, I will take up below.

It is obvious, I hope, that the two approaches, represented here by the work of Sabel on the one hand and Harvey on the other, would point toward rather different agendas for an anthropology of regions. We can, and many of us do, cut and paste bits and pieces from the one or the other, but I am not sure that we don't lose some critical insights as a result. The practice allows us to move into any room we choose – a bit of 'the social market' here, a bit of 'spatial fix' there; but it also allows us to move quickly on to another without exploring some of the closets before leaving. And the practitioners themselves encourage this. Strictly speaking, we could say that by adding various and largely unweighed-and-sorted causal factors to the original Marshallian model socio-economists undercut the principles and goals of the explanations they are trying to make. The general applicability principle, for example, which justifies the use of a model, diminishes as more and more factors (themselves incompatible with the market rationality that drives the model) are added. Likewise, Harvey provides us in his earlier work with a very powerful image of how the reproduction of capitalism impacts on the shape and form of places, but his more recent writings flirt uncertainly with the extent and distinctiveness of 'flexibility' and seem to throw up caveats to the iron logic he had hitherto exposed, caveats that seek to enrich but in fact undercut the power of the model. If the condition of postmodernity is to resolve and surround the limits to capital, just how limited does this make capital: just how conditioning of capital are postmodern trends and forces?

It turns out that it is the warm and fuzzy soft toy, 'culture', that enables the two approaches to keep faith with the ways of thinking that underlie their respective approaches – the dominant role given to the allocation of scarce resources to satisfy assumed needs in the one case, and the logic of capital in the other. This seems to obscure rather than highlight the multiple and complex set of templates and forces that arise from the evidence of particular historical and local cases.[19] If this is so, then these approaches would be of use us in so far as they either dispense with use of culture as a component of their explanations, or clarify what they mean by use of the term.

Perspectives on Culture

Both Sabel and Harvey understand capitalism to be taking on a modified form. Sabel sees this as a radical break (Piore and Sabel 1984), while Harvey sees it as a new wrinkle on an old cloth (Harvey 1989: 191ff.). In both cases this suggests changing relationships between economy and culture – between the culture of production and the production of culture. And hence a changing research agenda. Yet from the different epistemologies of these two approaches emanate quite different understandings of economy, society and culture, and hence quite different sets of priorities and problems.

For the socio-economists, interest in the regions has been generated by a perceived novelty or modification in capitalist industrial organization and technology, labour markets, and consumption patterns.[20] Central to this discourse is the assertion that we have moved from the hegemony of an intra-firm command structure to a process of regulation encompassing wider geographical areas and hence penetrating more deeply into society itself, beyond the factory walls, as it were. Much of this novelty was demonstrated by the empirical observation of the region of Emilia Romagna in Italy. And Bagnasco's original observation that the market was as much a social as an economic institution (cf. Polanyi 1957), was subsequently extended by people I have called 'socio-economists', so as to make their models more accurately reflect these new social arrangements.

The steps involved are as follows: (1) The impetus to render a model more sophisticated came from the empirical evidence (first for Marshall in Sheffield; later for others in the Third Italy). (2) This took the specific form of obliging socio-economists to explore the implications of *social* forces for economic action. But (3) Since 'the social' itself tends to be negatively derived from a neo-classical understanding of what constitutes 'the economic', it remains undertheorized (see Chapter 5). This pre-empts the exploration of profound differences in, for example, the private and the public, the constitution of gender, or the social definition of 'ownership'. (4) Actual differences therefore become explainable in terms of 'culture' – a kind of historical deadweight.[21] The limitations of a synchronic neo-classical analysis become the stimulus for the turn to 'culture', but because culture is used as an *explanation* for local practices and strategies, it has to be kept distinct from them: either *back* in history (custom, tradition, and so on) or *up* in mental constructs (ideology, cognitive maps, and the like).

I want to try to illustrate how this imaging of the social world directs our attention in one direction and not another, setting up a realm of questions while rendering others unimportant or at least less important. Since I regard the issue of social inequality, be it between classes of people or regions in a country, to be necessarily a central concern to any legitimate social science, I will start from there. I will then turn to what I consider to be likewise necessarily of concern to a legitimate social science, the exploitation of labour.

We can begin by recalling Sabel's question, 'Does the [regional] community operate according to a single logic . . . or does [it] depend on the fusion of more fundamental distinct principles . . .?' As Sabel goes on to imply, how this question is resolved gives rise to a very specific research agenda, yet it is a very difficult one to answer. From a cultural perspective it is a question about the degree to which meanings, values and interests are broadly shared *and the manner through which – historically – this coherence has been reached.* Sabel, for example, talks about the past being redefined as traditionally harmonious; but this seems to imply a set of social subjects who can step out of the historical currents that brought them into existence and reinvent that past that presumably played some role in inventing them in the first place.

A potential answer comes from Becattini:

> The system of values . . . constitutes one of the preliminary requirements for the development of a district, and one of the essential conditions of its reproduction . . .
>
> This does not mean that there will be no clash of interests between the members of the district, or no perception of such clashes. Rather, they are experienced and defined in similar forms and within a framework of a sort of community-like superior interest which becomes an inner principle for the people of the district as a whole.
>
> All this may look like a description of a 'closed community', where people's lives are smothered by a multitude of rules. The industrial district is indeed a place where historical development has induced strong inward constraints to the so-called 'natural' behaviour of individuals. Among these constraints is, for instance, some quantity of 'resistance' against unconditional acceptance of values which prevail in the 'outside world', and a related tendency to use 'double standards' when treating [with] one's fellow-citizens – even the 'new' ones, provided they are 'integrated' – rather than 'strangers' (1992: 39).

Here we find that the system of values is a pre-requisite for regional 'success', but a rather tantalizing question escapes us: we have no inkling of how 'a framework of community-like superior interest which becomes an inner principle for the people of the district' comes into being. This, it seems to me, requires a more thoroughly historicized sociology than would be possible given the

frame of reference for this kind of enquiry: a deeper characterization of processes of social reproduction, for example, and the
emergence of collective groupings – of resistance and accommodation – thrown up within such a process. Yet, if this were done,
Becattini's answer to the either/or question – single logic or fundamentally distinct principles – does seem to me to be useful and
important. For it encourages us to take a thoroughly politicized
and dynamic view of regional culture. As he sees it, the reason
why 'clashes of interests' do not degenerate into irreconcilable
'distinct principles' is because resistance to the outside world
generates an umbrella-like regional culture that constrains behaviour (cf. Chapter 2). Rather than a static view of cultural values
and regionality, the suggestion seems to be that regionality is
analogous to a social movement in which internal dynamics are
dialectically related to what the movement is up against.[22] Regulation of internal differences is conditioned by the more urgent task
of confronting and dealing with differences with the outside. This
provides a useful point of comparison between my Central Peruvian
case, where such politics existed (as Becattini puts it: 'resistance
against unconditional acceptance of values which prevail in the
"outside world", and a related tendency to use "double standards"
when treating [with] one's fellow-citizens . . . rather than "strangers"'
(1992: 39)) and my Spanish case, where it didn't. Yet Becattini's
suggestion does not fit the latter case. The *sine qua non* for a
(successful) industrial district is here made to lie within the domain
of a certain kind of culture of collective resistance (apparently absent
in contemporary Bajo Segura); though this seems to be a tauto-
logical argument, begging the question of where such a culture
comes from. This reveals the extent to which explanations of this
kind tend toward an extremely superficial view of historical process,
since present cultural values become an explanation rather than
something to be explained.

The Bajo Segura example would suggest a slightly modified line
of argument about how insiders and outsiders get to be constituted
as such. Because 'flexibility' is used to refer to an ability (on the
part of an individual, institution, or region) to respond rapidly to
very *specific* situations (for example, market opportunities, product
changes and so on) it comes close to the situational adaptability
associated with 'informal economies',[23] and this becomes especially
so when the flexibility of labour is seen ultimately to rest on regional
family values:

The most important factor is lower labour costs which come from two sources. First in family run companies, family members are willing to work long hours for their direct stake in the firm. Secondly, wage-workers are willing to accept wages lower than in areas of older industrialization since they can count on a lower cost of living and on family support in the form of free rent and/or participation in agricultural activities (Cenzatti 1992: 201–2).

Flexibility, then, ultimately rests on a variety of informal relationships in which labour is mobilized through appeals that require something above and beyond the commodified labour contract. Here are the lines of contact between flexibility and informality, and the point where the two join is in a shared sense of the importance for social reproduction of *intimate, face-to-face relations,* or ideological extensions of this kind of intimacy to broader arenas (Smith 1990, 1994b). This offers a different view to Becattini's, of the region as a closed community in contrast to an alien world beyond. One very important element of 'culture' that Becattini has almost picked up on is its use as a particular element of social regulation – highly dispersed, widely diverse, uneven and elusive – appropriate in a regional context, because of the region's fuzzy and unpatrolled frontiers and empty centres of control (as opposed to those of a national state or corporate firm, for example). This understanding of the nature of social practices helps to explain how things with such fuzzy and unpatrolled frontiers and such moving centres can generate the magnetic fields that then come to be seen in cultural terms – as propensities to work, trust and so on.

  This, however, seems to produce a rather limited view of how social power works, confining it to the transactional power of individuals making (albeit socially and culturally complex) decisions. This becomes clear as we shift attention toward the history of the kind of social relations of production and reproduction that tend to be tied up within a region. This requires a rather different set of questions. Earlier I have tried to show how Harvey's work might help to throw light on the role of regional forces – be they local banks, or even local sentiments and beliefs in the area – in tying up capital in regional physical infrastructures that, in turn, make possible the increased circulation of more mobile capital. Harvey points out that, as the rate of circulating capital increases, more political interventions are required to make investments in regional infrastructure attractive or obligatory. Yet all this reveals the difficulty of separating the 'material conditions' of capitalism in a region, from local culture: culture understood here both in terms of the region's history and also in terms of the inter-communicative practice of ideas, values and beliefs about the future.

We can speculate on how these processes get translated into ideas about 'local culture'. Gazing from the present toward the past, the prior creation of these kinds of infrastructures is a pre-condition for a successful regional production process in the present. Since local social will – enforced saving and personal sacrifices in consumption, for example – is required to generate such capital for fixed infrastructures, local people's memories – of the straitened ethics and regional sentiment of their forebears – may not be entirely invented. Then, gazing from the present toward the future, fictitious capital is an investment in the belief that the combination it produces of physical and social infrastructure with the circulating capital and labour of a future round *will be more productive* than the present. Fictitious capital is a claim on future regional labour. As such it requires both faith in the region's future and/or power over the region's reproduction. In the long run investment in the future productivity of labour must be called in: put bluntly, the physical labour must eventually be found. Of course, one definition of a capitalist crisis is precisely when this faith in the future is not met: the future round cannot achieve the productivity that was anticipated for it. When this happens, once more some intervention above and beyond 'the natural laws' of the market is required. Circulating capital and labour must be rendered sticky in some way; they can't be allowed to drift off to other sites where rates are better.

One way to do this with respect to labour is to limit the way it is freed up through the use of the pure wage-relationship: either decommodify existing labour relationships or pushing work toward arenas not customarily commodified.[24] This of course not only tends to make labour more sticky in respect to place and person (you get and give jobs to those you 'love' and 'trust'), it also makes it cheaper. Hence we find Cenzatti noting earlier that the most important factor in regional success is lower labour costs based on family labour. With the help of pre-existing networks, forms of labour are extended from direct domestic production that uses family ideologies and patriarchal forms of control towards more extended versions of much the same things (what Harvey refers to as godfather or guv'nor relationships) in order to increase surpluses while limiting the need to invest in capital equipment. Labour is subsumed to the dictates of capital accumulation through a formal mechanism that is 'more favourable to the development of *versatility among the workers,* and hence to increasing the diversity of modes of working and ways of earning a living' (Marx 1976: 1026–7, *italics in original*).

Here we see a rather different slant on Becattini's 'strong inward constraints to the so-called "natural" behaviour of individuals'. While there is no question that many are the ways in which small family firms and other forms of intimate workplace are also the sites of inventiveness and technological change, it would be a mistake to separate such local worker skills from the way in which these 'cultural investments' relate to the requirements of regional circulating and fixed capital. Some kind of personalistic culture – and many are its actual manifestations – is essential for the reproduction of the relationships that generate absolute surplus value. As such, it is closely connected with the competitive threats to local capitalists, whose investments are tied up in regional fixed capital, such as land and plant. Whether through inclination or necessity local entrepreneurs use guv'nor relationships and the like as a regional substitute for the spatial fixes accruing to more mobile circulating capital. Sometimes, as in the Third Italy, it works impressively. Sometimes, as in the Bajo Segura, the results are rather more draconian.

In these two forms of capitalist relationship (formal subsumption and local fixed capital) we see the way in which culture is brought into play. The cultural sites of absolute surplus value make possible the increased extraction of surpluses from workers on the part of local bosses, landowners and so on, whose old capital is deeply buried in local infrastructure (physical, social and even 'political' – in the form of bribes, the cost of occupying political office, and so on). The more unfettered circulating capital becomes, the more primitive becomes local capital, in this respect. This of course provides a historical materialist explanation for why regional revivals occur simultaneously with the globalization of capital. These *social relationships* take on the appearance of a regional *culture*. In their appearance as authoritarian fathers, for example, or men of honour and women of shame, or colourful local political bosses, these can be read as elements of local culture.

This suggests that the two approaches imply two rather different ways of employing the idea of culture. Socio-economics seems to encourage us to draw a picture of culture as a form of ideology. Serving an important function as mediator and regulator of 'economic' behaviour, culture can be seen in terms of norms and expectations that pattern conduct. As such, they require some historical continuity, but are nonetheless subject to selection through the manipulation of 'history'. Harvey's interest in the sociogenesis of regionality, on the other hand, seems to push us away from the association of culture with the mental, the subjective or the blueprint for behaviour. His preoccupation with historical process encourages us, if not quite to dissolve, then to understand dialectically the distinction between 'objective' environmental conditions on the one hand and embedded social practices, on the other; between the forming of physical and social infrastructure on the one hand and the forming of social subjects on the other. Whether or not such an imaging of social process requires a notion of culture is, to my mind, uncertain.

Conclusion

As anthropologists have become increasingly interested in the new economic zones of China, the *maquiladoras* on the US–Mexican border, or the character of 'Asian capitalism', the need to understand local practices in the context of global forces makes the eclectic application of existing socio-economic approaches to new forms of capitalism, especially the study of regions, very attractive. They seem open both to local and global currents in seeking explanation and they show themselves to be open to *marxisante* and world systems perspectives while acknowledging a flattering debt to those who have concerned themselves with the study of culture. This trend will continue. The question is how it will direct attention – toward what kinds of metaphors and images of society and hence their attendant questions, and away from other metaphors and images, and hence other, still obscured questions and issues.

When we find socio-economists wishing to give greater weight to elements of local culture in their analyses, their discovery of culture is clearly reflected in the everyday world of regional economies, where local culture likewise has become an issue, and I have attempted to show why this might be so. Yet socio-economists are not very convincing in showing us that they have been able to move beyond their own limitations of neo-modernist apologetics for, or worse, celebrations of, capitalism. They persist in using 'culture' unreflectively to cover a very wide range of social phenomena. But, more importantly, they persist in ghettoizing culture. Kept in a laboratory phial, it is let loose to explain an analytically pre-cultural set of practices. Far from teasing out more interesting questions to ask, this practice forecloses them, and this is especially so with respect to their avoidance of a historical sociology that goes beyond hunting and gathering from the past to pick up isolated practices here or beliefs there that in some way explain current peculiarities of conduct. Harvey's work, at least in its earlier form, seems historically more rewarding. It gives us the *questions* we might want to ask of history – what kinds of factors and forces we should be looking for that give particular character to the way people think and act around the magnetic field of place. But the danger lies in the answers coming always in terms of the juggernaut of capital, rather than in the specifics of particular histories and specific places.

I began this chapter by contrasting the strong sense of place felt by the people of Huasicancha in Peru with a much more diffuse sentiment in a region of present-day southeastern Spain. Raymond Williams was a firm believer in the way in which the immediacy and primacy of locality gives us an anchor on ourselves as stable *personas* with at least some kind of internal coherence. One has the feeling that Williams would have been happy in the locality of Huasicancha, its remoteness, its high mountains and its position on three provincial borderlines. But what makes Williams's writings so provocative and useful is that as he left the place of his growing-up and became a different and distant person from it, he began to understand too that the place he had left was changing – in a sense changing from the kind of place I found in Peru to the one I could hardly find in Spain.

Regions are about the historical ways in which people relate to one another through the medium of and by the use of place. Yet because there is a number of different dimensions to how people 'relate to one another' so there are many ways of thinking about social relationships. In the contrast between the Peruvian and Spanish cases, for example, it is not simply the fact that the Huasic-anchinos subjectively relate to one another as though they lived in a fairly knowable community of others, while for the people of the Bajo Segura there was a sense of floating that made this 'know-ability' more problematic. It is also that the sense of 'knowing' on the one hand and of 'floating' on the other are themselves the product of *an entirely other level* at which people relate to one another in and through space (Hudson and Sadler 1986: 173–4). What makes Huasicancha seem 'knowable' is not so much its size, but what appears to Huasicanchinos to be 'desirable and necessary to be known' . . . '[W]hat is knowable is not only a function of objects . . . It is also a function of subjects, of observers – what is desired and what needs to be known' (Williams 1973:165). And this in turn is a function of historical forces that have produced a particular sense of place among these people of highland Peru.

But the *knowability* of such communities and, by contrast, the alienating sense of knowing so little in places like the Bajo Segura, *are only apparent*, are only one dimension. As Williams would put it, a first way of thinking – a 'militant particularism'. For what is desired to be known and what needs to be known are not necessarily the same thing. The *huasicanchinos*' way of knowing place was an especially important component of their political campaign (Smith 1989), yet it does seem to be a rather special form of knowing. Indeed it is precisely the form of knowing that comes from the direct extension of local experience and intimate culture to a wider field. An extension that is tempting, but not for all that, analytically valid, 'insufficiently aware of the quite systematic obstacles which [stand] in its way' (Williams 1989: 115).

While I have tried to show why culture of this kind seems so crucial an explanatory device for regionality, there is a great danger of analysts themselves taking up this mentalist view of culture; what Augé calls 'the totality temptation' (Augé 1995: 48). This is dangerous, because the way people relate to one another through the medium of, and by the use of place, involves a range of levels. Though regionality cannot be understand without a historically grounded understanding of *social differentiation,* yet there is no *one* such process but many, operating with and against one another and at a number of different levels. As there is a material history – of machines and migrations, of buildings and bombs – and also a way in which people interpret their past, so too there are variations in the way people get distributed over a locale and a way in which they interpret their locality. So complex is such a process that no *a priori* model is likely to serve. One imagines that it can only be fruitful to study specific cases of the waxing and waning of regional magnetic fields over a historical period. Something like this is what I set out to do in the next chapter.

Notes

1. The chief influences on my first fieldwork and the metaphors it invoked were Bailey (1969), encapsulated and encapsulating; Wolf (1956), fields of power; and Godelier (1972) and Althusser and Balibar (1970) articulated modes of production.

2. Indeed, one of the most active elder political figures among the Huasicanchinos so deeply buried the fact that he was born and later inherited about 70 per cent of his landholdings in another town, that he told me of these holdings only fifteen years later and had kept the information out of public discourse throughout his 62 years in Huasicancha. As he said, when he told me, 'It makes not a bit of difference. I am more *huasicanchino* than pretty much anybody.' He told me this in his small watch-repair shop in Huancayo, eight hours from Huasicancha.

3. This is especially the case in the influential study by Robert D. Putnam (1993), *Making democracy work: civic traditions in modern Italy*. Here the culture of civic morality occupies the same explanatory position for today's Italy as Banfield's culture of amoral familism occupied in the 1950s. This work is too bereft of sociological or historical insight to make it worth inclusion here.

4. My use of the term *locales* here is much the same as Appadurai's use of the term 'neighbourhoods': 'life-worlds constituted by relatively stable associations, by relatively known and shared histories, and by collectively traversed and legible spaces and places' (1995: 215). No doubt there are points at which my discussion here overlaps with Appadurai's discussion of locality and neighbourhood. The question of how my argument might relate more to that of Appadurai, though important, exceeds the scope of this chapter.

5. The area to the extreme south of the País Valenciano is made up of pockets of municipalities that do not speak *valenciano*. The town of Catral does not, its neighbour Crevillente does; the town of Almoradi does not, its neighbour Guardamar does, and so on.

6. Though both socio-economists and historical materialists are concerned with 'backward regions' 'peripheral regions' and the 'rust belt regions' where capital has moved on, to use Raymond Williams's evocative expression, both can be said to work back from capitalism's successes in constructing places. Raymond Williams's essays, as well as the work of Hudson *et al.*, represent important reflections on the importance of place when capitalism has moved on (see Williams 1989: 242; Carney, Hudson and Lewis 1980; Hudson and Sadler 1986).

7. Sabel's piece follows in the path of his *Work and politics* (1982) and, with Zeitlin, his 'Historical origins of mass production' (1985). Harvey's article is an extension from his *Limits to capital* (1982); further extensions are made, with respect to flexibility and cultural perceptions

of place, in his 1989 and 1993 works.

8. I use the term 'socio-economics' to refer to a range of writers, including Granovetter (1985), Granovetter and Swedberg (1992) and Grabher (1993), who might be referred to more narrowly by the term; to institutional economists and students of 'organizational culture (Morgan 1986; Cooper and Burrel 1988) and to economists' studies of networks (Law,1986). I include here too the work of Storper and Walker (1989) and Sayer and Walker (1992) toward the sociologizing of geography. While much of the original work on the Third Italy was derived from a broadly Marxist-informed perspective (and indeed was often stimulated by the PCI), it has increasingly shifted into the dominant socio-economic discourse: see Pyke, Becattini and Sengenberger (1990).

9. Harvey's work (Harvey 1973, Postscript) follows in the tradition of Henri Lefebvre (1974), whom I would include in the 'sociogenesis of regions' school, as I would Castells (1977); N. Smith, (1984); Hadjimichalis (1986); Hadjimichalis and Papamichos (1990); and Soja (1989).

10. Authors vary in the precision they use for regional economies as distinct from industrial districts. Sabel would see a regional economy such as that of Emilia Romagna as being made up of a series of smaller industrial districts.

11. Throughout this essay I refer only to Sabel's use of Italian examples in the article.

12. Sabel correctly notes, in the last sentence of the above quotation, that features of the Third Italy are to be found deep in the heart of the old Italian 'North'. A number of Italian scholars now dispute the specificity of 'the Third Italy' altogether, noting similar features in widely dispersed parts of Italy (Mingione, personal communication). Fergus Murray (1983) and Michael Blim (1990a) in a different manner have disputed the peculiarity of many of the features associated with the Third Italy and described further below; see also Pollert (1988).

13. I discussed a similar phenomenon in work in Peru, referring there to 'confederations of households':

> Virtually all Lima-based multi-occupational enterprises and many of the better-off Huancayo-based units are involved in these complex ties. The degree to which they complement the operations of each enterprise is such that *the rationality – the developmental path – of any one unit becomes closely associated with the others to which it is associated.* Investments of time and money are crucially influenced by the imperatives not just of any one enterprise but of the confederation as a whole (Smith 1989: 109–10, *emphasis added*; see also 115–43).

14. Sabel goes on to elaborate the same argument with respect to the experience of cooperation in production (1989: 48–9).

15. In what follows I read Harvey with my own specific interest in regions. Occasionally I draw attention to this, placing *region* or *regional* in square parentheses.

16. Elsewhere Harvey notes:

> If space is indeed to be thought of as a system of 'containers' of social power (to use the imagery of Foucault), then it follows that the accumulation of capital is perpetually deconstructing that social power by reshaping its geographical bases. Put another way round, any struggle to reconstitute power relations is a struggle to re-organize spatial bases. It is in this light that we can better understand 'why capitalism is continually reterritorializing with one hand what it was deterritorializing with the other' (Deleuze and Guattari 1984) (1989: 238).

17. Sabel too recognizes this issue and proposes a state policy that will make possible the transfer of values in one region to stimulate development in Less Advantaged Regions. But this seems to avoid the striking fact that, as Gunnar Myrdal noted long ago with reference to India (Myrdal 1968), powerful classes whose interests rest in specific regions tend to use their power at the level of the state to ensure the continued flow of resources into their region.

18. Harvey does allude to this complexity :

> The same shirt designs can be produced by large-scale factories in India, co-operative production in the Third Italy, sweatshops in New York and London, or family labour systems in Hong Kong. Eclecticism in labour practices seem almost as marked in these times as the eclecticism of postmodern philosophies and tastes (1989: 187).

19. This leads many regional studies into a rather uneasy relationship to the work of ethnography and ultimately to what Ortner (1995), in another context, calls 'ethnographic refusal'.

20. For Sabel there is a caveat to this novelty. Similar features were to be found prior to what Piore and he (1984) refer to as the second industrial divide.

21. One example of this is the way the highly diverse and always uneven interpenetration of a commodified economy and other institutional forms (reciprocal, associational, and so on) is only incidentally understood in historical terms, so that attempts to theorize the relationship 'economy' and 'society' always end up reifying both.

22. This appears to be a very clear point of contact between the regional economies literature and the literature on regional nationalism (Mars-Molino and Smith 1996; Keating and Loughlin 1997) and new social movements (for Italy see Pizzorno 1978 and Melucci 1980; 1982).

23. Both Capecchi (1989) and Brusco (1982: 170) juxtapose the two.

24. Another is to import cheap, possibly illegal, labour.

CHAPTER FIVE

Towards an Ethnographic Method for the Study of 'Informalized' Regional Economies in Western Europe[1]

In this chapter I explore the challenges to existing social science concepts and methods created by the changing forms of capitalist relations *in* production (Burawoy 1985)[2] occurring in Western Europe. During the 1980s Anglophone sociology became increasingly concerned with those social relations of capitalist production that could not be studied simply as a variation on large-scale factory work. Arnaldo Bagnasco's *Tre Italie: la problematica territoriale dello sviluppo italiano*, had appeared in 1977; the substance of his argument came out in English four years later (Bagnasco 1981). Then, in the following year Sabel discussed contemporary Italy in his *Work and politics* (1982), and a steadily growing interest in 'the Third Italy' followed.

We have seen in the last chapter the kind of picture they drew. A group of firms in a zone would concentrate on one product. Each would have less than ten employees, and would not itself be vertically integrated; rather, the stages that went into the production of a finished item were integrated through the collaboration of a number of enterprises. Of these only a small fraction were involved in marketing the finished item, while others were subcontractors. The argument was that the radical break between rural-based agriculture and urban-based industry – usually considered a pre-condition of successful industrialization – was mitigated here, many manufacturing households having some link with agriculture, where there was a higher income per head relative to the rest of Italy.

Describing the garment industry around Modena, for example, Brusco (1982) noted that half the large firms manufactured only the samples they needed for promotional purposes, and were otherwise engaged only in packaging finished products. The bulk of production took place in three formats: small enterprises working for their own account, small enterprises subcontracted to these larger ones and – the vast majority – homeworkers. Yet such categories were not discrete: own-account enterprises themselves subcontracted out to homeworkers, and so-called homeworkers themselves often only represented the top of a pyramid of relatives, neighbours and friends. In addition, local political institutions, from municipalities, to chambers of commerce, to regional governments, played a crucial role in facilitating these forms of production.

These heterogeneous labour conditions were not seen as informal, so much as *flexible* – a feature that came into growing prominence (and controversy: see K. Williams *et al.* 1987 and Pollert 1988) as the decade progressed. Yet, as Brusco remarked (1982: 170) 'However defined, black labour is extremely common in Emilia Romagna, and underpayment, tax evasion and the extraordinary flexibility of labour are all important features of the productive system.' So there was a fuzzy line between flexibility – a good thing – and a general informalization of the West European economy – probably not quite such a good thing. Writing at the end of the decade Castells and Portes (1989: 11) described what they called 'the informalization process' in the West as follows:

> The process of institutionalization of economic activities is slowing down. Horizontal networks, not vertical bureaucracies, seem to be the new models of efficient organizations. Subcontracting prevails over union contracts in various industrial sectors . . . New legions of would-be workers are entering a casual labour market, where a new breed of entrepreneurship is on the make. The informal economy simultaneously encompasses flexibility and exploitation, productivity and abuse, aggressive entrepreneurs and defenceless workers, libertarianism and greediness. And, above all, there is a disenfranchisement of the institutionalized power conquered by labour, with much suffering, in a two-century-old struggle.

Sociological Rigidities

In the face of conditions such as these, it appeared that the sociology of capitalist work had become increasingly narrow over the course of Western industrialization, excluding more and more elements of people's lives as relevant for social reproduction. What feminist students of capitalist society had been saying for years about women's labour now occupied the centre stage in sociological discussions of capitalist working conditions, as the hegemony of the mass-production factory was eroded. Once marginalized as interesting though unimportant, domestic labour, homework, sub-contracting, reciprocal labour-exchange, and any other forms of work that might offer capitalism at the core a new fix that would drag it into the new century, have now become the focus of attention.

I have argued elsewhere (Smith 1991b) that the survey techniques and mass enquiries of conventional sociology were developed at first as *appropriate* for the study of an increasingly homogenized (proletarianized) worker and (rationalized) citizen in the era of expanding capitalism. But then what they uncovered became *the* facts that gave shape to the image of modern society. Then, across the diminishing horizons of relevance within sociological discourse certain facts (domestic labour, peasant farming, and so on), though acknowledged, were deemed idiosyncratic within this increasingly teleological history of modernity.

Now we see the tables turning: for the older mass-consumer clone Western capitalism now seeks to substitute the heterogeneous citizen/consumer, ever demanding new varieties and thereby providing new niches to be filled by flexible new products. This in turn highlights those parts of society surveys can't reach, and the limitations of social knowledge derived from statistics.[3] This in turn would seem to enhance the value of ethnography, traditionally designed precisely to reach such nether regions of the social body; and yet the question arises as to what such an ethnography might look like. There are a number of traditions we might choose to draw on, by no means necessarily consistent with one another. We might, for example, take the anthropological tradition and try to think of such a world as a site or location – a 'community' to be studied, as certain regional studies have chosen to (see Chapter 5). Or possibly the world of informal relations and flexible personas might be studied as a sub-culture, much as anthropologists study drug 'culture' or youth 'culture'. There is the sociological tradition that produced the ethnography of work in urban, industrial society, from Sennett and Cobb's *The hidden injuries of class* (1972) to Burawoy's *The politics of production* (1985). And there is the ethnography that has emerged from the (principally feminist) discussions of domestic and other non-wage work.

One way of answering this question is to suggest that it depends on the purpose of the study – not just what you want to know about these forms of livelihood, but why you want to know it – to garner votes, gather taxes, reduce 'crime', or improve workers' safety. This would be true of studies of the labour process such as those of Braverman (1974) or Burawoy (1985), which emanated from a particular take on socialist politics in the West, and a similar comment could be made about feminist studies of domestic labour (Himmelweit and Mohun 1977; Molyneux 1979). And it is indeed true that studies conceptualized around industrial districts and flexible specialization have tended to be done to defend Western capitalism against the competition and/or offer 'new times' to the old left (Hirst and Zeitlin 1989; Hall and Jacques 1990).[4] Yet these studies do appear to argue that we are indeed entering a new period in history – post-industrial, postmodern or simply new times – without any convincing arguments that the *idiosyncratic forms of livelihood* to which they address their attention are indeed especially new.[5] This suggests that we need to go back and rethink some of the sociological categories that have become familiar to us, asking what purpose they were supposed to serve at their inception, before we can proceed further with fine-grained studies of these, albeit heterogeneous, kinds of livelihood.

Such sociological categories arose in the context of the rise and establishing of large-scale industrial capitalism in the core areas of Western Europe and the subsequent establishment of the welfare state. As industrial capitalism required 'economic man' [*sic*], so the welfare state required 'the rational citizen'; these in turn produced a model of social process that was based on an economistic understanding of actors' 'interests'. In this sense *all* sociology of Western society was economic sociology.[6] Now, by contrast, the socio-political context in which we need to understand recent approaches to late-twentieth-century capitalism is one in which corporations have abandoned Fordism, governments have retreated from Keynesian social intervention in the spheres of production and consumption, and a social democratic left seeks to discover a new basis for what Gramsci (1971: 348) called the 'cultural–social unity' that would weld together diffusely felt experiences of livelihood.[7] Such images of the contemporary scene effectively undercut the 'reality base' on which the older aetiology of social enquiry was built, so that, just as it had once become increasingly economic, so now its economics needs to become increasingly 'social'. We see this explicitly in the work of the new economic sociologists and the new social geographers (see for example Friedland and Robertson 1990; Granovetter and Swedberg 1992; Storper and Walker 1989; Sayer and Walker 1992). It also accounts for the renewed interest in the work of Karl Polanyi (see, for example, Granovetter 1985; Mingione 1991) and for the popularity of the works of Bourdieu and Giddens, both of whom attempt to dissolve the distinction between social structure and (economistically) strategizing individuals, through notions such as *habitus* and *structuration*.

And yet we gain little by simply moving the conceptual goalposts to suit the academic game. Merely remarking that the economy is profoundly 'social', or, conversely, investing social phenomena with economistic terms such as 'social capital', tends to divert our attention from the way particular arenas of interpersonal interaction are constituted as 'social' in a given historical epoch (Smith 1994a). Indeed, the very way in which monetarist discourse that refers to people in terms of 'human resources' is juxtaposed in the examples just mentioned with academic projects draws our attention to the historical variability of 'the social', which Polanyi shows performs very different kinds of a regulatory role *vis-à-vis* 'the economy' through history. Thus recently we have seen the ideology of monetarism propose that where the state, as the representative of 'society', was crucial for the reproduction of the Fordist regime, it should no longer perform this role under 'post-Fordism'. This raises the question: if the state is to be delegitimized as locus of the social in its capacity as regulator, what forms and sites for regulation will take its place?

If we must rethink the realm of 'the social', we must also rethink the rather narrow definition we have come to adopt for labour as well. This narrowing too – this compartmentalizing of what is and what is not to be deemed 'labour' – is the product of a quite specific political and sociological purpose. The original studies of industrial society were based on the observation that people spent much of their waking hours in regimented work, which threw them together in concentrated spaces with other people, forcing them thereby to share the same experience. Apart from its regimentation, this form of work had a mystifying quality to it, masking the specific manner and degree in which these workers had the value of their labour taken away from them, and giving them an alienated sense of their relationship to the product they were involved in producing. Out of such conditions arises a situation in which people begin to share an identity with one another, as well as a perception of the world: a particular consciousness. On this basis was built the political agenda of working-class parties of the early part of this century. Such a notion of 'labour' leads Gorz, for example, to conclude that social actors in the new economy 'form a non-class in the sense that they do not undergo social integration . . . [through] their common work situation' (quoted in Mingione 1991: 43 and Castells and Portes 1989: 31) to the view that 'the experience of labour and the emergence of stable class positions do not correspond to each other' in informal economies.

But these views are in stark contrast to those of Marx, who believed that 'labour' was synonymous with human life, and thus the only starting-point for social enquiry into *any* historical period (1970: *passim*; 1976: 47). Of course, Marx also pointed out that under capitalism that which distinguishes humans from bees, namely the ability to conceive a project before working on it, gets broken up into separate parts – mental and physical labour. Marx made a distinction, then, between a transhistorical notion of social labour – the starting-point for all human sciences in his view – and its historically specific form as industrial labour (cf. Postone 1993).

This, then, speaks for the category 'labour'. But while Marx concentrated his attention on the kinds of compartmentalization that occurred within factories between manual and mental labour, and then in ever more detail within the manual labour process itself, Weber addressed the processes of compartmentalization that occurred within cultural production in the society at large. As Habermas (1979, 1984) has pointed out, Weber noted the way in which the initially discursive and directly intersubjective elements of cultural production relating respectively to the objective world, the normative order and the subjective world became 'rationalized' into compartments in modern society – science, law and art. Moreover, because experts developed professional authority in each of these spheres, so the (rest of) society became increasingly alienated from its 'cultural senses'. And, just as ever more sophisticated machinery and more 'rational' divisions of labour in material production alienated the Fordist labouring population, so, too, ever more sophisticated language and divisions of expertise in cultural production alienated the Fordist citizenry from cultural production of any hegemonic significance – i.e. in scientific discoveries, legislation or high art. Under Fordism extensive rationalization of this kind has become indistinguishable from the process of social regulation itself. Hence we see here how 'the social' has taken on a historically specific meaning.

Over time, then, that which we take to be 'the social' and that which we take to be 'labour' has each become so bound to specific sociological projects and hypostasized images of the social world that it needs rethinking. Taking together 'social' and 'labour', the task becomes one of discovering *the form social labour takes under historically specific conditions*: in this case, historically specific conditions of particular cases where heterogeneous and dispersed livelihoods prevail. While we would therefore accept, with Polanyi, the 'social' as a regulatory impulse over economic relations,[8] and while we would also continue the tradition of industrial sociologists who saw the experience of work in large-scale factories and the reduction of significant differences among a de-skilled, proletarianized workforce as the principal components giving rise to the *formation* of a working class, the realm of 'the social' would need to be problematized, just as 'labour' would have to be wrested from its association with a factory system which confined it to regimented, monological and instrumental activity.

To perform the beginnings of such an exercise I turn now to work I have been doing in the extreme south of the País Valenciano in Spain. So the case study that follows can be used only as a provocation, whose implications I then try to address in the final section of the chapter.[9]

Aspects of Livelihood in the Southern País Valenciano

In the past two weeks, Federico, fourteen, has been in school just two days. During the same period he has: opened the irrigation gate on to different fields farmed by his father; taken shoe batches delivered to his mother and sister at the house, to three different neighbours, since Susana and Almudena, between them splitting a day's work on the farm, have been unable to complete their batches; worked both in family-farmed fields and on others' as an espantapájaros *(making noises to keep birds off the seeded fields); and acted as apprentice passing canes to an artisan broom-maker. His father got work three weeks ago, at a hotel 23 miles away. He goes there each morning on his* mobilette.

* * *

One time I was driving along the autopista *just south of Beziers, when a Citroen pulled up alongside and started beeping his horn. I looked over and saw it was Francisco G. We pulled over at the next bar and were soon discussing the various broom enterprises back in the fieldsite area.*

'When I was very young, my father ran our shop like the other two.[10] *We had artisans working there. Now it is different. Before the 'capital' was all in* la destreza *(skill, craft, dexterity) and in the brooms themselves. Now the capital is in the machines and the skill is all in the marketing. Before, we sold brooms. If we had made a lot of brooms we had to sell a lot. If we had made a few, we only sold a few. The selling was subordinate to the making. Now the machines can make anything. The skill is in the marketing. I am going to Belgium now. We sell split-bamboo blinds there. We started making them for the hotel carparks on the coast for the tourists – you know, as shades from the sun. Now I am trying to sell them in Belgium for holding down the earth embankments beside the autoroutes.*

That's the difference between the artisan system and the capitalist system: it is we, the capitalists, who have to be the craftsmen now, and it is not the production that tells us what to do, it's us the people in marketing. It's the market. You have to learn about the market. That's the new way.

Superficially, the area of the País Valenciano to the south of the city of Alicante is not dissimilar to the Italian case. There is a long history of prosperous agriculture and alongside it small manufacturing, which, as in Italy, is concentrated by product: Crevillente is associated with rugs, fishnets and rope, Alcoy with blankets; ceramic tiles in the towns of Castellón, and toys in the towns surrounding Alicante. But the largest such concentration is that of shoes around Elde and Elche, in the south of the País.

Moreover, this pattern of pockets of product-specific manufacturing centres interspersed amid prosperous commercial agriculture goes back a long way in Valencia's history. Though to the visitor Valencia may appear 'like Catalonia; just a little less so', retaining like Catalonia a strong sense of regional distinctiveness from Spain, speaking a version of Catalan and having a stronger tradition of commerce than the interior regions of Spain, the similarities can be misleading. Valencia's development[11] through the last century was closely tied to export agriculture – especially wines and oranges. Dependency on foreign markets and on imported agricultural inputs put Valencia sharply at odds with the persistent tariff protectionism of the Catalan bourgeoisie. Meanwhile, the demands of commercial agriculture in the region were never sufficiently great to drive up rural wages and thus eliminate artisan production;

rather, the evidence suggests that often stimuli for items such as packing cases and irrigation machinery gave the impetus for development of manufacturing less directly tied to the export agriculture sector (Nadal 1990).

Like small, dispersed manufacturing elsewhere, various sectors of Valencian artisan production frequently fell to competition from elsewhere, be it the silk works of Lyons or the textile factories of Catalonia. And (whether as the cause or effect of scale) there was always a lack of venture capital, especially as, during high periods of the economic cycle, agriculture always offered better returns.[12] Nevertheless, as we have seen above, various forms of dispersed manufacturing did persist, and, in doing so, underwent a variety of transformations (Bernabé 1976).

Nonetheless, unlike Catalonia, neither Valencian agriculture, nor its industry, developed an effective power bloc (Palafox 1987). Valencia's distinctiveness as a self-conscious region is therefore ironic: it arose *against* protectionism and without an effective leadership to press its interests at the level of the Spanish state. Even so, perhaps because of its distinctiveness, on the one hand *vis-à-vis* regions such as Catalonia and the Basque country, and on the other *vis-à-vis* the pre-eminently uncommercialized interior, the País Valenciano evolved a regional identity and regional institutions quite as vibrant as the other peripheral regions of Spain.

There is, then, *a significant history* of interlocking agricultural and manufacturing production here. Put in precisely the kind of orthodox language I want to distance myself from: the separation of industry and agriculture, town and country, was rather indecisive. Moreover, for both the male and female population, experience of geographical mobility, small-scale manufacturing, large-scale factory and service work were variously experienced. We are not talking, therefore, about a pristine peasantry or artisanal class, now turning to pluriactivity, but one with greater or lesser experience of industrial routines. Indeed, the whole metaphor so central to modernism of *the radical break* seems inapposite here: be it the *radical break* of the migrant from rural community to urban *anomie*; or of the artisanal master to the routinized and de-skilled factory worker. These kinds of sweeping away of the past are by no means an imagery familiar to the pluriactive household. A more familiar image would be one of *the continuity of flexibility, adaptability and transformations*, alike in skills, tools[13] and the package of household livelihoods. To this 'pre-existing mode of production' came the demands of the new international division of labour first, and with greatest influence, affecting local shoe production, as the production of cheap shoes moved from Italy to Spain (and thence to Brazil); but, as we have seen in the vignettes above, also taking in other activities.

In the year I was first introduced to this region (1979) official figures showed there to be over 1,800 firms producing shoes in Spain, with an average size of 30 employees (Benton 1990). Over half of these were in this region, and of course these are only the *official* figures: there were clearly far more. Throughout the 1970s a production structure emerged in which a family-owned firm took a contract, from just one large US or northern European customer, thereby establishing a relationship of extreme dependency, the buying firm sometimes providing injections of capital and getting involved in managerial decisions, yet not thereby developing principles of loyalty. The local firm then met the orders with a workforce located in its legally-registered factory, plus a much larger workforce spread out in a 'putting-out' system.

José, a work distributor in shoes, comes from a town of 5,000 some ten miles from Elche. He describes his induction into the job as follows: 'After I had been working at the factory for about three years, I began to take work home during the lunch break. We had an old Seat 500 then, and I'd pile in the work, rush home, leave it with the wife and try and get back to my place on the line. It was a frantic business. But that way I got higher piece rates.[14] Maria did the work downstairs in the garage. After a while, I exchanged the Seat for a second-hand van. I got more work home that way, and Maria started getting her sister and a couple of friends in on the work. But the pace was awful. I started having accidents at work. And anyway, half the time the pieces [the women] did turned out wrong and got rejected, so I lost my rate. Other fellows were working full-time taking work from the factory and giving out [to subcontract homeworkers]. I started getting an old bloke who'd worked on the machine before to take my place a couple of days in the week, so I could work more with the pick-up and at the taller at home. Well you can see me now: I haven't been working at the factory for over two years, but it's just as frantic, because now I have to get work from a whole bunch of factories, not just the one. And you have to keep them happy or they pass the consignment on to somebody else' [What about the taller?] Maria [his wife]: 'I won't let him in there!' José (shrugs): 'It's true. She runs that place. I don't set a foot in there, except on Sundays maybe, if we have a lot of upgrading to do.'

Meanwhile, in the home, from the initial wife's contribution, we move – through her already-established network – to an extensive set of subcontract, subsubcontract, etc. homework. And the distributor and his wife are likely now to have a small full-time *taller* or 'workshop', employing one or two people solely to upgrade work coming through the chain.

As for women lower down in the chain, they are likely to be part of an agricultural household and, as a result, under extreme pressure. In another paper (Smith 1990; see also Sanchis 1984 and for Catalonia, see Narotzky 1989 and 1990), I describe the situation as follows:

> The demands for work on the family's own farm are erratic – the husband/father for example, may get a day's work and, finding a task on the farm incomplete, will put pressure on his wife or daughter to put aside the home work in favour of the farm. . . . [Meanwhile] work distributors, anxious to minimize the amount of travelling and contacting they have to do . . . encourage women to take large batches by paying geometrically higher rates up to the last item completed. To acquire these rates, home working women, already under pressure from their farming husbands, may speak for excessive batch sizes with a view to off-loading some to a neighbour.

Such a complex set of social relationships is built upon a long history of extensive interpersonal networks through which intertwined agricultural and artisanal activities were reproduced. Over time, personal claims extending outwards from immediate family, to extended family, neighbours, community members and ultimately other 'Valencianos' became an institutionalized component of everyday life, in the manner described well by Sider (1986): 'By 'claims' I refer to the rights people have or assert not just *over* other people or to the product of their labour, or their labour itself, but *in* other people – the structured and conscious co-involvement in other lives, whether friendly, hostile or both.'

Such claims, of course, account not just for the lines of subcontracting, but serve also to relieve pressure from other quarters on a wife and mother:

> *We looked after Pilar and Primitivo today. Concepción arrived at the house with her mother. They were engaged in quite a vocal argument. Concepción's mother wouldn't have the children today. She had to go to the hospital in Elche, she said. Concepción said she could always go another day. Today was an emergency. Her mother replied that she had been putting off going for too long, and every day was an emergency. Why didn't Concepción send the children*

to the guardaría *as she had in the past? The essence of the reply had to do with 'payment' for the* guardaría*. Despite its official-sounding name, the* guardaría *is a private house where some thirty children are cared for by a single woman and her ageing mother. Usually payment is in cash but, owing to a cash-flow problem (or something else?) Concepción had made 'other arrangements' with the two women, which she didn't care to discuss. But they had reneged on the arrangement and now refused to have the children. Concepción says that they made the excuse that, 'My children are too* malcriados *[poorly behaved] and disrupt the other children. But everybody knows that place is a disgrace. I wouldn't send them there anyway . . .'.*

The Franco years ensured that the tradition of municipal support for the local economy noted for the Third Italy (Blim 1990a, 1992) has no historical basis here. An especially important institution for the channelling of claims of the kind Sider refers to, however, is the *cuadrilla* (Cuco I Giner 1990), a group of perhaps eight to twenty people who form friendships in school and then continue them as they grow older, extending to include their fiancé(e)s and later, marriage partners.[15] It can be said without exaggeration that these groupings constitute *the* body of significant others beyond the family for a person – leisure activities such as drinking in bars, going to dances and football games and so on take place within this group, and political identifications are almost always uniform throughout the group:

Ana took work in a shoe factory when she was 17. She worked there nearly five years but, she says, she had trouble getting to the factory if she wasn't on the day shift and she hated the authoritarian atmosphere. She quit over a dispute with her supervisor and helped her mother on her machine at home for a few months that turned into nearly a year, her mother says. Then she helped out a friend of her mother's at her house on her machine. Her mother persuaded her to get her own machine and now she works in a small glassed-in veranda off the kitchen. She works on average from 8 to 12 and from 4 to 6, except Fridays and sometimes Thursdays, when she works longer to make up on the batches to meet her quota. Ana doesn't rely on a single distributor. She picks up batches from two or three women, all of whom are part of her cuadrilla.*

She used to take work from Pablo S. She says he was good to her because he is her father's cousin and in his* cuadrilla, *and she tried to do good work for him but, she says, he had a bad mouth and a short temper. 'At first I was glad to have him but, you know, I didn't like it too. I worked slower for him. I was worried about making mistakes – but I was just starting then. He was family. Anyway, I got no special deals from Pablo! Once I was off for two weeks and when I asked for work again, he gave me half, saying he was using somebody* *else now. He teases me about not working for him when I see him in the street. It's difficult to find work this way. You have to be nice to everybody, no? But it's better this way.'*

Another institutional mechanism besides these is 'cooperatives'; but back into the Franco era various forms of government-recognized cooperatives have effectively evoked images of bureaucracy and government interference rather than reciprocal and interpersonal linkages:

America and Claudia have a small, unregistered workshop doing finishing work on bras – adding clips, etc. and packaging them. They usually have three to five women working for them, depending on demand. They pay by the hour and say lots of women like to come and work a few hours. They have a pool of people who 'know the work'. The operation runs out of a garage. Usually for every two adults there are three school-age girls working.

The business has been going for nearly a year now. America says it is her third business and she doesn't expect it to last more than a year or so more. She says she did this one because she likes working with Claudia, who is a close friend of hers and in the same cuadrilla.

I asked her if she had any experience of worker cooperatives. 'There are cooperatives and cooperatives, in my opinion,' she says. 'It's a word. It doesn't mean anything. You can hear just anybody talking about "cooperatives". Anybody! The [home-working, shoe-]stitchers, the politicians, even Francisco G. will try to sell you on cooperatives! Frankly I don't understand them [cooperatives]. There's a lot of tramites *[red tape], I do know that. I like to work with these people around here [her neighbourhood].'* [Me: Are they good workers? Can you trust them to do good work?] *'Aye, they're people like any others. There are some like this and some like that. Work is everything to people around here – you know that. They're real workers around here.* Locos. *Anyway, they know me.'* [Me: And you know them . . .] *Ah yes. I know them!'*

When competition grew from the period I have just described, through the 1980s, this already thoroughly 'informalized' economy was made still more informal, and a prevalent means by which this was done was by use of regulations governing worker cooperatives.

When I returned to the field in the late eighties I found myself one day with four guys drinking in a bar on the road between Crevillente and Elche. The topic of conversation was worker cooperatives. All four men were themselves entrepreneurs: three were in shoe production, the fourth was Ricardo, Francisco's (marketing) brother. The two brothers are now in the 'export–import' business.

Ramon, who used to run the shop, has been invalided for some time; it is unclear whether he has had a nervous breakdown or is suffering from acute ulcers; possibly both. Much of the machinery has been dispersed, but Ricardo, together with two others at the bar, is explaining to the fourth man how to set up a workers' cooperative to provide a shell around the productive machinery that's left, after the 'thinning diet', as they describe the process of stripping down the enterprise.

The pattern is a familiar one: while officially registered firms and employment figures in the industry declined, overall shoe production increased. Registered firms declare bankruptcy and close one day, opening the next, with the original shell-firm now operating entirely in a merchant capacity, leasing the old machinery either to a 'cooperative' or to a now wholly illicit subcontract shop made up of workers, who agree to reduced wages, safety and benefits to get the contract from their old boss. Superficially, this looks like a response to recession, but in fact the atmosphere of 'crisis' and 'disorganization' is both *produced by* bankruptcies, etc., and – more importantly – is ideologically constructed so as to justify forms of labour regulation hitherto deemed unethical by *all* parties involved, and to delegitimate collective action by people in their capacity as workers (cf. Ybarra 1984).

Rethinking Labour and Society

What little has been said here about southern Valencia makes it obvious that much work remains to be done toward distinguishing different sets of social relations – from highly rationalized interfirm forms of just-in-time production to the casual labour of the (officially) unemployed. And the same thing needs to be done in characterizing different kinds of regional clusterings: what have come to be studied as 'industrial districts' (Gertler 1992; Cooke and Morgan 1991). Clearly, the extent to which what follows is relevant to one or other of these conditions will vary: the objective is not to provide a universally applicable blueprint, but to provoke a rethinking of issues *prior to* a more extensive comparative agenda. It is for this reason that I have begun by venturing out from the Valencian experience on the one hand, while testing the limitations of categories previously generated for the study of the mass collective worker on the other.

The case material presented here evokes an image of manipulation, spontaneity and anti-structure – in a word: informalization.
Even so, the real complexity and challenge of this local and present
reality should not divert an ethnographic enquiry from the less
immediate: both past history and non-local shaping forces. In this
case it is especially evident that – historically and contempor-
aneously – the Valencian social economy has been profoundly
shaped by external forces. Export agriculture in the last century
and the imperatives of the postwar international division of labour
more recently make this necessarily an open economy, often despite
the Spanish state's contrary policies.

These very concrete abstractions then provided the material
conditions through which emerged historically specific social
relationships that, over time, became sedimented in institutions of
a particular regional character (Valencia's historical articulations
weren't those of neighbouring Catalonia to the north nor those of
Murcia to the south, and they were only partially those of Spain as
a whole). Out of the interaction of the present with such a past has
sprung a selective tradition requiring the tools of cultural analysis
for its proper study.

Then, as we turn to the present, we are immediately struck by
the role of daily, weekly, yearly – possibly even generational –
strategy in the reproduction of livelihood, i.e. local *agency*. Such
agency is made up of a number of components: fragmented, situationally generated and hence multiple forms of attention, possibly
even *consciousness* on the part of an individual; a second component
of *identity*, which implies a set of perceived relationships to various
collectivities of relevant others; and finally *praxis*, individual and
collective. Moreover, to make the issue still more complex, we must
note the heterogeneity of social actors – in their present insertion(s)
in social labour, in their life histories and in their varied mobility
in and beyond the region – all of which give rise simultaneously to
shared and differentiated interpretations of reality.

Of course, it is striking how far this kind of social world is from
the sociological construction of the urban worker and modern
citizen; but the problem for anthropologists is that we should be
just as struck by how far this world is from the anthropological
construction of the habitual practices of rural folk. The result is a
challenge to social enquiry. Features such as those just described
encourage us to collapse the old distinctions – between structure
and agency, the social and the economic, even the idiographic and

the nomothetic. Nevertheless, faced with the pragmatics of ethno-graphic enquiry, for analytic clarity we find ourselves forced back to one or another 'point-of-departure', albeit temporarily – an explanatory framework that then tends to dominate the entirety of our subsequent analysis.

As a result, three paradigms are pervasive in the literature that attempts to explain the informalized settings of regional economies. First there are *structural approaches*, in which human beings engaging in the practices of daily life are pretty much absent. Then there are the approaches that focus on [relations between] individuals engaging in *social practices*, to find within those practices strategies that are made to derive from a more or less sophisticated under-standing of 'rationality': the more sophisticated adding 'social' factors, such as 'cultural capital', to rationality. Here a concerted phenomenological methodology to expose different actors' maps of meaning is downplayed in favour of an etic understanding of the emic.[16] Finally, and usually in a utopian or entirely politically disengaged mode, there are studies in which maps of meaning float off in a serendipity of culturalist images and allusions/elisions/illusions devoid of people and material conditions, the extreme form of which is exemplified in the turn to postmodernism.

Yet I would like to propose that the kind of world we have been discussing might best be studied by intentionally dovetailing these paradigms. Such an ethnographic project will have to evolve *a series* of possibly mutually incompatible methods that would allow us to tackle the inter-relationship between the dimensions of social reality monopolized by each of these paradigms.[17] In the more instit-utionally established 'modern' society discussed, for example, by Habermas (1984), the compartmentalization of social conduct encourages a sociological approach appropriate for the study of each such compartment. Hermeneutic theories might appropriately be employed to study literature and art, phenomenological approaches to study the interpretative attention and communicative ploys of actors, studies that employ 'interests' to explain conduct in market transactions, and so on. In so far as any 'informalization' process involves the decomposition of these distinctions of practice and institution, so an appropriate sociology must self-consciously face off a range of methodologies to help us to muddle through these kinds of ethnographic sites. The unfamiliar fuzziness of conditions in regions like southern Valencia, where idiosyncratic forms of livelihood prevail, implies thorough intertwining of these dimensions: the cultural production of material conditions, individual and collective practices that, through history, structure material conditions in the present, and maps of meaning whose compass-readings are profoundly embedded in an actor's situated daily and longer-term projects. These require different lenses for bringing forms of reality into analytic focus, and hence the design of methodologies appropriate for their study.

These different dimensions of social reality should not be confused with different scales of operation: the image of external (macro) determinants as the *structural and material conditions* faced by regions, communities, households, individuals, who then (internally) respond to them through *strategies*, would be one example of this kind of confusion. Rather, we have to interrogate the larger formation – world system, national economy, and so forth – each time through lenses of enquiry that bring into focus its material conditions, and at another time its social relations of reproduction, and at still a third, its appearance in cultural forms. And the same exercise, though in a different ordering, would apply for locally situated phenomena. The effect of such a research agenda would be to problematize categories from one paradigm through exposure to another.

The entry-point for such an agenda and the way in which one methodology is articulated with another will be a function of the analyst's purpose-at-hand. I have already made clear that the power of earlier analyses of the working class, from Marx and Engels to Thompson to Braverman, derived, partially at least, from their concern with the sources of collective organization and political leverage (see especially Thompson 1978b). Here I retain their assumption that the experience of historically specific forms of social labour provides the principal *starting-point* for the ever-incomplete and ongoing process of the coalescing of collective identity and political will that we might call class formation. But to engage in such an enquiry we must generate categories of 'labour' appropriate to the subject studied – rather than the routinized, de-skilled drudgery of the mass collective worker. And we must likewise rethink the realm of 'the social' – beyond the compartmentalized 'rationalities' that provide the principal means of regulation of the 'modern' social system, as noted by Weber and formalized by Habermas.

From the point of view of the Valencian study, for example, it might be suggested that Fordism made the state the arena *par excellence* for regulating the outcome of negotiations between classes over accumulation versus consumption. Flexible accumulation represents an incipient attempt to generate modes of regulation that by-pass both the institution of the state, in a general abstract sense, and specific States in terms of their sovereignty over the regulation of capital. While flexible accumulation *appears to be* an 'informalization' of the economy, in so far as this is made possible precisely by the development of technologies for more sophisticated and extensive regulation across vast spaces,[18] the term is confusing. Rather we have to explore the shifting of regulation to new forms and social spaces. The historically specific character of the social realm in a region like southern Valencia emerges from such overlapping, conflicting, and inconsistent modes of regulation, which manage to stabilize for any length of time as a result of the balance between these more dominant regimes. The unfolding field of force that results provides the material conditions within which this social economy operates. They are what David Harvey (1989) calls 'concrete abstractions' – the spatial configuration of factories, dwellings and roads, or the rate of inflation that results from regulatory practices in the other regimes – which are experienced as an ecological fact by such an economy.

In so far as these *concrete abstractions* 'determine the distributional pattern of opportunities and thereby the interest structure' (Habermas 1981: 264) of people in informalized economies, they *are* inevitably a component of the social world that has to be studied in an ethnography of idiosyncratic forms of livelihood. So the place to *start* is to record these *systemic components* in the region. This involves mapping out the relationships between institutions and assessing the organizing weight of, let's say, a local Fordist factory (in Valencia literally: the Ford Fiesta plant), as well as of course, the study of the *history* of these articulated structures as they impact on the region.

Such a lens highlights the systemic component of the study, yet 'informal economies' are, almost by definition, exemplars of how institutionalized social regulation is sidestepped, manipulated, even resisted, just as such regulation nevertheless conditions and provides much of the arsenal, even the language and ideological space, through which this *agency* is expressed. It is here therefore that the methodology must switch gears toward an approach that can attend to the *consciousness-identity-praxis* of participants while remaining sensitive to the fact that *any* economy evolves, albeit contesting, social spaces for its regulation.[19]

Here I confine myself to some observations turning around the need to rethink what we mean when we use the terms 'labour' and 'social'. The two are not easily separated. Literature that tries to chart the transition from Fordism to something else, for example, has addressed the issue of 'hierarchies and markets' (Law 1986). Within a large firm, social relations can be gathered under the rubric hierarchy; beyond them lie market relations. Often at issue is the question of whether a task can be done more productively by employing the hierarchical structure *within* the firm, or market (subcontract) transactions *beyond* it. New economic sociologists have shown that such a distinction isn't quite as nice as this; elements of market relations can be found within firms, and market relations may have a strong organizational component to them, as many subcontract relationships demonstrate. And recent work on industrial districts like the Third Italy has sought to introduce a third category: the network, where boundaries between firms are not very clear – Sabel (1991) talks of 'the Moebius strip firm' – and linkages are horizontal, and may even be more cooperative than competitive.

Were anything like this to be the case, it is quite obvious that we would have to rethink the ideological construction of labour and society. Capitalist democracies rely on the ideological carving up of social space in such a way that, *within* the social space of the Fordist corporation, managers' legitimacy derives from their visible ability to *supervise*. Departures from this command structure are referred to as *delegating* authority, and resort to democratic work teams can only be justified in so far as they achieve managerial goals. A very clear boundary-line encompasses this arena; beyond it, the employee becomes a *citizen*. In principle in *this* arena is to be found a rationalized and modernist democratic society in which the citizenry reverse the corporate hierarchy by delegating their civil authority to *representatives* who occupy positions within the state. It hardly has to be pointed out that conventionally the former arena is that of labour, the latter that of society. Nor do we need to dwell on the obvious fact that practices in the one arena run over into the other. For what we are referring to here is an *ideological* image. The fact that Americans with jobs live the major part of their waking lives under conditions less democratic than those of their Swedish competitors or their pre-Gorbachev Cold War enemies, and yet can continue to feel that the principal feature of their own society is its democratic character, exemplifies the power of this ideology.

The radical division created within individuals and families that reflects this distinction between the closely 'managed' corporate arena of social interaction (itself internally divided between mental and routinized labour) and a second arena characterized by the more dispersed regulation of 'civil society' has to be reformulated (but not necessarily abandoned) in the context of the kind of idiosyncratic forms of livelihood found in southern Valencia. This is what I mean by a need to problematize 'the social'. Yet it also means problematizing 'labour', which is not just directed to changing objective conditions, but also embraces a process of intersubjective communication in which actors form 'new powers and new conceptions, new modes of intercourse, new needs and new speech' (Marx 1964: 92–3).

In Valencia dispersed regulation, following the contours necessary for the reproduction of *livelihood*, has, through a long history, taken on regionally specific *cultural* forms. Even so we don't see here the kind of regularities anthropologists have traditionally associated with the 'culture' of a rural area. Rather cultural practice needs to be deeply imbricated in our reconstitution of the arena of 'the social' under these kind of labour conditions. Unlike their bureaucratic counterparts, a high percentage of institutions here are egocentric and situationally invoked. A failure to invest time, charm, memories of past events, possibly even money, in any one of these *daily-activated institutions* will mean that the institution – that friendship, that orally-struck contract, that loan of help – will be lost. To borrow money, retain a client, induce a cousin to work overtime, people have to make claims and counter-claims, and to do so they must use and invest in *an ideology of shared identity*, a stretching of the bounds of intimacy through the use of metaphors of blood and physical place, and appeals to religious, racial or regional identity. To refer to this merely in terms of cultural and social 'capital' is to miss entirely its implications for the reconstitution of social membership and, by extension, citizenship.[20] Political theorists who talk of the charms of community and new forms of citizenship might wish to ponder what kinds of contours of *différence* – we-ness and they-ness – are constituted when social reproduction relies on *these* kinds of ideological calls.

Conclusion

The industrial sociology from which existing studies of informalized regional economies is drawn has remained locked in the *material production* component of social labour, precisely because it was developed for studying industrial societies in which that component was figuratively stressed as *bona fide* 'labour' by being physically placed in a specific social space: the factory. This was the internal element of Fordist regulation – Taylorism – designed to secure consent at the point of production (Burawoy 1985). When various social practices in the shadow economy cannot then be read off from this very narrow instrumental view of labour, it is a mistake to declare the whole project of viewing society in terms of social labour to be unworkable. Rather, we have to bring back a more synthetic view in which cultural production becomes an inherent part of our understanding of 'social labour', and, conversely, 'culture' must be understood in the same terms as we understand any other artefact of human activity (Williams 1961, 1977). 'Labour processes' of the kind we have seen for Valencia require not just the rational-instrumental components of social labour associated with the factory. They also require intersubjective work on an ideology of shared identity, the reproduction of which cannot be left to the fixed institutional spaces in the social world to which Weber drew attention. This in turn invokes its own forms of regulation. Here social power is negotiated interpersonally from day to day in a manner not unlike that invoked by Bourdieu (1977) under the rubric 'habitus' for Kabyle society. Yet the heterogeneity of livelihoods as well as the enforced discontinuities in people's life-experiences in this highly volatile world make the notion of habitus not quite appropriate. It is not 'tradition' *per se*, but the way in which components of tradition are called upon and interpreted by very different participants.[21]

Moreover, Bourdieu tends to focus emphatically on the mechanisms *toward conformity*. Yet what we find are coextensive forms of regulation in a particular regional economy resulting from its specific situation within other, overarching regimes. Once we have some grasp of these 'concrete abstractions', the challenge becomes just how 'traditions' in Raymond Williams's (1977) sense are selected. What stimulates the call on a certain experience and buries another? I have suggested here that it is far too pat to find an answer in terms of instrumentalist views of actors' rationality, derived from extending the orthodox focus on spatially concentrated material production in the factory to the more dispersed social relations found in idiosyncratic forms of livelihood.

After all, the process by which material production was severed from the intercommunicative components of social labour was itself a political project aimed at the design of a quite specific mode of social regulation. If we were to re-examine the fine-grained political disputes through which this was established, we would find a whole series of other exclusions and divisions that both gave form to those disputes and then resulted from them. 'Domestic spaces' in society were reformulated, women's places in the reproduction of this regime were carved out, 'free speech', too, was banished from the corporation and consigned specifically to bourgeois-controlled media and so on. The point is that these were not, as is often asserted, directly a result of their 'function for the reproduction of capital'. Rather, they are specific cultural forms produced by a whole series of disputes and overlapping fields of force that, in the process of their enactment, *select out from and reformulate various patterns of tradition.*

In turning to these kinds of livelihood, therefore, we have to recognize that the intercommunicative component of social labour – i.e. cultural production – has re-emerged as a major component of potential regulation (communal membership, social memory, 'kindness', 'dignity', etc, etc.) and therefore becomes as much the site of struggle as the arena of material production itself. Moreover, if we learn anything from history, it is that these *political* projects are open-ended. In Chapter 2 I have tried to show how collective political engagement itself often provides a hothouse atmosphere producing renewed and invigorated cultural categories ('traditions', in Williams's terms), which then feed back into that ongoing political trajectory. Here I have sought to think through the beginnings of a method for finding lenses into this kind of process. It is an incomplete project.

Notes

1. This chapter is a modified version of an article that appeared in the *International Journal of Urban and Regional Research*, 18(1) (Mar. 1994) with the title, 'Toward an ethnographic method for the study of

idiosyncratic forms of livelihood in Western Europe'. Various versions have been delivered and discussed in seminars. I would like to thank especially Enzo Mingione, Bryan Roberts and Gerald Sider for their comments. Support during various stages of the research has been gratefully received from the Social Sciences and Humanities Research Council of Canada and from the Small Grants programme of the University of Toronto.

2. Burawoy distinguishes between relations of production and relations *in* production. He has a straightforward Althusserian understanding of relations of production (Althusser and Balibar 1970), but the latter he uses to refer to the particular ways in which labour is organized, regulated, given technical tasks and so on. Thus, he suggests, even where relations of production may be vastly different, as was the case between the Soviet bloc and the West, relations *in* production in many large mass-production factories may be (and in this case) were quite similar.

3. One is struck by the burgeoning literature that surveys the field of informal economic activities from a bird's-eye view with the caveat that much of the phenomenon under study escapes attention because census data cannot catch it or because the survey categories used are not quite appropriate for this kind of social world.

4. Indeed Pollert (1988) has suggested that sociologists who favour an understanding of flexible capitalism as something new have, intentionally or not, bought into the language – and hence the way of thinking – of management, rather than labour.

5. I use the expression *idiosyncratic forms of livelihood* throughout. There is an intentional irony in its use since, as I have pointed out, I am unconvinced that, taken out of the context of a teleological history of industrialism, such livelihoods are idiosyncratic at all. I am also aware that the term is cumbersome, but I prefer to avoid the prior assumption that we are looking at an 'informalization process' or labour whose principle feature is its 'flexibility'.

6. For the sake of emphasis I have caricatured sociology, but the division of labour between it and anthropology *was* largely understood as one in which sociology took care of the forward march of history, while anthropology dealt with historical throwbacks (hunter–gatherers; tribes [cf. recent references to 're-tribalization', e.g. in the ex-Yugoslavia]) and contemporary idiosyncrasies (from drug cultures to peasant societies). Thus the new definitions of core sociology also effectively throw up new divisions of labour between the two disciplines and new tasks for anthropologists.

7. Mike Watts captures the spirit of the way in which political projects of this social democratic left are based on a particular reading of the state of the economy:

The new economy ... heralds a shift to flexible labour markets, privatization through subcontracting, product differentiation toward a self-conscious targeting of lifestyle, taste and culture, an explosion of service and white collar occupations, the rapid feminization of wage work, and an unprecedented globalization of productive and financial capitals. In its socio-cultural aspect, 'New Times' is taken to embrace a plethora of sometimes ill-defined tendencies, including political fragmentation, pluralism, new identities. a weakening of older collective (class) solidarities, and the rise of so-called new social movements (Watts 1992: 7).

8. What Peter Mathias calls 'non-economic determinants of cohesion' (quoted in Berg *et al.* 1983: 29).

9. The case material cannot claim to be 'representative' of idiosyncratic forms of livelihood generally, since, as I have already said, hetero-geneity puts into question the whole issue of representativeness. For the same reasons it cannot even claim to be representative of all kinds of labour conditions in the southern País Valenciano.

10. In 1979, there were three enterprises in the fieldsite making brooms of varying sizes and shapes from bamboo cane, cut from the marshes around the neighbouring *albufera*. Two of these retained an artisan system. A skilled broom-maker sits on a six-inch-high stool on the ground surrounded by materials. With him is a boy from fourteen to eighteen years old, his apprentice, who passes him supplies, keeps tools in readiness and does some aspects of the work himself. The third enterprise, referred to here, at that time produced brooms with the aid of machinery. It also produced split-bamboo blinds, very basic bamboo furniture and some tools. The enterprise was run by three brothers. The eldest, Ramon, ran the shop, the other two, Ricardo and Francisco, spent two-thirds to three-quarters of their time 'on the road' selling. Ricardo worked mostly in Spain; Francisco worked in France, the Netherlands, Belgium and Germany.

11. The nature of Valencian development over the past two centuries is the subject of intensive debate. See for example, Lluch (1976); Giralt (1978); Aracil and Bonafé (1978); and Martínez Serrano *et al.* (1978)

12. The role of family capital and local tied usury – as opposed to financial institutions – seems to have been large in Valencia. This would have the effect of making capital sticky in respect to sectors and regions.

13. Berg *et al.* (1983: 11) make this point – both the ability to specialize *and* the flexibility of the 'intermediate technologies' of small-scale manufacturing 'before the factory': 'Its hallmark was flexibility and application, according to the dictates of artisan skill, to the production of a wide range of different articles. But these new tools also provided the opportunity for ... extreme specialization of product.'

14. In most factories machine workers are paid a low basic wage conditional on their producing a minimum unit rate. Units above

the minimum are paid in batches, each batch being worth a geometrically greater rate than the one before. It therefore pays a worker to produce as many batches as possible.

15. While I can't speak for other areas of Valencia, *cuadrillas* in the Bajo Segura are *not* groups of male friends and their spouses. Rather, the friendships that produce the *cuadrilla* can be between three male friends, then the third man's wife and her two friends and their husbands, and so on.

16. We need to note that neither of these first two approaches rejects the idea of 'culture' as might be said of earlier French structural Marxists or the Manchester School transactionalists (cf. Long 1992). Rather it might be argued that culture performs here a crucial role: when all other explanations fail, use this. There is a danger that such an untheorized notion of culture transposes to 'regional economies' problems encountered earlier in American anthropological studies of national character in terms of 'culture and personality'.

17. Many of the reflections that follow owe something to Herman Rebel's discussion of cultural hegemony and class experience (1989), for example: 'the quest for experienced cultural hegemony does not begin with what people say or what theatrics we can observe them perform but with the deducible structured irreconcilables of their social relations that they have to speak about somehow' (1989: 132).

18. I am referring here not just to electronic technology but to the entire culture industry itself (J. B. Thompson 1990; Pred and Watts 1992).

19. Elsewhere (Smith 1992), I have illustrated this dialectic between escape from existing regulations and the emergence of new forms of regulation, by reference to the language of civil society as it emerged in England in the seventeenth century, a language that emerged *against* monarchical regulation, yet evolved a language of 'freedom' that then provided the principles for bourgeois regulation.

20. On 13 September 1992 the *Independent on Sunday* carried the headline '1.8 MILLION BRITONS DISAPPEAR'. The article begins: 'Almost 1.8 million people have disappeared from the official records of England and Wales . . . [They] are certain to remain in official limbo, unable to vote or claim benefits.' *Working* off the books also eventually means *living* a life beyond citizenship too.

21. Cf. Bourdieu (1977: 86): '[I]t is in a relation of homology, of diversity within homogeneity reflecting the diversity within homogeneity characteristic of their social conditions of production, that the singular habitus of the different members of the same class are united; the homology of world views implies the systematic differences which separate singular world-views, adopted from singular *but concerted* standpoints' (*italics mine*).

PART FOUR

Disciplined Practices

CHAPTER SIX

Overlapping Collectivities: Local Concern, State Welfare and Social Membership

> [T]he processes that position people as citizens of nations *and* as members of larger, smaller, or dispersed units of agglomeration need to be conceptualized together. Citizenship ought to be theorized as one of the multiple subject positions occupied by people as members of diversely spatialized, partially overlapping or non-overlapping collectivities.
>
> — Akhil Gupta (1992: 73)

> On the one hand, all of us belong to communities that speak the same language, inhabit a common territory, have certain shared memories, and follow the same customs (this is the sense in which anthropologists use the word 'culture'). . . . On the other hand, all of us belong to communities that guarantee our rights and impose obligations on us – communities of which we are citizens . . .
>
> — TzvetanTodorov (1993: 171)

> Civil society and the state are separated. Hence the citizen of the state is also separated from the citizen as member of civil society. He must therefore effect a *fundamental division* within himself.
>
> — Karl Marx (1989: 117)
> [Italics in original]

Introduction

In Chapter 4 I started on an exploratory expedition in search of ways in which we might get a more acute sense of how patterns of locality are socially produced – a sense of locality more appropriate to our contemporary world than the sense we might derive from an earlier tradition of anthropological ethnography. The exploration began with a journey through various non-anthropological studies that discuss the relationship between changing capitalist forms and the emergence (or not) of regionality. Then, in the last chapter, I have tried to push my way through the ice-flows of older conceptualizations of work and industrialization to begin the job of recasting the way we do ethnography in a social world where every form of work seems to be idiosyncratic. I now want to shift to a somewhat different register, but one that arises very much from living and working with the people we have met in the previous chapter, and not only from that experience, but from my interactions with old acquaintances in the village where I grew up in England, and in the topics of concern and debate on the street-corners and in the bars of the villages in France I have lived in as my partner went about her fieldwork. The issue is the elusiveness of our sense of belonging, the persistent perception we have that we are inevitably tangled in the weeds of social membership, but that this shifting, rocking and unstable entanglement requires complicated and often awkward manoeuvres and sensibilities.

What exercises us – my informants and friends, my sparring partners and chastisers – is the issue alluded to above by Akhil Gupta, and taken up by David Harvey (1991) when he asks, 'To what space do I as an individual belong? Do I express my citizenship in my neighbourhood, city, region, nation, or world?'. On an almost daily basis these people, each of us in our different ways, are made aware of the fact that in some way or other we are citizens of a nation-state whose geography provides the horizons of our daily world; yet how do we situate this citizenship as just one of the subject positions that we occupy in a given locality? In the Bajo Segura in Spain or in the villages of England or France, we find ample evidence that the processes that position people as citizens and as members of local units of agglomeration need to be conceptualized together, as Gupta suggests; but how is this to be done?

In his Introduction to *Cultural intimacy: social poetics and the nation-state*, Michael Herzfeld notes that, 'There is a curious symbiosis between the state's argument that it must intervene to prevent a final collapse of civic morality and the rebellious Cretan sheep-thieves' view that the collapse of *their* morality is what necessitated the intervention of the state' (1997: 8). Herzfeld follows up with a rich and detailed argument about the overlaps and interfaces of intimate and national spaces in terms of cultural practices, or the practice of culture. In a similar way Anthony Cohen, in his two edited books *Belonging* (1982) and *Symbolizing boundaries* (1986), which focus on communities in the United Kingdom, wishes to explore the very different evocations of what is required of social membership, depending on which arena of sociality one is being enveloped in. He talks of state policies and local people's responses, and notes that the latter belong 'to that realm of phenomena which anthropologists label the "symbolic". It is in the symbolic that we now look for people's sense of difference, and in symbolism, *rather than structure*, that we seek boundaries of their world of identity and diversity' (1986: 2, *italics mine*). These two authors address very much the kind of overlapping to which Gupta refers, and which I have felt so strongly while living and working in Europe; but for my part I need to understand the kind of issues and concerns that my acquaintances in France or Spain discuss with me as being only in part issues about representation, symbols and a kind of deracinated 'culture'.

While I have no doubt that there is one sense of culture that embraces the entire realm of the way we organize our thoughts about *all* these various overlapping and confusing calls to social membership, I also think that there is another sense of culture that we need to attend to, which is captured in the picture drawn above by Todorov in the second of the two opening quotes, one element of membership being analogous to the kind of 'culture' to which he refers, the other drawing on his second feature of membership, citizenship. Indeed, it is this kind of language that provides the starting-point for this chapter, yet it seems to provide us with a rather too neat 'division of labour' – *cultural membership* nicely referring to that package of membership claims and responsibilities that seem to be mediated by habits and practices in some way beyond the politics of the state, and then *civic membership* seeming to involve simply a turning of the page to another set of more formal properties. One reason why this neatness is no longer tenable is that even though anthropologists continue to work in local settings, grappling with the complex world of people's daily lives, the works of such people as Elias (1976), Althusser and Balibar (1970), Abrams (1982), Foucault (1980) and Bauman (1987) have made us increasingly aware of the way in which the modern state's political project involved the shaping of social subjects, what Gramsci referred to as 'the "ethical" state', a process that would affect local culture from the outset of our studies, making it less tenable to work within a metaphor of social space in which more intimate communities (with 'cultures') interface with 'the state' metaphorically referred to as external.

Yet, once we take this move, we need to be especially cautious not to make rather sweeping assumptions about the ubiquity of a disciplining state and the way it has penetrated into the everyday world of local cultural settings. My hypothesis is that the kind of culture we find ourselves interpreting as we do our fieldwork in local settings is not innocent of the quite particular histories of *étatisation* from one country to another. This would suggest, then, that we might compare the spaces of 'locality' made possible by the state in one ethnographic setting to changing state projects elsewhere in Europe. For the way in which state projects have worked on the forming of the citizenry has been quite diverse throughout Europe. It can be captured in the following two questions: is the arena of the family, of neighbours, of local community, primarily one of awful privation, need and atavism – is the noble savage more savage than noble, and if so, should membership of the state protect her/him from such barbarism? Or is the arena of the family, of neighbours, of local community actually the principal source of moral fulfilment, of personal recognition, of the emotional perquisites that make life worth living and, being thus, shouldn't the state no more than guarantee that these 'liberties' should not be trampled upon? So even if we were to understand the disciplining state in terms of a rather top-down view, then these two ideal types would give quite different degrees of moral authority to the local.

And anyway, perhaps we should understand the emergence of citizenship claims less in these top-down terms, and more in terms of a series of struggles, possibly the by-products of other struggles over protection in the workplace and participation in the political process, for example. This would suggest that neither the idea of an overweening, disciplining state shaping the world of the passively receiving community, nor the idea of local attachments and claims existing in their own terms (state institutions providing simply contextual shapes over which they move) – neither of these two ideas would be especially tenable. Rather we would need to explore the specific histories of the dialectical relationship between the citizenship-forming project of specific states and the constitution of local-level collectivities. This would help us to understand how the two threads of membership I have alluded to interweave themselves quite differently through the lives of people from one social setting to another. Put in the form of a question, if we assume that through their work habits, the calls on their home life, the pleasures and tribulations of their friends and neighbours, people find themselves involved in daily claims and responsibilities that arise from their membership in these networks, then how are these claims and responsibilities modified by people's claims as members of a larger body politic?

In the cases to follow, while there is no absence of definitions of the situation that rely on local cultural mores and practices, these occur within parameters set by a vast and present state – not just today or yesterday, but for as far back as anybody's memory can go. Moreover, this is persistently pressed home by the people themselves, who perpetually juxtapose the claims and obligations of their interpersonal relations with the claims and responsibilities that come from what seem to them quite remote sources. In what follows I do no more than unthread the dense weave of these issues, trying to suggest a series of questions that we will have to ask if we are to continue to use anthropological understandings of culture in the setting of the late-modern state.

Scenes Between a Rock and a Hard Place

As we saw in the previous chapter, in the Vega Baja del Segura homework is a major form of livelihood. Small, 'informal' economic enterprises with a complex network of outwork have been actively encouraged by a government facing the highest unemployment rate in the European Union (22 per cent – *Independent*, 29 Oct. 1995). Effectively, this reconfigures the lines between the concern adults are expected to show towards family and neighbours and the state's own claims to provide 'welfare'. We saw in that chapter that one of the jobs that falls to the wife and children of a work distributor is that of quality control. An element of production largely taken care of through surveillance in the setting of the factory, quality control is problematic when work is dispersed. It rarely pays to return jobs to original workers, even assuming they can be identified. Far quicker and more efficient is to have a trusted partner – the wife or one or two older children (usually daughters) – go over the jobs and upgrade items. In three cases over as many years, women I have known in this job have faced especially gruelling pressure, as one or another of their parents or parents-in-law became so sick that they needed almost constant care in their homes. The pressures here, from overwork, from interpersonal tensions and from a growing sense of personal incompetence and/or loss of sympathy for dear ones, in each case resulted in physical illness.

There *are* other resources, some of which are covered by taxes; but these kinds of services are being reduced by the neo-liberal state, so that such things as local old people's homes or visiting nurses all require outlays of cash. But a major problem for work distributors is cash flow. They are in a weak position to demand payment from recalcitrant putters-out. This is not just because there are so many distributors willing to do the work; it is also because their relationships with these putting-out firms are unprotected by the state, so that the only leverage such people can have is through localized interpersonal sanctions and their own personal powers of persuasion (see Chapter 7). In the other direction from the putters-out, the work-distributors' homeworkers are taking in so little cash that any shortfall can bring them up against the baseline of necessity: they simply can't keep their machines running, their children cared for and so on.

By week's end, therefore, the work distributor habitually faces a potential crisis – one that is frequently resolved by use of the pension cheques of various elders. Apart from the kinds of draconian care conditions this results in, middle-aged adult sons and daughters live through weekends in guilt-ridden terror that a parent will fall sick and there will be no cash for basic needs. It is these conditions that provide the context for the kinds of emotional and physical exhaustion afflicting the three women I just mentioned.

For the second case I want to refer to a community on the west coast of Newfoundland. It is an area that has long suffered extreme poverty and hardship. Fishing was supplemented by work on a nearby military base, but over the past few years the fishing has declined to almost nothing and the military base has gone. There is a high degree of seasonal and longer-term out-migration, chiefly among men, and for the men that remain much of the year is spent eking out a living on unemployment cheques and welfare. In the community single mothers are also dependent on welfare and on getting work projects through the local employment office, which might bring in a small wage and then allow them to qualify for a short period of unemployment.

Because of the high proportion of out-migration, as well as other factors, being a single mother is not uncommon in the community. While local normative attitudes toward single mothers may contain a strong element of criticism, these are shot through with an accept-ance of the prevailing conditions that give rise to the situation. An unemployed man may co-habit with a single mother, thereby pooling their child-support, welfare and/or unemployment cheques.

Without wishing to play down the appalling stresses and tensions created by the condition, it might nonetheless be possible to say that among local people there is a certain resigned acceptance of single-parented families and the conduct that goes along with them. Within this context, however, lies the state and its agents, the local social workers. Single mothers are eligible for child-support pay-ments, making the pooling of resources at least a potential benefit. The state, however, makes support payments based on its own criteria of single motherhood, and seeks to enforce these through surveillance. Cohabitation with a man can lead to the severance of welfare payments, and women 'caught with the toilet seat up', as the saying goes, are threatened by the state with both economic hardships and normative sanctions, and then by the community with the indignities and victimizations following from the economic destitution that results.

This case is taken from the work of the anthropologist, Glynis George (1996a; 1996b: 121–65), and in my rendition clearly suffers from lack of detail. But the point I want to make is clear – while it would be inaccurate to say that the values of the state are pervasive in this community, it is clear that social relations and the expect-ations and values that go with them are thoroughly penetrated by the expectations of social membership dictated by the state. And of course, in the case of single mothers there is an invasion not just of the community but of the intimate spaces of their personal domestic lives. A pair of men's shoes left near the door, an extra beer mug on the table are no longer just idle items of the household scenery, but are potentially dangerous.

Glynis George makes it clear that there is much discussion and room for interpretation within the local community, giving rise to a distinctive local discourse: she illustrates this through reference to the heightened media (and state) treatment of child abuse and the ways in which a historically impoverished and peripheralized rural community has tried to cope with this relatively recent concern with one component in a whole web of societal abuse of these people. Nevertheless, as in the Spanish example, the agenda of the

dialogue and debate within the community is set pre-eminently by
non-local forces.

Cultural Membership

In studying people in the context of fieldwork anthropologists
see them pursuing their lives at the local level – making a living,
marrying, choosing friends, joining associations and so on. Conventionally we have tended to talk about these things in terms of
culture. Yet practices and institutions such as these are also referred
to, usually in non-anthropological literature, in terms of a quite
different notion – that of *civil society*. In so far as a state's formulation
of citizenship is mediated through complex understandings of this
civil society, as well as notions of (national) culture, we need to
situate these different notions *vis-à-vis* one another and thence *vis-
à-vis* particular understandings of citizenship. So I begin here with
a brief discussion of what we need to have in mind as we think
about culture in a local setting, and then, while retaining these ideas
about culture, I turn to the different, but, as it turns out, not
altogether disconnected idea, civil society.

If we go back for a moment to the way in which anthropologists
employed the term 'culture' in settings conceived of as integral and
isolated, we find culture, 'compris[ing] systems of shared ideas,
systems of concepts and rules and meanings that underlie the way
humans live' (Keesing 1981: 68).[1] In so far as they continue to work
in local settings, however much those settings may now be
embedded within a broader field of forces, the notion of culture
acts as an important tool for capturing features of this world.
Working as we do in local settings,[2] we become aware of particular
institutionalized practices that occur and recur mediated by a
local *habitus* having no immediate connection to state institutions.
Because these occur among an identifiable group of people and
often in an identifiable physical setting (the fieldsite), they can be
distinguished from similar institutionalized practices in other
settings. These similarities and differences are nicely embraced
by the anthropological convention 'culture'. In this sense, as
Bloch argues, some notion of culture is indispensable: 'Social
anthropologists are aware that they cannot study action, verbal or
otherwise, if they do not construct, probably in imagination, a
representation of the culture of the people they study, since this is

the only way to make sense of their activities' (Bloch 1991: 185).

Moreover, in so far as it includes the sanctions and expectations that go along with certain behaviour patterns, culture has the sense of a set of taken-for-granted *regulations* of everyday life, while, as a result of its referring to practices carried out over time, there is also a generative element to culture (Goody 1993: 6). Cultural expression, then, becomes a means by which people articulate their *participation in a group*: claims and responsibilities *vis-à-vis* the collectivity that are not directly mediated by formal state institutions[3] – 'Cultural traits are not absolutes or simply intellectual categories, but are invoked to provide identities *which legitimize claims to rights*' (Worsley 1984: 249, *italics mine*).

But – still within anthropological discourse – this local sense overlaps with a broader use of the term. It would therefore be quite wrong to assume that this spatial dimension of 'culture' exhausts the ways in which anthropologists use the notion, for 'culture' refers as well to the standards, norms and idiosyncrasies of a much broader range of people than those involved in daily interaction – Balinese culture, French culture, and so on. Thus we find Marcel Mauss (1969 [1920]), on his return from the First World War, recording his astonishment at the inability of British troops to use French spades. Interactions between these two perceptions of culture can then be referred to in terms of a folk–urban continuum, high and low culture, or culture and subcultures; but each of these generates a different idea of the respective fields being discussed and the nature of their interaction.

We need note two things about this broader idea of culture. The first is that, unlike the more spatial idea of culture, *this* notion of 'culture' tends to stress the sense of being a code to which people refer or conform, as against the way in which their practices generate cultural patterns. Culture here becomes hard to disentangle from history (see Chapter 7). The second is that it shares with the first notion the sense of having a life of its own irrespective of the state. By extension, this has often meant that culture, in both senses, has been understood as a prior set of patterns and ideas on which politics is then expressed, as though culture was *there, in situ*, and politics were expressed *through* it (Comaroff and Comaroff 1992: 28).

At first sight these first two perceptions of culture stand in contrast to a third sense of 'culture', one that is generally understood to have arisen outside the musings of anthropologists. This is because, in those settings where anthropologists originally used the term, the idea that culture expressed – was possibly the only means for expressing – social *membership* was so obvious as to be almost taken for granted. And yet, as we work in settings where people have clearly evolved a social world long integrated into national states with extensive and effective schools, lawcourts, police forces and national economies, we find ourselves having to ask how the specificities of a culture as 'a system of shared ideas, a system of concepts and rules and meanings that underlie the way humans live' *came into being.* 'Habit,' 'custom,' 'tradition' and so on, all seem to beg such a question. We can understand E. P. Thompson's major works (1968; 1975; 1978a) to be concerned with precisely this issue: culture as an element of identity that emerges from participation in collective struggles across a wide social canvas. They may indeed be struggles precisely over (among other things) the issue of collective and individual social membership.

Rather than seeing any one of these three perceptions of culture as sharply distinct, we need to see the way they inform one another. If the contours of local distinctiveness and identity, as well as the broader field of 'national culture', arise out of historically quite specific struggles within and between existing and emergent sets of collectivities, then any sense of culture – what 'culture' may actually mean at any given moment – must arise as a result of the nature of these struggles. This makes it impossible to rest with a neat distinction between anthropological notions of culture and the English 'Marxist' version.

The clear distinction, therefore, that George Marcus wants to make between older anthropological notions of culture and what he refers to as 'the Marxist emphasis' is hard to sustain.

> Anthropologists, specialists in the study of those on the margins of world historical trends emanating from the West, are accustomed to staging culture as an integral spatio-temporal isolate, not without its own internal contradictions, but at least with its own integrity against the world, so to speak. This is much different from the Marxist emphasis, which views culture as a product of struggle [No references cited]; there is no self-contained integrity entailed in the concept [No references cited]; it is a function of critique and acceptance in thought and action among those variously situated in a system of political economy, which is not finally monolithic, once viewed from the perspective of an ethnography of cultural forms, but rather a diversity of responses to the enacted principles of capitalist political economy (1986: 178).

Here Marcus has described very incisively the accepted differences between notions of culture supposedly emanating from two different schools – the anthropological and the Marxist. The clarity, of course, obscures much of the confusion and overlap between the two uses (as well as the dialogue within the two traditions). But it is important to note that, even here, with this kind of simplification-for-the-sake-of-clarity, we are able to see how deeply interconnected are the two ways of thinking about culture. And this interconnection has to do, not just with the supposedly pernicious role of the anthropological narrative in producing imaginary cultures with their own integrity – as the postmodern position would have it. The interconnection arises immediately we reverse the old order and place politics in front of, rather than after, 'culture' – not how politics finds expression through culture, but how cultural collectivities arise out of political engagement.

Far from standing in contrast to the first two perceptions of culture, this third perception provides a historical dimension to dynamic processes of 'culturogenesis' (to adapt Elias's term, 'sociogenesis'), allowing us to ask questions about the different ways in which historical processes produce cultures of locality of various kinds. We see this connection especially clearly for parts of rural Britain in Williams's discussion in *The country and the city* (1973), where he shows that, viewed over a long period, the actual character and meaning of rural 'locality' went through a virtually infinite variety of changes. We see how, in an almost unstoppable modernist sensibility, we read off these fraught, inconclusive experiences as coherent traditions of shared values (etc.). Then, in a nearly unremarked gesture, this backward glance is, by a kind of reverse logic, extended into the future, so that what 'remains' of rural life in the present is doomed to extinction in some proximate future – an always disappearing world.

Hence the image held by the romantics of an integrated rural village, where self-help and mutual aid were common currency, which is then subsequently destroyed by enclosures and the predations of the industrial revolution. Against this Williams juxtaposes the biography of *Ashby of Tysoe*, a neighbouring village to the one I referred to earlier where I grew up. Tysoe was made up of a set of occupations – craftsmen, traders, and labourers[4] – that carried with them more or less clear class differences. Indeed, the evidence is that by the mid-seventeenth century the divisions between rural gentry, surviving craftsmen and the then growing rural poor, were stark indeed. Here are Williams's reflections on Tysoe:

In Tysoe there was a revival of community, as the village came together in the nineteenth century, to fight for its rights of allotment in the Town Lands. In many parts of rural Britain, a new kind of community emerged as an aspect of struggle, against the dominant landowners or, as in the labourers' revolts . . . against the whole class-system of rural capitalism. *In many villages, community only became a reality when economic and political rights were fought for and partially gained,* in the recognition of unions, in the extension of the franchise, and in the possibility of entry into new representative and democratic institutions. In many thousands of cases, *there is more community in the modern village, as a result of this process of new legal and democratic rights, than at any point in the recorded or imagined past.*

That is *active community,* and it must be distinguished from another version, which is sometimes the mutuality of the oppressed, at other times the mutuality of people living at the edges or in the margins of a generally oppressive system. This comes out in many ways, overlapping with the community of struggle, or persisting as local and traditional habit (1973: 104, *italics mine*).

We need to note here how Williams places the perception of common experience (which need not pre-empt internal differences) into the context first of particular and local struggles, and then into a wider field of conflicts that inflected upon – provided the possibilities, idioms and opportunities for – local expression.

The point is, though, that, in any of its manifestations, culture cannot be disentangled from claims. And claims must be asserted collectively if the claims made individually *within* the collective are to be worth making. But collective and individual assertions of this kind take place within a larger, politicized setting where other currents, other particularities, other cries and silences are occurring. This in turn gives rise to competing interpellations of people's sense of who they are as *social persons*, and not all these are mediated through 'culture' or 'cultural membership'. This becomes clear in the distinction Hobsbawm (1990: 20) makes. He notes that what characterized the nation as 'a people' seen from below, 'was precisely that it represented the common good against privilege', a 'revolutionary-democratic point-of-view', and he contrasts this with the nationalist point of view (one to which Mauss alluded with his quip 'because the nation created the race, it was believed that the race created the nation' (Mauss 1969 [1920]: 159)). Hobsbawm continues:

The equation state = nation = people applied to both, but for nationalists the creation of the political entities which would contain it derived from the prior existence of some community distinguishing itself from foreigners, while from the revolutionary-democratic point of view the central concept was the sovereign citizen-people = state which, in relation to the rest of the human race, constituted a 'nation'.

What is emerging here is something that we need to superimpose on what we have so far said about cultural collectivity – a distinction between claims articulated in terms of a common culture versus claims and responsibilities that derive from participation in the state, specifically as 'sovereign citizen-people'. States have articulated their civilizing mission (albeit differently) through both these channels. And the arena of civil society is no less multifaceted than what has been said about culture, though the prisms are set differently.

It is hard to unravel the tensions in the civilizing process of the state and what the process was directed through and against, then, without moving beyond culture to civil society.

Civil Society

The problem we have at this point is that while the idea of civil society may at first seem poles apart from the ways in which anthropologists have used the culture concept (indeed, one version explicitly casts civil society as something above and beyond the affectualness of culture) the notion 'civil society' nonetheless relies on many of the components of culture that we have so far discussed, and hence overlaps with that concept. Chris Bryant, for example, talks of a sociological variant of civil society that 'refers to a *space or arena between household and state,* other than the market, which affords possibilities of concerted action and social *self-organization*' (1993: 399, *italics in original*), while Krishan Kumar, referring to Gramsci, notes that 'civil society is the sphere of culture in the broadest sense' (1993: 382). And just as some anthropologists want to avoid pre-emptive definitions of 'culture', preferring a more open-ended notion that will capture the multifarious manifestations of 'cultures', so John Keane argues that 'efforts to maximize the level of "concreteness" of the idea of civil society for political purposes should be resisted' (quoted ibid.: 387).

Indeed, it might well be that culture – as an arena of expression, interaction and practice beside, beyond or above the state – has served anthropologists so well that 'civil society' has hardly entered the disciplinary vocabulary at all. What, then, does the term embrace? The answer is not straightforward. This is partly because there are three tensions in the idea of civil society. Each of these has its analogue in discussions of culture. Firstly, we find in use of the term a confusion we have already seen in anthropological uses of culture: just as we might ask of anthropologists, 'Is "culture" a heuristic device you use to help you understand people's practices and beliefs, as Bloch seems to suggest above, or is it the thing you are studying, for which presumably you will need *other* heuristic tools?', so we might ask, 'Is the idea of civil society merely a blueprint, a set of attitudes and so on, against which we might measure the actual practices we find in society, or is civil society an identifiable space in the social fabric – or even a *potential* space in the social fabric that could, practically, be occupied and made to work?'

A second tension arises from the internal properties of a civil society and that which it is set against or to which it is to be an alternative. We have already remarked on a tension in the notion of culture between its sense as a relatively integrated and coherent arena and its sense as emergent from collective forms of resistance to hegemonic forces in the larger society. We see these same issues arising now with respect to civil society. The internal character of civil society is greatly a function of its position *vis-à-vis* what is not civil society; as, in Bryant's case, this seems to be the market, so market calculations and practices would not operate here. This might then be a world of non-commodified relations that distinguish the various forms of reciprocity from commodified exchanges. If so, then anthropologists would be quick to point out that far from producing a civil society of coevals, such reciprocal relations position people *vis-à-vis* one another in terms of variations in social distance. Yet, on the other hand, civil society may arise out of struggles against a state: the internal character of such a 'civil society', however, will necessarily be built against and upon features of that state (see below).

A third tension is analogous to the role of social institutions in anthropological treatments of culture (see Note 3). As we see in Bryant above, a defining feature of civil society is the notion of self-regulation, a need to bring society closer to itself (in the words of Pierre Rosanvallon (1988: 206)), without the oppressive and remote institutions of the state. Yet civil society keeps dirtying its own nest: spontaneous practices become institutionalized practices; institutionalized practices become institutions. If these institutions are to become democratic institutions, how are they different from the state? If they are to remain 'intermediate' institutions uncontrolled by the state (Beteille, quoted in Gupta 1997b) – such as [private] schools, [alternative] health care facilities and [local] lawcourts – to whom are they answerable (Gupta, ibid.)?

To sort out some of these issues then, our answer must be couched in terms of different prevailing historical conditions from one place to another. For Hegel civil society was to supersede the atavism and patriarchy of the family and inform the coming into being of the ideal state. Civil society was simultaneously a kind of community that lay above the family, supervising morals and settling disputes, and, as such, an incomplete form of the state. He talks of this as an 'early state', which educated and cared for its members, being superseded by a more advanced state, which adds to this, 'the external wellbeing of the subjects' (Bobbio 1989: 33). Yet Hegel did not see these in developmental or historical terms, but rather in terms of potentialities – potentialities, however, which had to be realized for the attainment of civilization. For Hegel, then, there is not an *a priori* separation of two autonomous entities – civil society and the state. This contrasts with de Tocqueville, who, in his study of America, concluded that *prior to* the coming into being of a modern state, there needed to be in place a civic culture (a conclusion that made him quite pessimistic about post-revolutionary France). We see how these two positions are to be played out in the interplay between local cultural concern and the welfare state, by recalling the questions I put at the outset: is the arena of the family, of neighbours, of local community, so awful, needful and atavistic that membership of the state should protect the individual citizen from such barbarism? Or is the arena of the family, of neighbours, of local community actually the principal source of moral fulfilment, of personal recognition, of the emotional perquisites that make life worth living, and, since it is thus, shouldn't the state do no more than guarantee that these 'liberties' should not be trampled upon?

We find Marx and Engels, who saw civil society as nothing but the commercial relations of the market, quite aware of two of the conditioning characteristics of civil society that I have mentioned as part of a real, identifiable historical situation. Civil society was not so much contrasted to the family; rather, as an arena of market relations, its 'freedoms' found their dialectical opposite in the rigidities of the old absolutist state.

> By civil society is meant, negatively, the realm of social relations not regulated by the state: which is understood narrowly and nearly always polemically as the complex of apparatuses that exercise coercive power within an organized social system. [Along with this notion of the state] is the group of ideas that accompanies the birth of the bourgeois world: the affirmation of natural rights belonging to the individual and social groups independently of the state and which limit and restrain political power; the discovery of a sphere of . . . economic relations whose regulation does not need the existence of coercive power because they are self-regulating (Bobbio 1989: 22).

So here Bobbio alludes to this unresolved tension: civil society arises out of a struggle *against* external regulation (by the old monarchical state), and yet reproduces within itself institutionalized regulatory practices.

Not surprisingly, Marx was supremely concerned with matters of social control under these very modern conditions; but, unlike Gramsci subsequently, he saw these largely in terms of a *compart-mentalization of functions* in which the state was to substitute for the older community. In feudal society citizens were always members of some branch of the society, and within this branch itself resided a regulatory function, be it the guild, the community or the feudal manor. After all these 'estates' had been penetrated by market and commodity relations, a realm of society had to be instituted that would perform the old political or regulatory function, by standing above all branches (see Sayer, 1987; also 1979). For Marx, then, civil society in this very specific sense is uniquely a characteristic of modern capitalist societies. So bourgeois/civil society – *die burgliche Gesellschaft* – was both a period that followed feudalism in which the social organization of society that best served the interests of the bourgeoisie prevailed (i.e. that described above) *and* an arena of society in which commodity exchange prevails and which requires a distinct arena, the state, because of civil society's *inability* to regulate itself, and still yet retain its necessary ideology of freedom and autonomy.

By the time Gramsci is writing, the state has considerably invaded the space of civil society as Marx understood it. As social relations within civil society became themselves more institutionalized, so the clear distinction between fields of regulation (the state) and non-regulation (civil society) broke down. The point for Gramsci was to understand the means by which civil society went beyond the Hobbesian world of Marx's concept to develop its own fields of power. Clearly such a process gave rise to organizations and institutions, and the form these took was largely to do with the specific character of the economic and state contexts within and against which 'civil society' emerged in any given place. But of particular interest to our discussion here is the way Gramsci links culture to the class-based project of civil society. Kumar writes that, for Gramsci,

> It is where values and meanings are established, where they are debated, contested and changed. *It is the necessary complement of the rule of a class through its ownership of the means of production and its capture of the apparatus of the state.* By the same token it is the space that has come to be colonized – the famous 'war of position' – by any new class seeking to usurp the old (1993: 382–3, *italics mine*).

Here in Kumar's reading, Gramsci sees culture as *the process* by which power is exercised through civil society. We do not see a sharp division between the state and civil society except in so far as the power bloc exercises power through the state in the form of domination and through civil society in the form of hegemony.

Let me recap here. I have suggested that at the local level we find claims, expectations of conduct and interpersonal responsibilities taking distinct cultural forms from place to place. I have suggested that in the European setting we have to situate these kinds of arenas within the frameworks of different states. But I have suggested that this juxtaposition is made especially complex by the fact that we are not talking about two relatively fixed templates or structures set side by side or superimposed on one another; rather we are referring to a dialogue of struggle in which different forces give voice and 'make history' and for which the 'civilizing' script is continually being re-edited, re-directed and re-produced by an *auteuriste* state.

In a sense tucked between these two are growing commercial relations, which, by the mid-nineteenth century, were being referred to as a 'civil society' in some sense set against older notions of both community culture and the monarchical state. I have then suggested that this arena of civil society was deeply contradictory. The hidden hand of the market was supposed to be left to its own devices, and for this to happen, such regulation as was necessary was to be compartmentalized in the state. Yet there was an inherent tendency within civil society itself for institutions of regulation to arise – from stock market rules, to guidelines for competition and for labour practices. At the same time the state itself remained distinct from civil society only in the most archaic of European societies (Tsarist Russia was most often cited); elsewhere regulation needed to become more pervasive and in doing so, in its allusions to 'proper behaviour', 'civilized conduct' and so on, it relied on culture.[5]

If confusions arise, then, as a person tries to sort out the local cultural and the civic ways in which she might mediate between herself and 'society', or express herself as a recognized and a recognizable, legitimate social subject, it is not because she cannot decide which clearly transmitted channel to switch on, but because the channels themselves are scrambled – both within themselves (*within* what it is to make cultural appeals or civic appeals) and between the one and the other (where the communitarian begins and the liberal-civic ends). This is made especially so by what the English call 'the Welfare State', the Spanish '*el estado de bienestar*' , the Italians, '*il stato assistenziale*,' and the French '*l'Etat providence*.'[6]

Historical Differences

If we now begin to explore the interplay between the civilizing process of the state and these other discourses of collective member-ship we need a much more historically enriched notion of the state (or more accurately *states*) than is provided by either a nexus of 'formal' institutions external to the daily habitus of local practices, or conversely a pervasively disciplining state that orchestrates the entire drama of life, moulding the characters and directing the plot in its entirety. We need to know both how the authority of state projects was built on accepted notions of civil society and local culture, and also how its colonization of these other social spaces influenced people's views of the way in which their claims and responsibilities might be articulated *within* the space of local culture.

In what follows I try to show how different histories of state welfare projects in Europe shaped both the relative autonomy of local memberships and the language of claims *within* those localities, i.e.: set the conditions for the authenticity of local culture.[7] I do this by setting the British case under which I grew up and whose principles I have tended to take for granted (as I believe do many other Anglophone anthropologists) alongside those of France and Spain, where I have lived and worked.

It was T. H. Marshall, in his (1965) review of the evolution of welfare policies in Britain from the latter part of the last century up to and a little beyond the Beveridge Commission of 1942, who produced the notion of *social citizenship*.[8] Marshall referred to *social citizenship* as 'the right to share to the full in the social heritage and to live the life of a civilized being *according to the standards prevailing in society*' (1950: 11, *italics mine*). It is important to note here that he adduces cultural criteria not so many miles from the kinds of thing we saw anthropologists referring to earlier, and we shall see that Marshall's historical narrative invokes the weaving together of the elements I have so far associated with culture and civil society. As Bryan Turner notes (1990:191), 'At the heart of Marshall's account of citizenship lies the contradiction between the formal political equality of the franchise and the persistence of extensive social and economic inequality, ultimately rooted in the character of the capitalist market place and the existence of private property' (Marshall 1972). Marshall saw the social citizen emerging as the result of a series of ordinary people's struggles – a series of evolving claims 'to be accepted as full members of society, that is, as citizens' (Marshall 1963 [1950]: 8).

I have already suggested that the local settings that anthropologists have usually worked in have often encouraged them to see 'culture' as the medium through which social membership is expressed. As Marshall sees it, social rights were originally vested precisely in such local communities and in various kinds of associations such as guilds or municipal bodies. These were forfeited during a transitional period in English history. As people moved out of their local communities and became indigent, their claims on the state for welfare, for example in the form of the Poor Law, could only be made *by sacrificing their status as citizens*. They were essentially outcasts. It was their struggle for claims to civilized membership in the overall body politic (no longer the local community, but now the state as a whole) that reversed the formula from

outcast, hence recipient of charity
to
*citizen, hence right to live according to the standards prevailing in
society*

Marshall saw this in terms of three successful victories on the part
of ordinary people, the first giving them the necessary forms of
free property rights to partake in the market, the second greater
access to democratic rights through the extension of the vote, and
the third rights to state welfare.

It is important for our understanding of the confusions and
difficulties that arise for people as they thread their way through
the claims and impositions of different fields of social membership
to see that the social citizen seen through this historical narrative
cannot be cleanly extracted from some kind of cultural referent –
be it an older notion of relatively integrated cultures shared within
local communities, or the more pervasive standards prevailing in
society at large, or even the changing cultural possibilities that
emerge through struggle. Based on the bedrock of an older rural
community, the claims a citizen can make derive from a set of
supposedly consensually held expectations (the standards prevailing
in society), claims that are seen to be the result of a series of identifiable struggles. Yet Marshall's rather whiggish view of progress is
deeply middle-class, English, male and white.

For Marshall struggles appear to take place among culturally
disembedded rational actors, so that 'struggles for claims' can be
made within an arena of commonly held cultural values and yet
not produce cultural *differentiations*. What is missing is how the
subjectivities of ordinary people were modified in the process of
the political struggles he describes; it is as though each time the
ordinary folk appeared on the stage of history to carry off some
political trophy or other, they came with the same (instrumentalist)
script and clothed in the same (liberal) garb. Yet read today,
Marshall's understandings of the role of ordinary people's struggles
evokes the way in which E. P. Thompson (1968) encourages us to
see how historical struggles give form to cultures of collectivity that
become written on the complex interweavings of present-day social
forms. Moreover, as we see from Williams's comments on Tysoe,
these struggles – for increased participation in the body politic,
for better working conditions in urban factories, and so on, were
not isolated struggles, but thoroughly enmeshed with one another.

Marshall's conception of social citizenship, then, arose from a quite selective understanding of British history, and then this 'selective tradition' became an active component that set the intellectual basis for state involvement in local provisioning, care and claims. Far from the past's being a deadweight lying heavy on the present, past history is selectively produced and, thus produced, is then used to direct its unfolding into the future. We need to note here just how Marshall formulated social citizenship by a conceptual extension of 'the standards prevailing in society' from the local community to the (welfare) state. As part of the modernist historical imagination the local community is seen here as the site of norms and values shared consensually by all members, a bucolic rural community that once cared for its sick, but can no longer. Yet this was a remarkable evasion of historical reality, specifically of the very real and practical presence of local social institutions and social relations (not just local 'culture') that existed in Britain prior to 1942, and not *just* at the margins of Britain but in the North of England, the heartland of industrial society – of coal, steel, shipbuilding, and textiles – where the making of working-class culture found expression not only on the shop-floor but in the practices of provision and care for people in local clubs, associations, cooperative societies, union halls and educational programmes. In the early part of this century many Labour-held local municipal governments ran electricity, water and transport rates at a profit so as to fund public housing, unemployment relief, and local healthcare schemes(Wright 1993). They were to be reformulated by a quite self-conscious programme on the part of the pre-war Labour party to dismantle these local initiatives in favour of a *national* party programme. Here we see a clear instance, then, of the way in which the 'local culture' an anthropologist might come to study in the present has been shaped by a quite particular political history.

Placed in the influential position he was in in 1949,[9] it is hard to believe that Marshall was unaware of this kind of local community, with all its carbuncles and confusions. Yet he chose to allude to a much more romanticized and sanitized *culture* of shared standards and to a 'community' in a remote past. We can speculate as to why this was so. The very cogency of the notion of social citizenship, its acceptance as a liberal political idea, lay in the way it replaced cultural differences and local specificities with 'the standards prevailing in society' while downplaying the extent to which the values prevailing in society were themselves the outcome of very real collective struggles – as Williams noted – with very real implications for local culture. The effect of the language of universal citizenship on local cultural membership in this instance is not so much effectively to erase the legitimacy of local cultural difference, but rather, by casting cultural specificity in just one – and that a highly romanticized – mould, to circumscribe the possibilities for much more *praxis*-oriented kinds of local expression.

My original hypothesis was that the kind of culture we find in local settings needs to be understood in terms of the different histories of *étatisation* from one country to another, so that the spaces of 'locality' made possible by the state in Britain in 1949 can fruitfully be seen alongside changing state projects elsewhere in Europe. Marshall's linking of social citizenship to a series of evolutionary and internally coherent collective demands by ordinary people doesn't reflect the history of the formation of welfare regimes generally. That people *should* rely on the market mechanism to allocate them a livelihood and to fix the wage they get and that welfare processes are intricately linked to *this* kind of 'civil society' is not a universal characteristic of welfare regimes. Indeed, it was by no means what motivated the earliest self-conscious state welfare projects. Such regimes were not just 'the flying buttresses that prevented capitalism's collapse' by catering to the demands of the masses (Schumpeter 1970 [1944]: 139). Rather, they emerged to head off the effects of capitalism *on pre-existing* hierarchies. They were a response to quite particularistic and differentiated understandings of social membership, which they then reproduced.

This was so for all the major European countries – Germany, France, Italy, Spain. Thus one of the earliest cases of a welfare regime – in Germany – reflected Bismarck's vision of *Soldaten der Arbeit*, workers as soldiers in a German economy functioning on the principles of an army. This was 'the principle of "monarchical socialism", an absolutist model of paternal-authoritarian obligation for the welfare of its subjects' (Esping-Andersen 1990: 40), in which rights were conditional upon the loyalty and duty of those occupying a particular status in society. Welfare was not here attached to a universal or social citizen, and 'the granting of social rights was hardly ever a seriously contested issue' (ibid.: 27). In France, too, welfare was frequently a discourse of the Right explicitly directed against the advances of democracy, which were seen to threaten the stability of *le lien social* (Cohen and Hanagan 1995; Silver 1993). Thus the very term *l'etat providence* reflects the inter-war Catholic right's association of welfare with a corporate, non-democratic state (Silver 1996). But more important is the fact that as early as the 1870s, and more aggressively through the inter-war years, French industrial development relied less on the stripping of the French countryside than on the use of immigrant labour. Between 1911 and 1926 the foreign-born population of an industrial district like Saint-Etienne increased by seven and a half times, while in Paris the foreign-born population increased by almost 50 per cent (Cohen and Hanagan 1995: 100). 'By 1931, [the national percentage] had risen to 7%; 40% of all coalminers, 35% of all metalworkers, 26% of all quarry workers and 24% of all construction workers were emigrants' (ibid.: 101). Here the process of *étatisation* was not linked to an ideological goal of offsetting the inequities of the capitalist market, so much as regulating the labour market while at the same time trying to protect the sanctity of the French imagined community in terms of the Republican idea of the homogeneous, universal citizen. Such a regime is, from the outset, concerned about complicated criteria of categorization.

Today's Republican ideology, therefore, of *solidarisme*, in which disadvantage and distress are phrased in terms of 'social exclusion', must be seen in the light of a history in which a 'mobile population' of immigrants both bore the brunt of unemployment and were seen to threaten the 'privileges' of organized labour. As a result *citizenship* as a cultural kind of social membership (Silver 1996: 111) became the site for popular struggle over and above the citizenship of social rights and protection. Moreover, by its distinction between a mobile and a settled population, and its use of local-level organs of government for the purposes of social regulation, the French state produced its own quite specific resonance to (cultures of) 'locality'.

As with the British case, this mandarin view of what constituted local communities was undoubtedly at odds with ordinary people's various experiences of local culture (see Lem 1998; McDonald 1989; Rogers 1991); but my point is that these mandarin views did affect policy, and policy did affect the local experiences. As Noiriel acutely observes, 'the state directly contributes to the making of personal identities by codifying the main elements that define them' (Noiriel 1996: xviii) – and by the late nineteenth century, as the social restructuring made necessary for French industrial development combined with the stabilizing of France's external frontiers, 'an increasingly rigid line of demarcation established divisions within the internal social space' (ibid.: 272, see also Cross 1983) – divisions that were codified by ever more elaborate uses of the identity card.

In 1912 the 'anthropometric identity booklet' was introduced, which, along with entries showing civil status, included the following entries: 'the height of the waist and the chest, the size, length, and width of the head, the bizogamatic diameter, the length of the right ear and the left, middle and little fingers, and the colour of the eyes' (Noiriel 1996: 61). As Noiriel suggests, this system of *bertillonage* (named after Alphonse Bertillon) 'was not simply a technique; it was a new state of mind, a perception of the world and of others' (ibid.: 69), and, very soon after being applied to foreigners, techniques of identification were extended to the population at large.

> As soon as owners began . . . to keep track of foreign workers, it became apparent that the whole enterprise would be impossible unless French workers were required to carry ID's; how else could one unmask an imposter, who claimed to be French and who looked French but was not? . . . The mining company of Courrière inaugurated the anthropometric identification of its workers in 1905 . . . For owners, this was a convenient way of identifying and dismissing trade unionists (ibid.: 273).

Though the physical anthropology component of cards was gradually dropped by the 1930s, identity cards began to take on an almost bizarre complexity of classification. Agricultural and industrial workers were distinguished by different coloured cards, and artisans' cards carried a quite specific description of their trade. They were valid only for that trade and within the stated *département:* 'As social categories were diversified, so was the palette: yellow for agricultural workers, greyish-blue for industrial workers, green for non-workers, blue with red ink for artisans, orange for shopkeepers' (ibid.: 70).

The particular forming of social membership through citizenship and the way in which the state became involved in the providing of welfare, then, were very differently inscribed in France than Marshall's historical narrative suggests. Neither the active population nor political radicalism were drained out of the countryside in France between 1870 and 1939, as they had been in England. Meanwhile, the use by French industry of immigrant labour and the prohibition by the French state on collective political expression of cultural distinctiveness on the part of those immigrants coloured the nature of collective demands on the state. Citizenship as political

and cultural inclusion dominated the struggles of organized collectivities, while 'welfare' was chiefly confined to social Catholicism.

It is quite impossible to unravel these French social policies
without reference to two immensely powerful loadstones, the one
referring to culture (and nothing but), and the other referring to
civic membership (and nothing but). The first of these was an idea
about society in terms of a peculiarly French civilization – *la France
profonde*; the second was the Republican idea of society that was
the heritage of Jacobinism, 'an effort to establish citizenship as the
dominant identity of every Frenchman – against the alternative
identities of religion, estate, family and region' (Walzer 1989: 211).
Lebovics sums it up as follows:

> In the first half of this century . . . there were two conflicts about the
> identity of French culture. The first was the long-burning dispute
> inherited from the French Revolution . . . as to what was the French
> *patrimoine* and who had the right to speak for it. By the 1920s and
> 1930s the candidates of the right and of the left, respectively, were
> *peasants alone* and *both workers and peasants* . . .
>
> The second and in the long run more important issue . . . was
> whether, for all its regional diversity, France was an essential whole
> that had been created over time but that by the twentieth century
> embodied a fixed identity, as the conservative paradigm had it . . . Or
> . . . was French civilization a cosmopolitan, multicultural, syncretic, and
> ever-changing product of the lives of diverse populations, a world not
> usefully understood under the rubric of a single French 'identity' or
> 'essence'? (Lebovics 1992: 139–40).

Needless to say, parties of various political hues placed different
weight on one or the other side of this latter pair; yet it is important
to recognize that both were always present in all utterances pro or
con *l'etat providence*.

If, then, the disputes and struggles over what constitutes social
membership at the level of the state affect the idiom of claims and
responsibilities at the local level, then this French example would
imply quite different notions of local cultural membership than
the British case. We have seen how working-class struggles over
citizenship in France were quite different from the history of social
citizenship laid out by Marshall, and we might similarly surmise
that struggles between local communities and the state were also
articulated differently, giving rise in turn to a different constitution
of what might constitute authentic local culture. In her work on an

area of southern France that has a long socialist and/or communist tradition Winnie Lem, for example, shows how collective struggles of resistance – in fact usually either directed *at* the state, or requiring that the state listen to what they are saying – tied allegiance to the local soil (which, given hegemonic discourses of Left and Right, might have been misinterpreted), to participation in the working class, by placing the term *exploitation* into a pivotal position in their discourse (Lem 1994).[10]

So: anthropologists have used culture as a tool to get at people's structures of feeling and have accessed these through expressions as they have encountered them in the local settings of their fieldwork. But these constituting processes have occurred within the contexts of a wide variety of state projects that have impacted on the people in these settings. These in turn draw on mandarin understandings of the relationship between the state and (civil) society, in which the latter is suffused with some feature of 'deep culture', from notions of older, now-lost communities of caring, to those of *la France profonde*.

We can see the way in which the policies that thereby result then affect the kinds of claims people make on local bodies by turning to Spain. Under Franco the mandarin image of the state saw it to be not one consistent and rational body, but rather a series of relatively autonomous spheres or command structures. Thus, the original *Fuero de los Españoles* of July 1945 characterized the Spanish citizen as simultaneously a member of 'the national community', the Church, the family, the vertical syndicate, the municipality and the company where he or she worked (Garcia 1994).[11] Any and each of these was responsible for its members' welfare. This in practice gave a great deal of salience for a person's livelihood to local-level social relationships, and hence shaped the kinds of claims that could be made therein. A common practice in the Bajo Segura, for example, was what was known as *hipoteca humana* ('human mortgage'). Since day-labourers were never able to get their immediate employers to sign their social insurance books, they always needed at least one putative employer as a patron. Should the day arise when they needed to collect insurance, they could rely on this patron to backdate the book for three months' worth of work. The palms of such patrons, of course, had frequently to be greased.

Various criteria laid out by the European Union encouraged the Spanish state to modify the character of social membership, evoking a new dialectic between local cultural practices and this new vision of the state. One example of the more pervasive social policies the Socialists sought to enact was the introduction of a *Regimen Especial Agrario*. A worker who could provide evidence that he or she had worked the land for three months would qualify for a nine months' *subsidio* to cover the period in which they were out of work. What happened now was that local mayors began to perform exactly the same role as had the old landlords, by signing false affidavits that villagers had done their three months' work. The new 'social democratic' state, however, was marketing a quite different image of the relationship between social membership, locality and the state, and the *Regimen Especial Agrario* became a national scandal. Even so, seeing nothing scandalous about it, mayors continue a practice that they see as the proper protection of local people.

This provides a good illustration of the point I am trying to make: that we have to take great care not to superimpose our own particular understanding of the modern state and the role of citizens within it on any modern state where we happen to be doing our ethnographic work. Coming from Britain and then Canada, for me the welfare state embodied a liberal progressivist project, but from the perspective of the people I was working with in this area of Spain there had never been a (convincing) pretence that the Francoist state was journeying toward the construction of ever more widespread institutional mechanisms for their participation as citizens; moreover *state* welfare provision was ostentatiously *not* extended to them. As a result, local resources had retained an important role in the reproduction of livelihood when the increasing informalization of the economy began to occur in the 1970s.

I have argued in Chapter 5 that one reason why this area of Spain was especially attractive for the 'flexible production' regimes of late capitalism was that the institutions, the networks, the knowledges and so on that went along with existing self-provisioning were already in place. This is the 'economic' side of the local 'political economy'. One element of the 'political' side was the old practice of *hipoteca humana*. Now, however, the heightened demands of the new production regime that has been superimposed on this older one are experienced *at the same time* as quite new, unfamiliar and possibly locally maladaptive state welfare institutions are being put into place, supposedly as the flip-side to the new democracy. But the old practices, the old expectations, the old 'investments' in social membership haven't been suddenly curtailed overnight. To the contrary, in an often insidious back-room way, demands to be 'good friends', 'responsible Christians' [*sic*], respectful children, and so on have been escalated by both the new economic regimes and the state's endorsement of the barely legal practices that go along with them. Under these circumstances, it is not democratic part-icipation that is the most striking flip-side for the citizen of the new welfare state, but the payment of taxes, which appear as a kind of second rent to be paid for social membership. The experiences of inner personal turmoil, of family tensions and of social contrad-ictions that result are thus quite unique to this particular interplay between local membership and social citizenship.

I began this chapter then, with my very common-sense feeling that the ordinary people I had interacted with in my personal and professional life – in Britain, in France and in Spain – spent quite a bit of their time trying to figure out the different opportunities and responsibilities with which they were presented by their over-lapping insertion into local and wider fields of social membership. It now seems that there are quite a few links and connections, assumptions and assertions, arguments and indignations that we would each of us interpret quite differently given our various experiences of the state.

Conclusion

As we have become increasingly aware of the overt or covert ways in which the actions of the state give form to people's sense of who they are and how they are inserted into the body politic, so this perception creates an echo in an earlier concern in anthropology. Culture has been understood in various ways, but all of them somehow have to do with the way in which people's perceptions (of themselves) are interwoven with their social membership. In so far as anthropologists have studied culture through fieldwork they have seen these processes at work especially at the local level, and here I have dwelt on the ethnographic encounter with culture. This chapter has been motivated by my belief that a growing awareness of the historical lengevity of the 'cultural revolution' engineered by modern states (Corrigan and Sayer 1985), together with our recognition that these subject-forming processes were and are pervasive throughout society, obliges us to reformulate the way in which we seek to understand claims and responsibilities articulated through local culture. The physical metaphor in which the 'local' and the 'wider setting' are juxtaposed alongside one another is no longer apposite; for one thing, what different states establish as the criteria for making claims and taking on responsibility as responsible members of society is bound to condition similar criteria in the possibly less institutionalized and legalistic settings of the neighbourhood, the informalized work 'place' and the community. These latter settings are often glossed in the non-anthropological literature as the arena of 'civil society'. Projects toward the formulation of Gramsci's '"ethical" state' were predicated on assumptions about what civil society really was – for example, should the state protect people *from* civil society or protect civil society itself? Nevertheless these various definitions of civil society all resorted to some kind of cultural baseline, whatever way we choose to define 'culture'. Effectively, this brings us full circle or, put another way, completes the dialectical process. Settings where assumed cultural claims and responsibilities and so on do serve as a form of sanction are influenced by state projects toward similar ends, yet those same state projects are built upon assumptions about, first, civil society and then the realm of culture.

We have seen that this 'realm of culture' can take on various manifestations, from Marshall's nostalgia for an older *local* culture of caring and concern, to the distinction Todorov makes between culture and citizenship (which is echoed in *La France profonde* and the France of the Republic), to the sense of a collective culture arising from the historical experience of struggle in adverse conditions. While each of these senses is distinct – calling on different imagery and alluding to quite different assumptions about society, and possibly even about the fundamentals of being human – I have sought to show that they crucially overlap, and that this is what makes so hard our job of exploring the threads and tendrils of a 'disciplining state' and the various more localized and intimate calls on our social membership. Because I think that sweeping general statements about the power of *the* invasive, pervasive, and so forth disciplining state run the risk of generalization and of allowing anthropologists to deal with 'the state' in rather too vague a way; and because, on the other hand, I think that studies that focus pre-eminently on the level of sociologically deracinated symbolic utterances run the risk of becoming far too anecdotal and idiographic, I chose to explore some of the issues of this problematic around one particular element of a state's activities: different welfare regimes. This has the advantage of talking about quite specific and visible state initiatives directed at or toward the citizenry as well as often well-articulated expectations of what that citizenry should be and do. By looking at different welfare projects we are able to get some sense of the assumptions about social membership that underlay them. But a given welfare regime should not be taken as coeval with the state itself. Nor should the state be understood simply in terms of its institutions and policies. The state can't simply be reduced to a package of institutions, or of elite actors plus those institutions. There is a cultural compent too. The state itself has to be understood in cultural terms. We need to include within our understanding of any particular state, the ideas to which the forming of that state is directed. Included here are the mandarin intellectuals who provide visions of society, the state and the relations between the two, and we saw, for example, that, even limiting ourselves to welfare provision, these ideas are quite different whether we are talking about Britain, France or Spain. But included here too are the ideas that ordinary people hold of 'the state', and these too need to be interrogated – both in their specifics, i.e. particular dealings with the state, its schools, lawcourts and police forces; and in their more abstract and general understanding of 'the state'.[12]

Yet I feel that we have to avoid the temptation to answer the question Gupta poses at the outset of this chapter in the terms delimited by what what Herzfeld calls 'the politics of mereness' (1997: 94)[13] or to follow Anthony Cohen's (1986: 2) suggestion that local people's responses should be studied as though they occur in 'that realm of phenomena which anthropologists label the "symbolic"'. Attempts to understand the way in which people talk about, manipulate, play with and remain confused by issues of social membership are not usefully kept separated from the conditions necessary for the reproduction of livelihood. In Chapter 2, for example, where the focus was on people in the central Peruvian highlands, we saw how cultural membership could not be disentangled from the way people reproduced their livelihood. Among the Huasicanchinos one is especially struck by the extent to which the defence of the resources and social relationships upon which livelihood depended required the invoking of cultural membership. Culture was far from being just a quaint set of dance and dress practices, or the propensity to enjoy certain forms of joking; people defended local culture because local culture defended them.

Thus we can see how very limited an understanding of 'local culture' would be in this instance if it were confined to the *interpretation* of symbolic expressions. All this should caution us against an anthropological bias to celebrate cultural difference, and impel us instead toward a comprehension of the entirety of processes of social and cultural differentiation. This in turn would impel us toward critical attention to the way in which the utterances of professional anthropologists enter the political arena beyond academia (Stolcke 1995). As non-anthropologists increasingly seek to promote an autonomous space within society where 'politics' can occur (Laclau and Mouffe 1985; Arato and Cohen 1993; Bryant 1993) they evoke an imagery not unlike a much earlier anthropological idea about the culture of rural communities, so that anthropologists need to respond with a much more historicized and processual understanding of how cultural differentiations take place. Those who believe, for example, that the ravages of capitalism can be assuaged, possibly even overcome, through a rediscovery of 'civil society' or of 'comunitarian' sentiments in local settings that are in some unspecified way disconnected from the dictates of capitalist reproduction can do so only by reading a highly selective body of anthropological literature.

It is important to situate these particular recipes for contemporary *angst* in the context of today's political economy. As states become less and less capable of attending to the requirements necessary for the reproduction of capitalism within their own polities, so they are threatened with a legitimacy crisis. The reproduction of the labour force remains one component of those requirements; yet if issues essential to ordinary people, such as caring and concern, can be unloaded on to non-state collectivities, then questions of legitimacy can be diverted from the state toward those collectivities. The question becomes: Are these, often local, settings the potential sites of civic morality, as establishment mandarins like Amitai Etzioni (1997) or Robert Putnam (1993) would have it ? Or is the sense of locality more frequently the result of a form of cultural belonging that is almost by definition exclusive, particularistic, categorical and – either from the outset or as it becomes more refined – frankly racist (Cento-Bull 1996)? Local cultures and civil society cannot float off into a heavenly space in which they take on form and substance untrammelled by the policies of the state, the dictates of capitalism or differences of class. These are not questions of only marginal importance to anthropologists studying culture in local settings, even if they wish to keep splendidly aloof from political engagement. And this is not made less true when the people being studied have themselves retreated from politics, resorting instead to ever more private expressions of 'resistance'; rather, the role of political intellectuals becomes especially important at such times. In the next chapter I take up the issue of intellectuals and political engagement with which I opened the book, but now expanding the concern from issues of organization and interpretation to practical uses of hegemony.

Notes

1. I have chosen this textbook definition intentionally. I don't wish to caricature what Keesing has to say about anthropological notions of culture, about which he has been very critical (1994).
2. For the sake of clarity I refer to 'local settings', thus evoking the village, city neighbourhood and so on. What I have to say is meant also to refer to groups that evoke some similar sense of the face-to-face nature of interaction to refer to membership, such as ethnic groups, friendship networks and so on.
3. As Ortner (1984) has pointed out, there was a period in American cultural anthropology when culture was understood without reference to social institutions at all, and was kept conceptually separated from 'the social structure'. Thus Geertz, in a well-known formulation, distinguishes between 'the framework of beliefs, expressive symbols, and values in terms of which individuals define their world, express their feelings, and make their judgements' and 'the ongoing process of interactive behaviour, whose persistent form we call social structure' (1973: 144–5).
4. Landlords of course lived in 'country houses', a key theme in Williams's study.
5. Thus we find Arato and Cohen (1993: 201–2), in a much-quoted article, speaking of the '"modern political culture" that valorizes societal self-organization'.
6. The point about listing these different expressions in their original language is that each seems to allude to a quite different kind of activity on the part of the state.
7. As will be seen in the next chapter, by 'setting the conditions' I don't mean a one-way flow of power from the state and a passively moulded local community. I do mean that the terms of reference for struggles over social membership were largely set by the state.
8. While the British welfare system was put into effect by Attlee's Labour government after 1945, its actual initiation took place in the context of the wartime national government, in which the Conservatives traded domestic policy for management of foreign affairs and the colonies.

9. The social citizenship paper was his inaugural speech as Professor of the Department of Sociology at London School of Economics, the post-secondary institution most closely associated with Labour Party mandarins.

10. *L'exploitation* can be used to refer to the farm, as a shorthand for *l'exploitation agricole*, or to the nature of the relationship between workers and owners.

11. I say 'company where he or she worked', but the fact is that the earlier Fuero de Trabajo of 1938 had prohibited the employment of married women in workshops or factories (Garcia 1994).

12. I remember some years ago driving in France and being surprised by road-repair signs that read (roughly) 'We apologize for the delay. The state is working for you.' It struck me that the term 'the state' would never be used in that way in the Britain I grew up in. I have no idea if New Labour have now managed to produce an idea of the state that would make such signs more taken-for-granted in today's Britain. Michael Herzfeld's recent (1997) book notwithstanding, I don't think we still know very much about how different people envisage the state in which they live.

13. 'What I wish to suggest is that the anthropological demand for intimate access to the body politic violates state monopolies of representation in ways that reveal how those monopolies operate, what they control, and why they matter ... [I]t is the very mereness of what anthropologists mostly describe – the 'stories' of everyday life – that breaches the sense of unitary History that nationalist ideologies promote' (Herzfeld 1997: 91). I hope it is clear from my arguments here that, like Herzfeld, I am interested in the way in which 'state monopolies' operate, and that I would agree too that what anthropologists mostly describe are the local experiences of everyday life. But I am nervous that contemporary anthropology has become too focused on 'state monopolies *of representation*' and decriptions of the everyday mostly in terms of local people's 'stories', the result being that we risk losing the opportunity to see the way in which such things are imbricated within social relations and very real economic and political practices.

CHAPTER SEVEN

The Dialectics of History and Will: The Janus Face of Hegemonic Processes

> In Marx's analysis, social domination in capitalism does not, on its most fundamental level, consist in the domination of people by other people, but in the domination of people by abstract social structures that people themselves constitute.
>
> — Moishe Postone 1993: 30

> [I]t is not by lavishing generosity, kindness or politeness on his charwoman (or on any other 'socially inferior' agent), but by choosing the best investment for his money, or the best school for his son, that the possessor of economic and cultural capital perpetuates the relationship of domination which objectively links him with his charwoman and even her descendants.
>
> — Pierre Bourdieu 1977: 189–90

Introduction

In this chapter I turn to a concept – hegemony – that I have found useful in the past. The way in which I used the term, and the way in which a number of other anthropologists have used the term over a similar period (Sider 1986; Rebel 1989; Boddy 1989; Smith 1989; Muratorio 1991; Comaroff and Comaroff 1992; Roseberry 1994, 1996) has helped us to situate our ethnographies (as produced texts), as well as the subjects of our ethnographies, within the history of power relations. Indeed, it is precisely because of the importance of the notion, that we need now to explore some of its rather different, though interlocking dimensions. Here I do this by exploring hegemony as it threads its way through a set of interwoven social processes – the various forms through which capitalism is reproduced, the accumulated history of power struggles, attempts to *produce* hegemonic fields, and hegemony understood as a cultural field of that which is taken for granted.

To anticipate what I am about to say, my argument is that hegemony is not just about any one of these. It is especially not *just* a cultural phenomenon. Hegemonic processes don't operate only at the level of culture, even when we accept that there are a number of different ideas about what 'culture' is. We need to be able to talk about the reception of historically produced hegemony and we need also to be able to talk about praxis in the present and predicaments where hegemonic projects are being attempted now, without immediately casting all this into the realm of culture, whether culture be understood in terms of cultural *theory* (Culler 1997: 43–54) or whether it be understood in its aspect of recorded and immediate experience (Williams 1988: 87–93; 126–9). Put another way, we will only be able to interrogate the shape of what 'culture' is taken to be in any given setting, and we will then only be able to explore how or why hegemony may at some points operate through that medium or channel, if we resist the temptation of starting our enquiry with assumptions about culture and its role in power relations. If we can perform this exercise, then we can turn back and re-examine the moments where 'culture' does indeed play a decisive part in the historical acceptance and the practical production of hegemony.

But this can only be done if we approach hegemony with the intellectual tools that were sufficiently a part of Gramsci's way of thinking for him to take them largely for granted. I try to do this by pointing up particular perceptions of his that may not be so obvious to us, and I then turn to history and praxis. But in doing so I separate what cannot be separated. I disconnect one dimension of hegemony from another in such a way as to jeopardize our sense of the dialectical dynamic between a backward look at the way hegemony as history is consumed on the one hand and a forward look at the way it is produced in the present, on the other. So in one section I insist that the process of social reproduction itself provides an essential bedrock for historically ongoing hegemonic processes; then in a following section I insist that any comprehensive notion of hegemonic process must include the agency of political actors – intellectuals, leaders, class fractions and emergent blocs – in attempting to form hegemonic fields. Yet acceptance of the two gives rise to a tension in the way we understand hegemony to work

(Anderson 1976-7). Rather than seeing this as a theoretical impasse though, I see it as a highly fruitful feature of Gramsci's idea.

One way of seeing this is that, rather than simply infiltrating 'hegemony' into the albeit sophisticated ideas that anthropologists now hold about 'culture' to thereby render the latter still more sophisticated, precisely the issue of how hegemony *appears as culture* needs to be addressed. Rather than taking for granted that hegemony acts at the level of culture and then making the analysis of hegemony an almost entirely cultural analysis, we need to begin by tackling Gramsci's two different, but interacting elements of hegemony, neither of which is fundamentally a cultural process, but each of which ultimately has the effect of producing a cultural process. There is – obviously – a very strong tension in these two elements. Yet because 'culture' can be understood simultaneously as past history *and* present practice, the effect of understanding hegemony as almost exclusively a *cultural* process is to obscure this tension, and the dialectical relationship between these two moments or elements. I therefore proceed by problematizing the cultural moment in hegemony.

Throughout this book I have tried to use the counterpoint of my experiences in Peru with those in southern Europe. One feature of my shift from work in Peru to work in Spain (and subsequently Italy) has to do with the relative tightness of interpersonal relations among the Huasicanchinos and the relative looseness of those relations in the case of the people I was working with in Spain. This tightness and looseness may be expressed in numerous ways; from the virtual monopoly on collective identity engendered by militant localism in the former case, to the dovetailing of various interpellations of social membership in the latter cases; from the very different ways in which individual agency was practised within, against, or despite calls for collective responsibility on the one hand among Huasicanchinos and on the other among the people I have lived with in Spain . . . and so on.

When I shifted my fieldsite from the highland setting of the pastoralists of Huasicancha and the large *haciendas* that surrounded them to the shantytowns and inner-city slums of Lima, my reading of the literature encouraged me to turn a page in my conceptual points of reference. I had been thinking about resistance and rebellion in the context of a rural and agricultural setting; I now found myself in an urban and commercial beehive, and I began to think in terms of 'informal economies' and the haphazard, fragmented unpredictability of getting by in the city. But in fact *huasicanchino*-ness played a very powerful role in people's social construction of reality and the way they placed themselves in that reality. It was, in these circumstances, relatively easy for me to think about these people in terms of hegemonic processes, and in doing so, of course, my attention was shifted – repositioned – *vis-à-vis* the literature on 'informal economies', which had not been phrased in terms of hegemony.

Once I began work in Europe, it quickly became apparent that informal economies were far from being confined to 'the Third World'. As we have seen in Chapters 4 and 5, one way of thinking about what was happening to Western European economies was precisely that they were becoming increasingly 'informalized', in the language of Castells and Portes (1988), or 'disorganized', in that of Lash and Urry (1987). In the actual fieldwork experience itself, the temptation to see this situation simultaneously in economistic and individualistic terms was quite similar to the earlier temptations of the informal economy literature that had caught my attention when working in Lima. Initially, moreover, there appeared to be no counter-call from the field-situation itself analogous to what had happened with the Huasicanchinos. Yet it became increasingly clear to me that a great deal was being missed in the non-anthropological writing about disorganized capital, regional economies and marginality, because of a failure to formulate what was happening in terms of historical and contemporaneous hegemonic processes. Then, once having begun to 'read' this reality in these terms, the change in venue had the effect of making me explore much more thoroughly the implications of hegemonic processes than I had done in Peru.

Three things seemed especially striking about the new context I found myself in. All of them obliged me to fit the lens of phenomenological social enquiry over the more historical reading I had hitherto used in my understanding of hegemony. In doing so I realized that this more hesitant and politically fraught perception very much concerned Gramsci in *his* reflections on the present. The first was that hegemonic forms take their shape in and around quite specific projects toward the constitution, and reconstitution, of collective political expression. Put another way, we run the risk of purging hegemony of its political force, if we continually talk about it beyond the context of identifiable collective projects. But the second thing was that, working in the kind of post-Fordist social and economic conditions that I was, it became obvious that attempts to form, reform or deform hegemonic processes are thoroughly enveloped in a pervasive logic of capitalist reproduction. The very language of daily acts was threaded through that awful fact, just like the need for breath vacuums in the contaminants of a polluted environment.

The third characteristic is especially evident as one works with people caught in the inconsistencies, unpredictabilities, and contortions of informalized livelihoods; and yet it is the most difficult to talk of in the language of social science. It has to do with the need, in trying to understand the way hegemony works, of recognizing the incompleteness of the way we approach our worlds and our lives, and yet our desire for completion: our desire to cease becoming and finally be what we *are*: the *work* of social authenticity. I see it linked to a Hegelian sense of the *potentiality* of truth, which Gramsci saw in terms of the way in which 'concrete historical acts' unite contradictory elements of our selves that effectively transform us into new historical agents (1971: 372). I also see it linked to an endless process of interpersonal negotiation in the constitution of the self, something especially apparent in the endlessly negotiated fields of power that contour informal economies, as I tried to show in Chapter 5. In Charles Taylor's words, 'a great deal of human action happens only insofar as the agent understands and constitutes him or herself as an integral part of a "we"' (1993: 52). This anxiety of incompleteness seems to be essential to an understanding of what hegemony offers and hence how it works.

In what follows I do not pretend to any Gramscian orthodoxy, and, some of my language notwithstanding, my foray comes with very limited pretensions toward advancements in theory. Indeed, I quite acknowledge the discomfort many of my more deeply Gramscian colleagues may have with the way I attempt to push the notion of hegemony to my purposes. Perhaps it is apposite, following the last paragraph, to emphasize the tentativeness of what I am trying to do here and to remind the reader that, abstract though these reflections may occasionally appear, they are my attempt to come to grips with reality; not with theory nor with mundane everyday life, but with the unforgiving crucible of political praxis. In this at least, I believe I follow in the spirit of Gramsci.

Anthropologists, Fieldwork and Hegemony

When doing fieldwork most anthropologists are likely to find them-selves dealing with cultural expression, the agency of social practice, and then a variety of factors that act as constraints on both. Our training in different schools of anthropology may encourage us to stress different components of these, configure them differently, and invest importance in different elements of one or another of them; yet most anthropologists who do fieldwork are likely to attend to each of these issues and the interrelationships between them. Close to the setting of everyday life in which individuals are able to act voluntaristically to take advantage of local conditions, we are made daily aware of the limitations of materialist or cultural deter-minism; working as we do with people who often have quite limited resources of power, we are likewise made aware of the extent to which ordinary people are constrained by social forces both at the moment and through the *longue durée* of their history; finally, the combination of people's situated daily practices with their material history makes us aware of the way in which 'agency' and 'structure' come together in quite specific cultural expressions.

The spirit of this particular version of 'holism' is caught nicely by Gramsci's reflection quoted in the first chapter: 'If it is true that man cannot be conceived of except as historically determined man ... is it then possible to take sociology as meaning simply the study of these conditions and the laws which regulate their development? Since the will and the initiative of men themselves cannot be left out of account, this notion must be false' (1971: 244). Not surprisingly, therefore, his notion of hegemony appears to come to our rescue. It appears to offer us a linchpin providing some sense of leverage between the historical role of power in giving form to human subjectivity on the one hand and the will and initiative of women and men on the other. It appears to politicize the more sanitized notion 'culture' by planting the asp of power within its breast. It allows us to 'explain' the particularity of forms of conduct – cultural specificity, cultural difference – while retaining a faith in the dignity of the (subaltern) subject: formed by yesterday's power, constrained by today's.[1]

A fieldwork experience from Peru I think carries many of these features: The political mobilization to which I was witness was closely associated with people's need for land to make a living. Not surprisingly, land *title* was therefore a much-discussed and disputed issue. Quite apart from the fact that even with freehold contracts to land ultimately might makes right, these disputes were also the result of the fact that land tenure in the Andes has long been a complicated and rarely and exclusive right. The system of vertical ecology often meant that valley settlements with proximate arable land controlled pasturage in higher zones through dependent families who lived most of the year there. In many cases, these latter families developed a sense of independence from their lowland 'centres'. Since this may not have pre-empted the continuance of reciprocal arrangements for grazing; since many valley communities were becoming increasingly involved in merchant activities and the less agricultural economy of towns like Huancayo; and since live-stock grazing was often relatively unremunerative – for all these reasons, many valley communities allowed this process to become quite developed. But, in the area surrounding the Mantaro Valley, it was this pasture land that was especially attractive to the large livestock farmers, who sought to expand on to all accessible land, resulting in ensuing conflicts.

In Huasicancha there were many accounts of these events, nearly all of them involving, besides the chorus of the Huasicanchino villagers, key village figures, the *hacienda* owners, managers or personnel and the army or police. One such story went as follows:

> It was the custom to invite the gamonal (hacienda-*owner*) and his manager to the village fiestas. We played music, danced and drank. One time, after the village authorities had become thoroughly drunk, the gamonal and his people took out some papers and got these older men to sign them. They turned out to be deeds of sale [or rent] handing over the rights of our pasture to the hacienda. Martin, who was just a young man then but cunning as a fox, told the elders what they had done and was sent to Huancayo to solve the problem. There he met his friend Antonio, who was finishing his high-school education. Martin stole the deeds from the Land Registry office and hid them on Antonio. They fled from Huancayo, pursued by the police, and arrived in an estancia in the high puna, where the woman who was the shepherd there hid them. Eventually they made their way to Lima. Antonio went to the market area and began to look for work, but Martin just went to the Plaza San Martín, sat on the ground, and started weeping and wailing, telling all the hombres grandes what had befallen him and how unjust it was. People started throwing money into his hat, and he soon became rich . . .

Some time after my first fieldwork in the highlands, I found myself reading about the history of various 'peasant communities' and their disputes either among themselves or with neighbouring *haciendas*. Though often complicated, convoluted and indecisive, these stories invariably involved the same *dramatis personae* as the Huasicancha stories.

> *In one case, for example, a valley community tried to 'invade' the pasture of a highland community, claiming it was land to which they had 'title' and that the highland villagers were their 'dependants'. The highland village 'authorities' were thrown into confusion by these challenges, but a highland villager who had become a schoolteacher encouraged the villagers to seek restitution in the courts. As a result he was captured by the lowland villagers, who hid him in their village. After the intervention of the local* gamonal *on his behalf, the police intervened, rescued the imprisoned schoolteacher, and obliged the lowland community to accept a settlement in favour of the highland shepherds and their protector the* hacendado.

Antonio, often a key figure in the stories I was told, had, by the time I was doing fieldwork, become a local representative of APRA. Albeit a remote figure, he was available for interviewing, though villagers were unanimous in assuring me that he was a compromised man who had long since lost his spirit of independence and pride in the community. Martin, on the other hand, remained an elusive character whom I found so hard to locate that I began to think he was a mythical, though essential, part of the story, until some twelve years later when we finally met. Prepared neither to confirm nor deny the stories about him, Martin was only too willing to bring me up to date on other exploits, in which he always took the picaresque part – hoodwinking railway personnel, acquiring a job as a *hacienda caporal* and then outwitting the peasants who worked for the *hacendado* . . . and so on.

I begin with this reminiscence because it seems to contain a number of dimensions of the social world that we most of us encounter during fieldwork. It contains information about prevailing social conditions (with respect to land distribution), which exhibit quite clear power differences, and play a determining role in actors' conduct and perceptions. It also contains evidence of people's ability to act in response to those conditions, both collectively and individually, and thereby modify these conditions. Finally, the example I have given is cast as history and as people's accounting of and for that history (including, of course, my own).[2] Philip Abrams (1980: 7) put it all together nicely when he wrote,

It is the problem of finding a way of accounting for human experience
which recognizes simultaneously and in equal measure that history and
society are made by constant, more or less purposeful, individual action
and that individual action, however purposeful, is made by history and
society. How do we as active subjects make a world of social objects
which then, as it were, become subjects making us their objects?

Gramsci sought to address precisely this set of problems through
his unfolding thoughts around the idea of hegemony, and Abrams's
riddle serves well to suggest that the notion is likely to be a difficult
and possibly even contradictory one.

Yet the fact that we are all of us clearly enmeshed in insidious
fields of power in which we learn over time to live has made
'hegemony' an idea that is almost ubiquitous in contemporary
anthropology and cultural studies, though in fact it is less one idea
than a number of ideas. For actually there are a number of
'common-sense' ways in which we use the notion of hegemony, all
of which have validity, but each of which, taken alone, is problematic. The first of these refers to hegemony as a *cultural field*. This
might be put as follows: each of us lives in a society, which, over
time and through habit and socialization, becomes a cultural field.
Certain 'facts' about the physical, social and even personal world,
are accepted within this field as being natural. It is quite normal
for access to land to be controlled through the use of contracts
and to be expressed in terms of freehold. Quite normal, too, for
the police to step in to settle disputes between members of civil
society. And, faced with the pandemonium of the city it is quite
normal for an *Indio* to humiliate himself in public and for *hombres
grandes* to take pity on him. There are of course whole collectivities
of people who refuse to accept the contractual terms for access to
land, just as there are individuals who refuse to humiliate themselves, or do so for quite strategic reasons. To the extent that these
appear to be out of line with the norms of the broader cultural
field, they might be understood as sub-cultures or even, possibly,
counter-cultures. There appears to be an element of refusal, rejection or possibly even ignorance of the norms of the broader cultural
field, and all this *could* be spoken of in the idiom of hegemony,
counter-hegemony, and even resistance. Indeed, it often is. But it
does seem that the processes at work here could easily be talked
about without any reference to hegemony: it is not certain that
hegemony adds anything to our understanding.

Secondly, there is the role of power. One doesn't have to be a disciple of 'dominant class theory' or of Foucauldian historiography or even of Weber's sociology, to suggest that one component that makes historically quite specific forms of social relations and culture appear to be 'natural' is the component of power. Disputatious peasants are kept in line by the forces of order, and elements of power are at work too in the scene in Plaza San Martín. We don't even need to be structural Marxists to accept the fact that relationships expressed through control over land have important effects in determining the field of actions, and even actors' self-perceptions. Again, though, the question is: does hegemony add anything to the picture?

A third feature captured in the notion of hegemony is precisely its limitations in terms of complete determination or constraint. In the balance between my own always (*because* my own) heterodox views of the world and those that prevail in society at large I, as an individual, am generally obliged to bow to the more generally accepted rules of the game. I vote in elections for one of two, possibly three, parties, and in doing so accept at one level that there is a real difference in the way each of them will govern, while knowing full well at another level that a broadly liberal and uncritical view of capitalism is common to them all. I fret at this difference, and possibly even see it in terms of the 'hegemony of a liberal democratic capitalist discourse' into which I am fairly deeply incorporated, though never fully: I remain, in my own eyes at least, an individual. This relationship between the larger cultural field and my own sense of freedom and, albeit limited, agency might also be seen in terms of hegemony. We might see it as analogous to Martin's rather manipulative use of accepted practice. Yet, taken on its own, I have to insist once again, that the notion of hegemony is not essential to such a view of the social world.

Finally, there is the entire rickety contraption made up of the institutions of society, from 'ideological state apparatuses' to capitalist corporations, as well as the networks of market and reciprocity that mediate between them: of family, union, hospital and so on, into which I am embedded by need. These catch me in the thrall of their daily insistences: that I have a good credit rating, that I stop smoking, that I strive to retain my job or, having failed, conduct myself so as to appear to be seeking another. In so far as these practices become obvious (at least for most of the time) they acquire a hegemonic character, and we don't have to look far in the vignette from Peru to find schools, lawcourts and so on that serve a similar purpose.

Each one of these overlapping characteristics of our existence within a distinctively *social* world has elements in it that are called up by the use of the term 'hegemony'. Each one, taken alone, could probably be analysed quite adequately without its use. Taken in combination, they add up, nonetheless, to quite a lot of what is usually meant when the term hegemony is used by anthropologists; yet a concept made to do so much is likely to lose much of its analytic utility. In fact, the emphases on one or other of these characteristics vary. Where anthropologists have used the term 'hegemony' they have either tended to do so in *historical* ethnography, where hegemony can be studied retrospectively in terms of its effects, or they have tended to see hegemony as a cultural phenomenon catching people unaware in its web. Yet what we need to do is to reveal the 'dynamic tension between *discursive* fields and *social* fields of force' (Roseberry 1996: 77, *italics added* see also Roseberry 1998). And this can only be done by looking at the historical and the phenomenological perspectives that Gramsci uses and exploring how each effectively *produces* a field of 'culture' that anthropologists have then studied by reference to 'hegemony'.

Gramsci employs the idea of a hegemonic process to comprehend social domination in terms of the interconnection between *the determining characteristics of capitalist social relations through history* on the one hand and *the willed practice of agents seeking control over history* on the other. Though 'culture' is a component of these processes – in the way in which social relations are experienced and in the specific form agency takes – it is not the basic element of hegemonic processes, but their effect. In what follows, therefore, I try to avoid starting with culture and taking hegemony to be synonymous with 'cultural domination'; rather I believe hegemonic processes are far more complex and multi-dimensional than that. To try to unravel this my argument is laid out in a rather schematic form. After setting out important elements of Gramsci's way of thinking about the social world I take as my point of departure the proposition that he introduced the notion of hegemony as a pivotal concept used to work through the distinction he makes between what is 'inherited from the past and uncritically absorbed', and 'the practical transformation of the real world' (1971: 333). What makes hegemony effective is the way in which these two elements are deeply embedded in one another. Yet for analytic purposes, I begin by envisioning them as two distinct processes. As I discuss these, I find that there are limitations to each of them. I raise these at the end of each section and then, in a subsequent section, I explore how we might address these issues and thereby produce a deeper understanding of hegemonic processes.

Gramsci and Hegemony

I begin, then, by enumerating features of Gramsci's thought that I take to be especially insightful and important in understanding social and political forces.

1. Gramsci's point of departure was Lenin's usage of the term 'hegemony'. Where Lenin had used the term to refer to a much stronger element of force, and the need for the party to capture the vanguard role in the revolution, Gramsci felt that the different conditions prevailing in Italy called for less brute force and more persuasion: a war of position, rather than a war of movement, in Clausewitz's terms. This simply remnds us of the obvious: hegemony is about power, but a kind of power that is contrasted to sheer brute 'domination'. Gramsci alluded to Victorian England in contrast to Tsarist Russia.

2. Most of the major social theorists of the nineteenth century were concerned with the repressive functions of the state and its ability to bring on board opponents – from Marx's discussion of Bonapartism, to Weber's understanding of *herrschaft* (Lüdtke, [n.d.]: 2–3). What Gramsci did was to shift the focus of attention from the legitimation functions of 'the State' to those of the entire arsenal of bourgeois society, of which the state was one (albeit central, organizing) component.

3. Hence, for Gramsci, hegemony has to be understood specific-ally in the context of a quite particular kind of society: bourgeois, capitalist society – its ideology, its institutions and its intellectuals.[3] One crucial feature of civil society, moreover, was not its appearance as restrictive but as *enabling*. So any sophisticated understanding of hegemony has to address this issue of how hegemony works through both conformity and enabling – moreover, conformity and enabling within a quite specific system of social reproduction: that of bourgeois, capitalist society. Here not just actors but particular *institutions* play their role. Gramsci himself was concerned not only with the role of the Church and schools in

the most obvious forms of ideological work, but also with such institutions of bourgeois society as the market and the large-scale 'Fordist' factory. The implications for method, here, would seem to be that we have only a limited view of the way hegemony works if we address issues of political compromise and cultural manipulation in isolation from the contradictions in capitalist reproduction. This is what Gramsci refers to as 'the necessities of the continuous development of the economic apparatus of production' (quoted in Hall 1996 [1986]: 428).

4. Crucial to any use of the idea of hegemony is also a recognition of the fact that it is a continual ongoing and active *process of negotiation* within the context of existing relationships and social forms. The role of active hegemony formation and maintenance is taken up variously by Raymond Williams (1977), Chantal Mouffe (1979) and Stuart Hall (1996). Initially, rather narrow groups of people recognize their common (occupational) interests, but then there is a 'corporate' moment, which, in the context of bourgeois civil society, Gramsci saw as being the acknowledgement of class interests expressed only in 'economic' terms.[4] Hegemonic processes proper arise as economic and political compromises and persuasions are extended to moral and cultural issues 'posing all the questions around which the struggle rages not on a corporate but on a "universal" plane' (1971: 181–2).

Though hegemony can emanate from other practices, then, it nonetheless requires persistent engagement of at least some actors who have a hegemony-forming and reconstituting project. The implications for method here would seem to be that all reflections on hegemony or, more strictly speaking, hegemonic processes must be understood in terms of *an identifiable social-political project*. To try to understand hegemony or to use it to describe certain features of foreign cultures, cut and cauterized from what these projects are, is bound to be a fruitless exercise. Rather, the value of sociological concepts must be judged in terms of their contribution to the formation of organized, collective social subjects with effective political will to struggle toward identifiable political goals.

5. It is here that the role of intellectuals becomes important; and Gramsci talks of their mastery over a series of 'positions'. Though this can be taken at its fairly obvious face value – the role of intellectuals in *the institutions of cultural production*: churches, schools, theatres, novels and so on – it is especially important to recognize that Gramsci sets up a series of cross-cutting categories

for intellectual work. He certainly talks about *professional intellectuals* who would occupy these kinds of institutions and would be involved in the propagation of ideology. But he also talks about a moment when the ordinary person becomes a philosopher, a kind of intellectual dimension to practical thought. This provides the setting for what he says about *organic intellectuals*: intellectuals who reflect the ideas and perform the functions appropriate to their class. And of course it is entirely likely that such intellectuals of the bourgeoisie would be found in bourgeois cultural institutions (cf. my discussion of bourgeois 'culture' in Chapter 1), making *these* traditional intellectuals also (bourgeois) organic intellectuals. But we need to understand these as categories that cross-cut one another, so it becomes fruitful to think about the way in which an 'intellectual or philosophical attitude' might serve to make a person into an organic intellectual among non-dominant groups.

6. Yet the way in which Gramsci sees these intellectuals (or this intellectual side of ourselves), taking a philosophical or critical stance toward the way reality appears as common sense, has to be understood in terms of his phenomenological view of social enquiry. The dialectical tension between the *historical conditions* that give us our specific social subjectivity and *the central role of our will*, Gramsci understood by means of a phenomenological reading of Marx's view of the relationship between history, praxis and truth. This Gramsci explicitly contrasts to a positivist and empiricist social science, which 'is taken root and branch from the natural sciences, as if these were the only sciences or *science par excellence*' (1971: 438–9).

Rather, hegemonic processes can only be understood in terms of a notion of truth that makes it emergent from social praxis (*verum ipsum factum*). It does not lie out there to be discovered, *pace* traditional understandings of the natural science model (though there may be good hegemonic reasons for making 'truth' appear to be of this kind). Rather the image is one of truth's *potentiality*. 'We know reality only in relation to man, and since man is historical becoming, knowledge and reality are also a becoming, and so is objectivity etc.' (Gramsci 1971: 446). Reality offers us latent truths, praxis actualizes them. 'To realize the truth' now means 'to make it happen'. It thus becomes crucially an issue of power, and the two senses of power discussed in Chapter 1, the one referring to power *over* things and people, and the other referring to the energy-power of an engine, become reducible in this sense to one.

The implications here for method are that, if we wish to argue that what is inherited from the past as well as the practical trans-formation of the real world are pre-eminently *cultural* processes, then we will have to understand 'culture' through this frame of 'the phenomenology of praxis'.

7. This perception lays a great emphasis on *incompleteness*: not just the incompleteness of history, but the personal sense of incompleteness felt by the social subject, captured in the word 'partiality', which refers simultaneously to the part of a whole and to a particular perspective: one's *partiality*. Hegemonic processes work on and through this sense by offering and yet circumscribing a unity and potency that can never be achieved in such a way that it would end our social or political projects.

8. Finally, we can reverse the process of thought to reflect not on hegemony as produced, but hegemony as received. Hegemony eventually both plays on common sense and produces common sense: if effective it provides the sense that what is happening is obvious, normal and natural. It is taken for granted. This is the dimension of hegemony that Jean and John Comaroff highlight:

> We take hegemony to refer to that order of signs and material practices, drawn from a specific cultural field, that come to be taken for granted as the natural, universal, and true shape of social being – although its infusion into local worlds, always liable to challenge by the logic of prevailing cultural forms, is never automatic. It consists of things that go without saying: things that, being axiomatic, are not normally the subject of explication or argument (cf. Bourdieu 1977: 94, 167). This is why its power seems to be independent of human agency, to lie in what it silences, what it puts beyond the limits of the thinkable. It follows that it is seldom contested openly. Indeed, the moment that any set of values, meanings and material forms comes to be explicitly negotiable, its hegemony is threatened; at that moment it becomes the subject of ideology or counterideology'(1992: 28–9).

They contrast this with 'ideology:'

> Hegemony consists of constructs and conventional practices that have come to permeate a political community; ideology originates in the assertion of a particular social group. Hegemony is beyond argument; ideology is more likely to be perceieved as a matter of inimical opinion and interest and hence is more open to contestation. Hegemony, at its most effect, is mute; ideology invites argument (ibid.: 29).

The position taken here seems to me to be one that focuses especially strongly on the way in which hegemony is *consumed* by ordinary
people, rather than the way hegemony is secured by intellectuals
and leaders (the latter an especially unfashionable idea in anthropology). It will become clear later in the chapter that the view that
hegemony 'is seldom contested openly', and that once it becomes
'explicitly negotiable' it shifts into the realm of ideology, is strikingly
at odds with non-anthropological writers, who tend, if anything, to
overstress the other side of Gramsci's idea – the degree to which
political manoeuvring alone can secure hegemonic rule. While I
think that the Comaroffs are the anthropologists who have used
the notion of hegemony most fruitfully in their (historical) ethnographies, I also think that this view of hegemony has the unfortunate
effect of shifting it entirely into the realm of culture – its production
and its consumption.

For me the notion of hegemony has to have analytic power across
both the terrain of what comes to be taken for granted, i.e.: the
reception of hegemonic processes, *and* the terrain of the active
production of identifiable hegemonic fields. It is the interlacing of
these two foci that might steer us toward an appropriate methodological programme for ethnography. We have to find a means for
understanding how individual and collective actors create and
maintain hegemonic fields: fields that enable their own willed
practices within and by use of the interlocking fields of others (who
are doing the same thing). Here Gramsci's phenomenological
understanding of sociological method provides a useful point of
entry. But we do not enter such projects with a *tabula rasa*. Rather
we enter them both as historically formed social subjects and as
actors capable of selective memory *vis-à-vis* history, and it is this
that requires some reflection on the implications of Gramsci's
reference to what is 'inherited from the past'.

Combining the two in this way generates a different imagery from
that normally used. The common understanding of hegemony sees
it in terms of a broader *cultural field* historically constituted, on the
one hand, and various kinds of *counter-hegemonic practices* set against
this prevailing cultural field, on the other. I am making an analogous
but different distinction, suggesting instead two rather different
kinds of 'fields' – the one having to do with the history of (capitalist)
reproduction and the institutions and cultural forms that crystallize
around this process, and the other having to do with individual
and collective subjects' mastery of social practices both within and
against this history.

History and the Philosophy of Praxis

So I now need to explore further these two compoents of hegemonic processes, the one looking back to historical conditions and
attending to the reception of hegemonic forces and the other
looking forward and referring to hegemony in terms of the practical
transformation of the social world. While neither of these can be
rejected, each is, I believe, limited and, to that extent, flawed. The
first is flawed because it either obscures or minimizes the link
between the reception of hegemonic conditions resulting from
political domination, and the reception of hegemonic conditions
that arise from people's necessary imbrication within relations of
social reproduction – Postone's (1993) 'domination of people by
abstract social structures that they themselves constitute' (quoted
at the outset of the chapter) or Gramsci's 'necessities of the continuous development of the economic apparatus of production' (Point
Three, above). This then, exposes a limitation to the way hegemony
has increasingly come to be understood, that is as separable from,
discussable with only passing reference (or no reference at all) to
the way capitalism has to be reproduced.

The second way in which we might understand hegemonic
processes brings us to a much more microscopic scale of social life
and has less to do with these historically ongoing 'givens' in our
lives, and more to do with our own attempts at hegemonic control
– of agency, will and praxis. Here I explore the possibility of
methodologizing Gramsci's insights by means of a phenomenological sociology (to which, as I have said, he himself alludes).
Again, though I find this useful in offering us insights into
important dimensions of the way in which hegemony works (and/
or could be made to work), I believe it has limitations that reduce
the importance of history and of power. These limitations derive
from the reliance of this kind of sociology on ahistorical rationalist
psychology and an individual subject whose social identity is always
understood in terms of goal-oriented 'necessities of the continuous
development of the economic apparatus of production', rather than
being understood to be formed out of his/her relationship to
(and embeddedness within) historically formed power differences
between actors; in other words: a failure to deal with the way in
which historical forces form and deform individual and collective
social subjects, not just at the level of their ideas, perceptions and
values, but at the level of their ability to affect their social world:
their praxis.

History, Experienced and Otherwise

In this first approach I want to look at the broad sweeps of hegemony that Gramsci referred to in terms of that which is 'inherited from the past'. Much of Gramsci's discussion of this dimension is couched in terms of enquiries into Italian history, and reading these reflections is quite analogous to unthreading Marx's agonizing over *The Eighteenth Brumaire of Louis Bonaparte* or *The Civil War in France* (Roseberry 1994, 1997): one feels the need for a potted history of the period to decipher the problems, impasses and relationships that fascinate each author. Nonetheless, the discussion here is of hegemony in its larger, embracing sweep of an historical period and a large national setting. While Gramsci's initial motivation may have been to ask *how* certain social shapes, figures and landscapes became taken for granted as in some way 'natural' or 'the way things really are in a normal world', much of the overall exploration gives us a strong sense of the *effects* (on subaltern people) of how this was done.

This is picked up by Raymond Williams in his reference to hegemony as 'A lived system of meanings and values – constitutive and constituting – which as they are experienced as practices appear as reciprocally confirming. . . . a sense of absolute because experienced reality beyond which it is difficult for most members of the society to move, in most areas of their lives' (1977:110), and we have seen how it is picked up by Jean and John Comaroff, who describe hegemony in terms of its reception by subaltern people. This effect may be the intended consequence of elite strategies, just the fall-out effect of a whole range of lesser policies aimed at various immediately perceived problems and crises, or the result of social and economic imperatives in which all are caught up. Within this frame, we can only impute such things. What we are made aware of is that much of hegemony is *consumed* without the consumers reflecting too much on the process. Thus Williams again:

> [The concept of hegemony] sees the relations of domination and subordination, in their forms as practical consciousness, as in effect [*note*: he is talking of 'effects' here] a saturation of the whole process of living – not only of political and economic activity, nor only of manifest social activity, but of the whole substance of lived identities and relationships, to such a depth that the pressures and limits of what can ultimately be seen as a specific economic, political, and cultural

system seem to most of us the pressures and limits of *simple experience and common sense* (1977: 110, *italics mine*).

Yet by talking about hegemony in terms of its effects – of making certain social phenomena appear to be natural, 'the way things are', – we run the risk of obscuring just how power blocs attain hegemonic leadership. Is the entire patchwork quilt of hegemony in a given setting (say, Thatcher's Britain (Hall, 1988)) reflectively stitched together by these dominant groups, or are we looking at separate tactical forays to secure hegemonic dominance in one or another quite specific project – an educational policy here, a crime-prevention policy there – the overall effect of which is to produce an apparently coherent taken-for-granted hegemonic field?

Yet Williams joins Mouffe (1979) in being quite clear about the conscious attempts on the part of elites to secure hegemony. Less concerned with issues of 'culture' than Williams,[5] Mouffe addresses specifically the politics of bringing about hegemony. She stresses the role of 'rearticulation', as she puts it: the reworking of older alliances and relationships to serve new political projects. Yet neither author makes it clear whether the self-conscious pursuit of hegemony refers to the overall broad field of hegemony or the pursuit of specific projects, the long-term *effect* of which is to produce a general acceptance of what is understood to be beyond question.

Here Stuart Hall goes into much more detail. His stress on the importance of the strategic hegemonic projects of those with power is the result of his uneasiness with the rather monopolistic position that Marxists have often given to the role of capitalist reproduction in explaining everything that occurs in society – the idea of capitalism as *an expressive totality*, a structure in which all social phenomena can be explained in terms of their function for the iron logic of capitalist reproduction. Hall prefers to regard the relationship of one element of a social structure to another, as well as its determining weight, as historically variable (or, in more technical terms, 'overdetermined'). This he refers to as 'Marxism without guarantees'. By shifting attention away from the iron logic of capitalism, Hall obliges us to attend to the way in which quite particular social and political battles are entered into, shaped, lost and won.

It is within this kind of social world that ideas, consciousness and culture emerge; yet it would be quite wrong to conclude that the result is the indoctrination of less powerful people with 'false consciousness'. Rather, the dominant group are just as mistaken as the subaltern group about the fundamental processes of capitalist reproduction, by seeing it in the practical terms of market relations and values. Ideas of the market are not false in the sense that they don't work, since clearly for capitalists they do; rather they are false because they are partial, uncritical common sense. Yet crucial to the work of Gramsci, Williams and Hall is *why* such ideas work – what it is that makes them practically true. The answer lies in power: 'To say that "men" define and shape their whole lives is true only in abstraction. In any actual society there are specific inequalities in means and therefore in capacity to realize this process' (Williams 1977: 108). We are reminded here of Gramsci's stress on the potentiality of 'truth' (see Point Six, above). Hall refers to this process as 'articulation', emphasizing the way ideology *articulates* with political and social forces: 'No ideological conception can ever become materially effective unless and until it *can* be articulated to the field of political and social forces and to the struggles between different forces at stake' (1983: 80, *italics his*).

What this means for Hall is much the same as what 'cultural analysis' would have meant to Gramsci. It means that the critical deconstruction of particular cultural expressions or indeed whole panoplies of interconnected cultural visions and insights into and on to 'reality' – the entire project of trying to understand the potency of such versions of reality – has to incorporate a sophisticated and exhaustive analysis of the historically specific social forces in which they are produced, i.e.: 'articulating this process of ideological de-construction and re-construction to *a set of organized political positions*, and to particular sets of social forces' (ibid., *italics mine*).

Using these authors, then, allows us very seriously to *politicize* the idea of hegemony understood in terms of history. I began by suggesting that in so far as history can be a reading of the past, we can often be induced to see that face of hegemony that has mostly to do with its effects. These effects are to give a historically specific form to social interpretations of what is supposed to be normal – both about the larger society and also about the social person, and that person's expected conduct. We may wish to read the outcomes of such historical processes as particular 'patterns of culture' or 'structures of feeling'. But, by pursuing the work of these various authors, I have tried to show that we need to be cautious about disconnecting the hegemonic *conditions* we find in our fieldsites ('*cultural* hegemony'?) from the issue of *articulation* as Hall sets it forth here; that is to say the quite conscious efforts for securing hegemony in any given project.

Yet this is still not sufficient. For Hall such projects only really come into play, or perhaps become visible for scrutiny, at moments of crisis in previously established balances of power – such, for example, as Thatcher's confrontation with the miners' union or (in my small vignette earlier) the Huasicanchinos 'invasion' of *hacienda*-controlled land. Yet the effect of this view, a view that has increasingly become popular, following Hall, is to reduce, often to complete obscurity, the way in which certain relationships, certain conduct, certain social persons must be in place and must be reproduced (in however distorted a form) for capitalism to continue its cycle.

Hall's autonomy of articulated moments in a complex capitalism is increasingly achieved by losing sight of the *active* basic relationships by which capitalism reproduces itself. The latter Hall wishes to see only as 'limiting and constraining' in relation to 'the categories in which the circuits of production are *thought*, ideologically, and vice versa' (1983: 82–3). The effect of this 'determination in the *first* instance' as he calls it, actually is to cast these processes off into the realm of the inevitable, rather like the forces of God and Nature in a premodern way of thinking. As a result, we begin to lose sight of these processes as we dwell on the attempts to establish domination and authority through active and conscious leadership – making these the only evidence of hegemonic processes, as though the power of political elites could be disconnected from the social forces and relations inherent to capitalist reproduction.

Yet we don't have to abandon the one to take stock of the other: we don't have to choose between the careful historical analysis of how particular social forces came to establish a hegemonic field, thereby shaping and contouring particular national and regional 'cultures' *and* at another level, a percipient and rigorous understanding of often far less visible, far less consciously experienced (though always thoroughly experienced at some level of consciousness) features of the reproduction of capital. Indeed, perhaps the most insidious effect of seeing hegemony as an entirely or preeminently *cultural* phenomenon is that this quickly leads to the compartmentalization of these latter processes and relationships as 'material' and 'economic' factors – precisely what Gramsci was trying to avoid.

This, then, is where I think there is a potential limitation on this particular facet of hegemony. It has to do with the way the analyst employing the notion configures the idea of history. I have already proposed that Gramsci critically accepted Marx's understanding of history (just as he critically used but rejected Croce's liberal understanding). Broadly speaking, we might refer to this as the way in which dialectical relationships emerge in the process of social reproduction. Now of course, not all people regard 'history' in terms of social reproduction; yet the way we understand how social reproduction occurs in a given society will greatly influence the way we understand the hegemonic process – the way in which hegemony forms our selves, our views, our actions and our relationships. We may, for example, regard the historical process as so happenstantial that the notion of social *reproduction* really does not grasp anything very useful about the social world. Though this need not be an entirely synchronic view of social relations, history here remains a descriptive idea, something that can be added on to the present, like hitching a trailer to a car. Within this set of ideas, hegemony can become a very broad, all-embracing concept, especially useful in explaining the way in which elites exercise control through gaining some measure of acceptance of their ideas by subaltern groups through their instrumental selections from history.

Or we may go a little further toward the idea of social repro-duction, by writing about the role of certain powerful historical blocs, class forces and so on in shaping the conditions of the present. Here we may also attend to crucial confrontations and their out-comes to arrive at a kind of political history that forms the necessary backdrop to contemporary hegemony. This time the history becomes more than descriptive, being a necessary component for explaining forces and relationships in the present; but it doesn't situate the victories and defeats of the past within the particular social and economic fabric of those times, and so it runs the risk of becoming too narrowly *political* history.

A third alternative might be to explore the way in which the dialectics of social reproduction give shape to emergent forces and social phenomena (from institutions, to classes, to kinds of social persons). Thus in Chapter 4, we found David Harvey characterizing capitalist reproduction as depending on 'the production of commodities produced through a system of circulation of capital that has profit-seeking as its direct and socially accepted goal' (Harvey 1985:128). Certain principles of the capitalist process cast up certain structures and social collectivities – from property relations to financial capitalists – that are inherent in the way these kinds of societies reproduce themselves. Here again, we can see that the space in the social fabric we give to hegemony, the way it relates to other historical processes, the various possibilities of its shaping – these will all need to be understood within *this* understanding of history.

Even if we wish to use hegemony to refer to pretty much every element of the way in which social subjects become culturally formed through history, then, the way in which we understand this cultural forming to operate will depend on what we understand history to be across a spectrum from history as one damned thing after another, to a quite acute political history, to a crude kind of technical determinism, and finally to a more nuanced combining of the dialectical forming of social phenomena with the particular histories of struggle from one setting to another.

The point is that each of these understandings of history allows for a different understanding of the the way hegemony works. For my own part, I believe that hegemony becomes an especially misleading and politically liberal concept, if it is separated entirely from the way in which the elements necessary for the reproduction of capitalism themselves have the effect of domination.[6]

It is a mistake, therefore, to talk of the historical element of hegemony as simply 'a broad *cultural* field'. To do so can either lead to a kind of cultural determinacy – as though it were just culture that was forming social subjects, rather than a far more complex, far deeper, process, and yet one that may well produce the sense that culture is reality and reality is truth: both manifest and potential. Or, ironically, it can lead to a kind of base/superstructure issue that authors are usually anxious to avoid. As I have argued in Chapter 4, to ask how 'material conditions' get translated into cultural forms is misleading because it obscures the way in which, through history, cultural expressions become inscribed on the landscape to form the material conditions of subsquent generations – who then access those conditions by interpreting them culturally. Too strong a distinction between processes of reproduction in a social formation and a looser, more expressive notion of 'culture' (Marcuse 1968) are therefore to be avoided, as Williams sought to emphasize by use of the term 'cultural materialism' to describe his own process of thought.[7] Yet, as Jameson notes,

> [T]he ideology of the market is unfortunately not some supplementary ideational or representational luxury or embellishment that can be removed from the economic problem and then sent over to some cultural or superstructural morgue, to be dissected by specialists over there. It is somehow generated by the thing itself, as its objectively necessary after-image: somehow both dimensions must be registered together, in their identity as well as in their difference (1994 [1991]: 278).

The objectively necessary after-image that is not some supplementary ideational luxury was of as much pressing concern to Marx as it is today for social analysts who seek to understand capitalism through consumption and the social life of commodities (Miller 1995; Appadurai 1986). At various points throughout his work he discusses how capitalist reproduction generates a dialectical relationship between structured material processes and experienced culture – from money, to alienation, to the valuation of labour power. Precisely in the area to which Jameson refers, when Marx describes the processes of circulation under capitalism and then the relations of *production* that underlie it, he is providing the elements for the way in which broad processes of social reproduction are necessary and then seem 'natural' in a social formation. Indeed, he is perhaps most explicit precisely in his discussion of the way in which the market produces an objectively necessary after-image in broader arenas of society:

> This sphere of what we are deserting, within whose boundaries the sale and purchase of labour-power goes on, is in fact a very Eden of the innate rights of man. There alone rule Freedom, Equality, Property and Bentham. Freedom because both buyer and seller of a commodity, say of labour-power, are constrained only by their own free will. They contract as free agents, and the agreement they come to, is but the form in which they give legal expression to their common will. Equality because each enters into relation with the other, as with a simple owner of commodities, and they exchange equivalent for equivalent. Property because each disposes only of what is his own. And Bentham, because each looks only to himself. The only force that brings them together and puts them in relation to each other, is the selfishness, the gain and the private interests of each (Marx 1976: 280).

Gramsci takes for granted Marx's views here of the imprinting of market ideology on a broader discursive field, and this provides the base on which his more explicit discussions of hegemony take place. To extract hegemonic processes from this bedrock runs the risk of losing what is distinctive about hegemony, as opposed for example to 'social control' or 'dominant ideology' or a Parsonian understanding of consensus. We need therefore to resist the hiving off of a hegemonic *cultural* field ('the apparently natural way things are') from the way in which capitalist processes of reproduction manifest themselves. We may want to shift ground from the more mechanistic metaphors of social reproduction provided by structural Marxism to do this, but we should not as a result end up with boxes in which we place 'material conditions' (or 'economics'), attempted 'rearticulations' of existing lines of domination by changing power blocs or elites ('politics'), and the field of 'cultural hegemony'.

Williams makes the point in this way: 'Hegemony is . . . not only the articulate upper level of 'ideology', nor are its forms of control only those ordinarily seen as 'manipulation' or 'indoctrination'. It is a whole body of practices and expectations, over the whole of living: our senses and assignments of energy, our shaping perceptions of ourselves and our worlds' (Williams 1977: 110). And while Bourdieu is economical with his acknowledgement of the influence of Gramsci on his thinking ('It was Gramsci who said somewhere . . .' 1984: 386), his own characterization of what I am trying to get at here is apposite:

> Once a system of mechanisms has been constituted capable of objectively ensuring the reproduction of the established order by its own motion (*apo tou automatou*, as the Greeks put it), the dominant class have only to *let the system they dominate take its own course*, in order to exercise their domination; but until such a system exists, they have to work directly, daily, personally, to produce and reproduce conditions of domination which are even then never entirely trustworthy (Bourdieu 1977: 190).

In this section I started out by noting that, working in fieldsites where they are constantly made aware of the ways in which currently prevailing and historical fields of power give shape to a particular set of cultural meanings and practices, anthropologists run the risk of highlighting the *effects* of hegemonic processes through time, over and above the practices of identifiable agents with self-conscious hegemonic projects.[8] I then noted that writers such as Williams, Mouffe, and Hall, as well as Gramsci himself, do address this issue. Yet in moving in this direction another danger arises – that in concentrating on the way in which self-conscious projects to secure hegemony result, over time, in a particular pattern of cultural 'givens', we run the risk of freeing up these strategizing agents from the way in which the reproduction of the (capitalist) system itself shapes, renders 'natural,' and calls forth certain cultural meanings and particular kinds of social subjects. I used examples from Marx to illustrate how this was so, but we do not have to be restricted to his analysis of nineteenth-century capitalism; we need only take care to situate dominant agents and subaltern recipients within a clearly delineated process of social reproduction.

If we turn back for a moment to the brief account of events in the Andes, we can see that the attempts at hegemonic control on the part of the *hacendados* who confronted the Huasicanchinos on the one hand and the neighbouring communities on the other involved quite different strategies. These strategies might usefully be seen in the context of the different sets of relationships in which the two communities were involved – the ability, for example, of one *hacienda* to appear to come to the aid of one community in its conflicts with another was closely tied to historical circumstances. The lowland community that was claiming pasture had gradually loosened its control over its hitherto dependent highland annexe, and this in turn was related to the increasing involvement of powerful families in merchant capitalist activities facilitated by the commercialization of the Mantaro Valley around Huancayo.

This certainly provides us with useful historical material with which to understand some important social processes in the present. But I think we can say quite a bit more about the different characteristics of hegemony in the Huasicancha case (which I know better) if we begin to place this moment of hegemonic balance (as Hall would see it) within a process of social reproduction – one in which an *hacienda* was becoming increasingly enmeshed in a capitalist process of expanded reproduction, yet unable (or unwilling) to use technical means to increase relative surplus value. Faced with this situation the *hacienda* attempted to use all the techniques associated with the formal subsumption of labour to extract ever more surplus from land and labour. As I have argued elsewhere (Smith 1989), especially important for anthropologists is Marx's implied suggestion (1976: 1019ff.) that a variety of cultural pressures can be brought to bear so as to retain the *appearance* of existing labour processes, while pressing them toward an ever more capitalist logic. We see this in Huasicancha, first, in the way in which communal work on the *hacienda* was stripped of its 'uninstrumental' components (such as drinking and dancing), and yet continually demanded by the *hacienda* and continually referred to in ever more heightened terms as 'the proper tradition and custom' that the villagers were not respecting. And then we see a new moment, a new casting of the cultural mould, as, faced with the perpetual failure of this technique, the *hacendado* attempts to redraw the property map in the area.

Here are processes of capitalist reproduction as they affect the *hacienda*. Meanwhile, among the villagers too such processes are taking effect, but in a different way. As we saw in Chapter 3, through increasing use of the commodity form small farmers find themselves contradictorily engaged in the logic of simple commodity production. It's a logic that impels them toward a need for greater control over pasture for their livestock, thus setting them against the *hacienda*. But it is contradictory, because it too requires their use of cultural devices for the mobilization of unpaid labour within the community. The real actors we encounter in our fieldsites find themselves 'articulated', as Hall would put it, within overlapping discursive fields as they seek to give authority, naturalness, and historical credibility to the relationships, institutions and practices that they are involved in. In doing so they resort to selective accounts, which we see played out here in the conduct of the *hacendados* and the various (albeit conflicted) organic intellectuals who are the 'heroes' of these stories.

This is far too brief a discussion of the material to be decisive; but what I have described can fruitfully be understood, I think, in terms of overlapping fields of hegemony: fields of greater and lesser extension – from the commercial operations of Huancayo-based merchants to the more restricted arena of the *comunidad* – and invested with greater and lesser magnitudes of power, as well as forms for its expression. Such contours might normally be represented in terms of hegemony and counter-hegemony; but I want now to turn our attention to processes that might be occurring *within* and *among* subaltern people as they attempt to establish a degree of authority over history and the practical world. In the case material just discussed this would bring us among the Huasicanchinos themselves; but in actuality, as I explained at the outset, it was when working among people involved in a regional economy in Spain that I began to attend to this second dimension of hegemonic processes, so more relevant case material is to be found in Chapter 5.

The Phenomenology of Practice

It is noteworthy that those studies that have most effectively introduced hegemony into the anthropological literature have been largely historical ethnographies attending to the dimension of hegemony I have just discussed (Sider 1986; Comaroff and Comaroff 1991; Fox 1989; Carstens 1991). Yet at the beginning of this chapter I painted a picture of the anthropological fieldworker working in the present, who is attentively aware not just of the way in which historical fields of force constrain and give form to people's conduct, but also of the way in which people actively engage in instrumental and intersubjective work as they weave their way through the daily business of living. This second kind of attentiveness in our social enquiries is more often discussed in terms of informal economic strategies than seen in terms of hegemonic processes or projects, and yet it seems important that we link forward-looking 'practical transformations of the real world', such as we find in these settings, to the historically embedded dimensions of hegemony just discussed. So I turn now to this more uncharted terrain on which hegemonic processes operate.

I need to begin by establishing a kind of 'point of view' from which to take a perspective on the social field I am about to discuss. This is the idea of the everyday world, which I understand as a particular kind of social space (the here and now: distinct from a broader focus – historically or geographically – but only methodologically and temporarily distinguishable from it); and also as a kind of daily social practice, this latter being of broadly two kinds: instrumental and intersubjective.[9] Attention in such a social arena is formed through partial, fragmented and shifting common sense. Common-sense attention requires calls upon such things as assessments of the situation to hand and the ability effectively to characterize (categorize) the people involved and their relevance to the situation, as well as being prepared to modify previous assessments and characterizations. This particular understanding of 'common sense' helps us to clarify Gramsci's stress on the importance of intellectuals who can be understood as 'organic', in the sense that they seek to translate experience from the personal and situationally specific to the more generically shared. The issue becomes that of exploring the role of the 'intellect' (Gramsci 1977: 76) in the move from this everyday arena toward that of historical *praxis*. By 'praxis' I mean not just collective practices, but rather collective practices in which agents see themselves becoming the subjects of history – through their agency modifying social conditions.

Nonetheless, as with the earlier discussion of hegemony, this formulation is limited, and I try to overcome some of these limitations by moving, both from the space of the everyday and from the association of power with individual agency, toward wider fields of force and a more subject-forming understanding of power.

The way social phenomenology understands the social space of the everyday world provides us with four components that give insight into the practical pursuit of hegemony. The first of these is that we engage with the world in the pursuit of projects. These need not be grand schemes, but maybe simply ongoing engagements with the world we live in. From this the other three follow: the social distribution of knowledge; the always partial nature of people's understanding of the social world; and the unquestioned acceptance of some parts of this social world alongside the questioning of other parts.

While in the everyday world a person may find moments to pause for reflection – to explore the kind of persons we are, examine the world we live in and so on – most of the time we actually address ourselves to the project (or set of projects) at hand. Both our attention to this task, as opposed to some other, and also what we take to be relevant to its undertaking are functions of the cultural world in which we live. Yet this cultural world is not usefully understood as a consistent and comprehensive guidebook for action, perfectly indexed so that we can open it freely at the page of our choosing, because 'the outstanding feature of a man's life in the modern world is his conviction that this life-world as a whole is neither fully understood by himself nor fully understandable to any of his fellow-men' (Schutz 1971b: 120).[10] In other words, the common sense appropriate to conduct in the everyday world is characterized by its fragmentary and partial nature.[11] 'Partial' in both senses of the word: incomplete and partisan. In such pursuits we need to hold constant certain components of our cultural world, while exploring and testing out others. The purpose of social enquiry if formulated in this way 'is to investigate what motives prompt grown-up men living their everyday life in our modern civilization to accept unquestioningly *some* parts of the relatively natural concept of the world handed down to them and to subject *other* parts to question' (Schutz 1971b: 122).

Yet what is taken for granted about reality and what is questioned is not *just* a function of the culture taken as a whole – the overall cultural field, pattern of culture, structure of feeling, and so on, for members of a pre-given culture do not 'accept the same sector of the world as granted beyond question' (ibid.: 121). First, this is because, as groups engage in a task, so their horizons of relevance (what they can take for the moment to be obviously true and what needs to be questioned) are shaped by that task. Persistence in the practice of a certain life-project – be it as cook, cardinal or carpenter – generates patterns of knowledge; in so far as practices are socially distributed, so are the patterns of knowledge. Second, the distribution of knowledge is purposefully regulated. In other words there are those ('intellectuals') whose job is precisely the distribution and restriction of knowledge.[12] If a broad cultural field exists, then – possibly in some superorganic form – it is in actuality the subsets of this field that are experienced by different groups as that part of their culture accepted beyond question: what Bourdieu would call 'accepted as the *natural* order of things' (1991); what Raymond Williams describes as 'a sense of absolute because experienced reality beyond which it is very difficult for most members of the society to move, in most areas of their lives' (1977: 110).

There is nothing new about anthropologists trying to deal with the social distribution of knowledge understood as differing perceptions of an otherwise shared culture (see especially Keesing 1987). But it does seem to be a somewhat different angle to take *as a starting-point* the idea that participants conduct themselves precisely with this understanding – that the other people with whom they interact have an incomplete, sectional, or partial understanding of the social world.[13] This gives us a crucial insight into the social dynamics of hegemonic processes.

And this leads us from a person's interest in instrumental knowledge – knowledge directed toward the goal of completing an identifiable task – to another kind of knowledge. This has to do with the communication of our experiences to relevant others. To make this work we need to know something about the particular perspective a colleague has on our shared culture. A crucial element of intersubjective work is the translation of my unique (and partial) experience into terms that make it possible for others to recognize it. Requiring persuasive skills on my part, and empathetic skills on the part of others, over time the effect is to produce a pattern of common experiences. If culture is in some sense a 'structure of feeling', then this is the creative everyday work a participant performs in producing and reproducing it. It is precisely when the patterns of shared culture through which these daily practices are thus sorted out, typed and shaped, come into crisis that a moment for hegemonic rearticulation (in Mouffe's terms) arises. Such crises offer an especially crucial role to the intellectuals, who can secure mastery over a number of otherwise fragmented common-sense 'positions' (to use Gramsci's military terminology).

It is at this point that the *organic* role of intellectuals becomes clearer. What happens as our common-sense experience, deriving from our engagement with the real world – which we know quite well to be tentative and partial – shifts from its predictable normalness to something less stable? One of the first casualties is our ability, crucial for practical engagement in daily projects, to type things: *situations* as typical of a certain set and *persons* as typical of a certain set. More realistically: clusters of typical situations, and with them clusters of appropriate persons. Seeing a particular situation as typical, seeing the conduct of particular people as 'normal conduct for people of that type' – these are all a function of a prior hegemonic arena understood as the unquestioned perceptions of reality shared over what we have taken to be a common cultural field, i.e.: one that all those relevant to us refer to – to invert Williams: our feelings of structure. But people themselves ordinarily have only sectional and incomplete views of their social world, so that their categorizations and typing of people and situations are *ad hoc*. By bridging the space *between* the taken-for-granted world of one sector of project-oriented people and that of another, the intellectual performs an organic task in the hegemonic process: making connections between one set of common-sense ideas and another. To do this, such intellectuals have to call upon the authority of articulated hegemonic fields as I have discussed them in the previous section. Thus the Andean schoolteacher incorporated his colleagues into a larger society in which the forces of order and the established hierarchy prevailed, while Martin dissociated himself and the Huasicanchinos from such a field.

We can grasp this better if we shift from the simple picture presented so far to the more realistic one in which we recognize that we are never unproblematically engaged in just one 'project'. Hence what and who are relevant to us are made up of overlapping clusters, giving rise to what Schutz refers to (1971b: 126) as 'twilight zones of sliding transitions'. Added to our awareness that we need more than the knowledge of our own experience and that of those like ourselves who share a habitual set of similar experiences, we now become aware of different sets of people. As we move around across different fields of the social world, for example, we become aware that there are people who are like us or not like us depending upon the different settings we find ourselves in. Further, we also become aware – perhaps especially at times of crisis and unfamiliarity – that we need knowledge not just deriving from their or our experience, but from a world not directly accessible through our experience. Schutz suggests that at this point the 'well-informed citizen' will turn to two kinds of people: one whose opinion carries weight with me in so far as 'I am convinced of the congruity of his system of relevances with my own' and the other whose opinions, though based on the same sources as the first, are 'grouped according to a system of relevances considerably different from my own', and yet give me a clear idea of 'the underlying deviating system of relevances' (1971b: 132).

We have now moved from the rather narrow, confined space of the everyday world with which I started this exercise. To summarize what I am saying about the way in which the ordinary person interfaces with a variety of kinds of 'intellectuals': 1. We accept it as given that our own cultural knowledge is partial. 2. In engaging with the world, we transmit our own experiences to others as they do to us, giving rise to patterns of shared common understandings that, over time, become that part of the world we can take for granted as natural and beyond question. 3. To do this we characterize ourselves as being a certain kind of person through a process of interaction with others with whom we thereby identify – we define ourselves, in other words, through processes of dialogical action (Taylor 1993). 4. Yet we move across a social landscape engaging in different projects with different people, thus forming different, overlapping patterns of cultural relevance as we go – giving rise, in other words, to different arenas in which we engage in this dialogical action. 5. This can (though it need not) make us aware of the limits of experience (ours and our relevant others') as our source of knowledge. 6. As a result, we become dependent upon sources of knowledge beyond our daily experience.

We don't have to see a world clearly divided between ordinary people, career politicians, and professional 'intellectuals', but rather changing patterns of dialogical interaction shot through from end to end by differentials of power. This is the point at which we can re-examine Gramsci's reference to the reciprocal development of ordinary people and that of intellectuals. Just as a certain kind of intellectual interpretation of the world (that of the 'traditional intellectual') can do little to enlarge the critical awareness of ordinary people, so too ordinary people can either simply accept their experience of the world as all there is that is worth understanding, or they can 'consider [themselves] perfectly qualified to decide who *is* a competent expert and even make up [their] minds after having listened to opposing expert opinions' (Schutz, 1971b: 123). As we have seen, if anything, what a responsible ordinary person (Schutz's 'well-informed citizen') *experiences* is precisely how limited (sectional) her or his knowledge of reality is. Such people need to know that their experience is not enough: that we need knowledge of components of reality over which we ourselves have no power, but which are nonetheless relevant to the successful achievement of our goals. It is precisely at this interface, I believe, that we can begin to identify the role of the intellect(ual) – not, that is, the intellectual understood as a particular person or a particular profession, but rather as a particular attitude or positioning, and a particular role that a political actor can take alongside her or his other activities, yet one that provides a crucial linchpin for the forming of hegemonic processes.

A distinctively *organic* intellectual, then, refers to the ability, minimally, to render partial experiences in broader generic terms and, more extensively, to then tie those more broadly identified experiences to underlying systems of relevances that were not immediately available at the level of daily experiences: organic in the twofold sense of being able to show the organic link between apparently disparate and fragmented experiences, and also of being able to *identify* people – as workers, children, farmers, mothers – so as to give coherence to their common experiences in a distinctive way. This requires persuasively accounting for reality and at the same time thereby constituting it. We are once more led back to Gramsci's understanding of the potentiality of truth and to his reference to the role of the intellectual in 'mastery' over reality.

For a moment then, I want to propose an image of the everyday conduct of ordinary people as a series of interfacing hegemonic fields (cf. Roseberry 1994). In engaging in a project I acquire a set of interests, and in so far as I share with others this project I share these (sectional) interests with a like-minded group; as a group we interface with others having somewhat different sectional interests. Rather than thinking of these projects as personal and instantaneous, we might think of them as the longer-term historically institutionalized practices of collective agents. A hegemonic gesture is a reach from a type of person with whom I identify toward other people whom I have categorized as different from me, at least *vis-à-vis* the project or set of projects I take to be of most relevance. In effect I am working at generating hegemonic spaces around me – through my social power and my willingness to compromise my own sectional interests – and I am also doing this within a broader field of power that anticipates me and is more diffuse than my own field of power. Throughout this process I may move in and out of a practical attitude and an 'intellectual' one.

The extent to which these kinds of shifting dialogical processes might take place – the exchanging of perspectives, the empathetic exploring of diverse ways of ordering experience, the dialectical tensions between practical engagement and critical scrutiny – will vary tremendously. There is no particular reason, for example, why structural crises make people especially open to new interpretations of their common-sense views, as I suggested earlier; quite the contrary – such crises may effectively close down people's sensitivities. The point is, though, that the imagery I have tried to present here provides a set of questions we might want to ask to assess a given situation. As we have seen in Chapter 2, there is good evidence that as crisis followed crisis in Huasicancha and as people explored various forms of collective agency to direct events, so they retained a peculiarly open-ended, I would say 'dialogical', ability to interpret and re-interpret the world on which they were having a considerable effect. In fact, this may have given a rather limited shelf-life to any one person acting as an organic intellectual; and yet it was the way in which collective praxis moved against reality – shifted possibilities, reconstituted space, shaped groups, changed livelihoods – that produced this condition. Nevertheless, I would argue that the high value all this placed on *experience*, actually devalued another kind of knowledge. The strength of Huasicanchino knowledge was its militant particularism; its weakness lay in the limitations inherent in this kind of militancy that restrained it from being rendered in more abstract and hence organically more embracing form.

What I have tried to do, though, is to present everyday practices in such a way that we understand them as particular ways of intermeshing practical and intellectual work – the importance of experience and also the ability to communicate it; the need for persuasion and the ability to empathize – and all these are simult-aneously practical and intellectual skills. We may find moments when particular people occupy one or other of these positions; we may find moments quite inappropriate for any real hegemonic shifting of the patterns of habit: but we need to be able to under-stand the kinds of interpersonal conditions that might give rise to the one or the other.

Yet I have suggested that this can be a myopic, one-sided view of things if we don't raise our eyes to a wider horizon beyond which crucial things are made to happen or glance back to see how history constitutes the world we are now exploring. Even so, it does have the advantage of encouraging us to think of all interfacing hege-monic fields as themselves dynamic. This seems preferable either to an imagery that tends to highlight a dynamic subject and a *constraining* broader hegemonic field or, conversely, one that high-lights a disembodied hegemony looming out of the past *to form* docile social subjects. Instead, we understand these as interacting fields of action, both of which are dynamic.

'The Identity of Contraries in the Concrete Historical Act'

In the preceding section I have tried to use some elements of phenomenological sociology to provide insights into the way in which hegemony works at the level of everyday life, specifically by suggesting both that all intersubjective practices have a hegemony-securing component to them – the use of power and persuasion to bring others over into one's own version of a social project – and then suggesting too that the organic intellectual component of this consists of connecting up fragmented and disparate interests and identities to broader versions of reality. To some extent this gives us some useful elements for getting at the way the hegemonic process might work; but it is also misleading in a number of ways. One of these is that, despite its bow to the way a broader cultural field provides points of reference, a stock of knowledge, and so on for actors, the notion of the way social subjects engage in practices relies heavily on the idea of the *intentionality* of meaning – as though the world takes on a form we can understand entirely as a result of our 'interests', whether narrowly conceived (in terms of *a priori* assumptions about instrumental rationality) or more broadly conceived (in terms of the cultural relativity of interests). I have tried to address this issue by referring us to the earlier section, in which the forming of social subjects is understood not merely as an apolitical cultural matter, but rather as a result of quite specific histories of different people's ability to make 'reality' happen: not just to impose a certain narrative of the truth, but to constitute reality through the imposition of such narratives.

In an earlier section we have already seen Mouffe and Hall arguing that elites engage in hegemonic projects to overcome each structural crisis of capitalism through political rearticulations and cultural redefinitions. These projects provide a clear set of tasks for *their* organic intellectuals. But, at a quite different point in the social geography, we should be able to identify the kinds of tasks organic intellectuals might engage in to overcome the debilitating effects of subordination, victimization and the sheer barbarism of the 'civilized' world. Such intellectuals can certainly perform the role of reinterpreting familiar experience by reference to other features of experiences, thereby revealing new connections, shapes and categories. But to remain at this (re-)interpretative level (of 'the everyday,' of 'voice', and so on) is to limit analysis. For what people take to be possible, and hence what they set about doing, is influenced by what they take the real world to be – the historical dimension of hegemony. And because the politics of everyday life are reciprocally confirming in this way, so there is as much a need for *critique*, as for understanding. This means that understanding the specificity of historical conditions involves going well beyond the experience of culture.

A second limitation on the kind of social phenomenology I have been discussing is similar to a problem I raised earlier with respect to elites. There I suggested that we had to be careful not to overplay their voluntarism by disconnecting their hegemonic projects from the processes of social reproduction that gave rise to their subject-ivities. Among less powerful people, the effect of overstressing 'interest' and voluntarism is to play down the inner conflicts and double binds that arise from the social subject's insertion into contradictory institutions and relationships (Lockwood 1964). Yet, if I am to argue that the effectiveness of hegemony and of the role of intellectuals in forging hegemonic fields has much to do with the fragmented, partial nature of daily attentiveness, then the argument cannot stop with the unproblematic 'interests' of goal-seeking subjects, since it may well be that personal inner conflicts play a crucial role in the effectiveness of established hegemonies and the possibilities for potential ones. Indeed, it may be that, in the case of Huasicancha, one of the effects of a quite long history of willed resistance has been to (temporarily?) reduce the kinds of inner conflicts I am referring too.

They were, after all, engaged in a struggle to protect what came to be increasingly articulatable elements of their lifeways, livelihoods, institutions – possibly something that might look very much like their 'culture'. Yet we should not underestimate the debilitating effect of the fragmented knowledge and social identity, as well as the inner conflicts and resulting paralyses, that overlapping processes of social reproduction generate in social subjects.[14] Herman Rebel, who deals with this at length, reflects on Adorno's observation that the worst tormentors in the concentration camps were the younger sons of peasants: 'He speaks here of the destructive cultural ties produced when the need for "shelteredness" felt by an urban class of employees threatened with unemployment, is realized by "authentic" rural social formations that dispossess and expel children from shelteredness in order to achieve the stability in rural social appearance required by the dominant cultural projections' (1989: 121). Rebel explores the ways in which different processes of social reproduction *necessarily* produce victims, and then how the task of cultural hegemony becomes the forming of versions of the truth that satisfactorily justify this barbarism. Sennet and Cobb (1972), too, in their *Hidden injuries of class*, provide rich ethnographic evidence of the kinds of inner conflicts and turmoil that arise among male blue-collar workers from the way contradictions in the reproduction of US capitalism are played out at the level of American cultural stereotypes, a set of double-binds carefully unwrapped by William Connolly (1982: 63–89).

These may be much closer to the conditions in which the prevailing neo-liberal hegemony is able to assert itself: engaging people in social practices of survival that involve profound inner conflicts, a personal authenticity that denies the very social relations on which it relies for legitimacy (Taylor 1991), and a deep burying of our intimate knowledge of the victims we choose not to see.[15]

If this is so, then it calls for a much greater dose of realism in anthropology than the present reflective turn seems prepared to endorse.

Conclusion

Like the other chapters in this book, this one has not provided a detailed application of a set of concepts to a body of ethnographic data. Instead, I began by explaining how my confrontation with new ethnographic settings had provided a 'catharsis' (to use Gramsci's expression) for reflecting on hegemonic processes. What I have tried to do here is to provide a series of frames that could serve to highlight certain features in the social world. From such perspectives particular methodologies might flow, suggesting ways in which we might work toward the interplay between the different levels at which power works through society. In so doing I have found myself unhappy with certain stresses and emphases in the work of others who make use of the term.

I have argued in Section Three (Point 2) that, while most social analysts had concerned themselves with the issue of what Weber called *herrschaft*, Gramsci's work is especially fruitful in so far as he chose to explore the workings of power through what he called 'civil society'. It is this that has made his work of great interest to anthropologists in their studies of other cultures. As they have become increasingly aware of the different forms power takes, the different levels at which it works and the different agents that exercise it, anthropologists have sought to introduce these insights into their understandings of these 'cultures'. The effect has been to empower culture at the expense, on the one hand, of material conditions of social reproduction, and on the other at the expense of the hegemony-pursuing strategies of social subjects. Not only do we begin to get the impression that power is really most interestingly understood when we see how it works 'culturally', that is to say at the level of the meanings and forms available to our interpretative gaze, at the expense of understanding those forms in relation to the concrete abstractions of social reproduction, but we also get the impression that the intended and unintended consequences of agents' pursuits of power are really only of interest in so far as they affect 'culture'. Yet, 'in a postmodern epoch', notes Terry Eagleton, '. . . what keeps the system going is less rhetoric or discourse than, as it were, its own systemic logic (Bourdieu and Eagleton 1994: 267).

If by 'cultural anthropology' we are to mean a body of professional social scientists who make it their business to study 'culture', or perhaps still worse 'cultures', then we should attach a *caveat emptor* to what we produce. The contours that form social subjects, be they individual persons or collective groupings, derive from concrete abstractions and material conditions unamenable to *just* the interpretation of culture. This means that severe limitations, indeed profound distortions, will result from a discipline – anthropology – setting itself up as the source of experts (in Schutz's terms) who specialize in the analysis of *cultural* hegemony.

This book began with a discussion of the dialectical relationship between intellectuals' images of society and the agency of the collective subjects that took up their attention. It ends with the elaboration of a concept – hegemony – that explores that relationship further. It can easily be argued that the people discussed in Chapter 1, and now Gramsci in this last chapter, faced a quite different political conjuncture than the one we face today. While they drew confidence, possibly a quite false, indeed arrogant, modernist kind of confidence, from their pursuit of a socialist utopia, we can no longer so straightforwardly situate ourselves as politically engaged intellectuals by reference to such a modernist agenda. Yet we should be careful not to condense more than a century of revolutionary history into a single, dismissive and fashionable 'sound-bite' and then read off the ideas, intellectual disputes, and real political conflicts (not to mention the suffering and death of the losers) of those involved as though, in some hidden and devious corner of their minds, they knew all along what we claim to know today.

Doing so enables us to underplay the extent to which Gramsci, for example, was seeking to build upon the work and yet overcome the limitations and blind spots of prior engaged intellectuals, while himself working within (and hence against) the suffocating hegemonic discourse of bourgeois versions of history and of the present. He, and the other writers who have played so important a role in this book, did this on the one hand by an unceasing engagement with a political struggle that sought to learn from history while refusing to compromise with the existing conservative ordering of the present, and on the other by a critical distancing that distinguished their work from the instrumental tactics of established political leadership, which select only the possibilities provided within the framework of the existing order. Aware though we are of the singularity of the modernist goals of our forebears, we should not use the confusions that confront us as an excuse to abandon the responsibilities of intellectual work through a refusal to engage with the present in political terms. Far from abandoning the critique of the present inherent in a socialist stance, we need instead to explore and enrich the possibilities provided by the values of socialism in such a way that our hegemonic project begins with a refusal to play with the false opportunities of capitalism, a refusal to accept it as the natural order of things, and instead work toward a critique that, in its perceptions, helps formulate alternatives.

Notes

1. Of course, if all of culture becomes 'hegemony', then all voluntaristic acts become resistance. This seems to add only a veneer of politics to what is being said: a kind of politics without a position, something unlikely to have sat well with Gramsci, who was so especially concerned with 'position'.

2. I, for example, became particular interested in the fact that in the more remote community of Huasicancha, which, at the time the accounts were given, was engaged in a campaign of open defiance *vis-à-vis* the police, the army and the *hacienda*, the stories always had the police and the *gamonal* playing threatening roles, and the 'hero' was always an uneducated but cunning local, while in the more incorporated villages with more direct ties to the commercial Mantaro Valley and with little or no success in campaigns against the *haciendas*, the stories reversed the roles of the police and the *hacienda* owners and evoked leaders whose relevant knowledge and hence agency came from formal education.

3. Though it has become common, especially in anthropology, to apply the term to a wide variety of types of society, Gramsci himself reserved the term for relationships specifically in bourgeois capitalist society. This is not to say that the notion of hegemony would be inappropriate where used in other kinds of social formation. It is only to say that Gramsci understood that the way in which hegemony worked had greatly to do with 'the necessities of the continuous development' of historically particular social relations of production. So, to retain the analytic power of his usage, one would have to situate hegemonic processes within the identifiable necessities of social reproduction in each case. While the term may well be usefully extended in this way, I

restrict myself here to those conditioned by the requirements of *capitalist* reproduction.

4. The importance of this point lies in the fact that 'economics' *is* the language of bourgeois civil society, so that at this stage the class bloc can only take on those who buy into a kind of society that is determined by the rationality of 'economics'.

5. Williams's concern with culture, moreover, should be understood within the context of the conversations he was having – with Marxists on the one hand and with established literary criticism on the other. The one is a conversation with a kind of Marxism that has tended to marginalize the dynamic role of culture, and Williams is here trying to place culture far more toward the centre of analysis, though not, I would submit, absolutely dead centre (1977: 114); the other *vis-à-vis* literary theorists who wished to see culture in pre-eminently bourgeois terms, terms in which professional writers, artists, and so forth produce culture, which is then consumed rather poorly by inexperts, whose competence is measured in descending order as one moves down the social scale. Centring culture *vis-à-vis* this latter group means to a large extent reformulating what it means when taken out of this specifically bourgeois project, and this can be done by recognizing the role of power in (bourgeois) cultural production.

As I have argued in the previous chapter, Williams wanted to show how works of cultural production play a decisive role in producing and reproducing the material conditions of life, especially the way in which they do this by forming and reshaping the structures of feeling of any given historical period. One way he sees this being done is the way in which the bourgeoisie define 'culture' itself. Against this he tried to suggest another view of culture – culture as 'a whole way of life' – that was more appropriate for working-class people, in so far as it didn't differentiate social activities into what pertained to 'cultural' and what pertained to less 'cultural' pursuits. Seen within this context the nature of his contribution to our understanding of hegemony becomes clearer: as an examination of cultural practices as *just part* of the expression of the power of particular groups. In so far as the power at the disposal of different groups varies in its extent and in its character, so too does the actual sense of what 'culture' is.

But if we look from outside the perspective of narrow discussions of 'culture'; if we look back at Williams, not ourselves sitting within those two conversations he was having, we can see that what he is mostly concerned with are *the effects* of hegemony on people's 'practical consciousness'. This led him to place great emphasis on how history, tradition and so on are *experienced* (and hence how they can be selected from).

6. I am thinking here especially of Stuart Hall's association with 'new times' in the elaboration of what came to be the liberal political philosophy of New Labour, where the 'will to power' required the systematic occlusion of the relationship between capitalist reproduction and social inequality, poverty, crime, ill health, the destruction of the environment and so on.

7. Since Williams's method of analysis is so very different from that of Marvin Harris, his use of the term 'cultural materialism' to describe his approach should not be confused with Harris's use of the same term.

8. Fox, for example, talks about the way in which 'domination can infuse cultural meanings . . . It is now internalized and appears natural. A system of domination [that] can come to 'saturate' everyday life . . . [that] becomes culturally encoded . . . lodged so deeply in cultural belief – that it appears natural and inviolate (Fox 1989: 91, 267; quoted in Kurtz 1996: 121).

9. 'Instrumental' practices are not synonymous with 'economic rationality.' Though they are goal-oriented, the means for achieving goals need not follow the logic of the market (Weber 1978).

10. In the next few pages I use this particular essay of Schutz's as a point of reference. Nevertheless, though I make no specific references to any other of his works, my discussion derives especially from the papers collected in Volume I of his three-volume *Collected Papers* (1971a).

11. I have already distanced myself from an 'expert's' reading of Gramsci. I am aware that the following discussion is closer to his notion of 'good sense'. Yet his suggestion that common sense can be inconsistent and contradictory remains valid here.

12. Thus Schutz makes a distinction between intrinsic relevances, which are the outcome of our own selective intentions, and imposed relevances (1971b: 127).

13. It is for this reason that, as Graham Watson (1991) argues, anthropologists are misguided when they take informants' accounts as providing an insight into their 'culture', since such accounts are, as Charles Taylor puts it, '*a posteriori* islands floating in a sea of what is essentially an unformulated practical grasp of what has happened' (1993: 50).

14. Yet, rather as it is with 'everyday forms of resistance', so with 'the fragmented or multiple subject'. Just as everyday forms of resistance show the effectiveness of regimes of repression, and hence are a problem to be overcome, rather than a discovery to be celebrated, so we should see the role of the organic intellectual as the overcoming of fragmented subjectivities, rather than their celebration. This is far from the position of those who see the subject's multiple and

various identities actually providing the potential for new social movements. (See for example Laclau and Mouffe 1985; or Lloyd and Thomas 1998: 134ff.)

15. We are reminded here of Thompson's remarks quoted in the Introduction.

> When we encounter some sonorous phrase such as 'the strong ebb and flow of the trade cycle' we must be put on our guard. For behind this trade cycle there is a structure of social relations, fostering some sorts of expropriation (rent, interest and profit) and outlawing others (theft, feudal dues), legitimizing some types of conflict (competition, armed warfare) and inhibiting others (trade unionism, bread riots, popular political organization) – a structure which may appear, in the eyes of the future, to be both barbarous and ephemeral (1968: 224–5).

References

Abrams, Philip (1980) 'History, Sociology, Historical Sociology'. *Past and Present* 87: 3–16.

—— (1982) *Historical sociology*. Cornell: Cornell University Press.

Althusser, Louis and Etienne Balibar (1970) *Reading Capital*. London: New Left Books.

Anderson, Perry (1976-7) 'The antinomies of Antonio Gramsci'. *New Left Review* 100: 5–81.

—— (1980) *Arguments within English Marxism*. London: Verso.

Appadurai, Arjun (1986) *The social life of things: commodities in cultural perspective*. Cambridge: Cambridge University Press.

—— (1991) 'Global ethnoscapes: notes and queries for a transnational anthropology'. In Richard Fox (ed.), *Recapturing anthropology: working in the present*. Santa Fé, NM: School of American Research Press.

—— (1995) 'The production of locality'. In Richard Fardon (ed.), *Counterworks: managing the diversity of knowledge*. London: Routledge.

Aracil, Rafael and Mario Garcia Bonafé (1978) 'La no industrialización valenciana: algunos problemas'. In *La industrialización valenciana: historia y problemas*. Valencia: Tres I Quatre.

Arato, Andrew and Jean Cohen (1993) 'Civil society and social theory'. In Peter Beilharz, G. Tobinson and J. Rundell (eds), *Between totalitarianism and postmodernity: a Thesis Eleven reader*. Cambridge, MA: MIT Press.

Archer, Margaret (1995) *Realist social theory: the morphogenetic approach*. Cambridge: Cambridge University Press.

Arensberg, Conrad H. and Solon T. Kimball (1940) *Family and community in Ireland*. Cambridge, MA: Harvard University Press.

Augé, Marc (1995) *Non-Places: an introduction to the anthropology of supermodernity*. Cambridge: Cambridge University Press.

Bagnasco, Arnaldo (1977) *Tre Italie: la problematica territoriale dello sviluppo italiano*. Bologna: Il Mulino.

—— (1981) 'Labour market, class structure and regional formations in Italy'. *International Journal of Urban and Regional Research* 5(1): 40–4.

Bailey, F. G (1969) *Strategems and spoils*. Oxford: Blackwell.

—— (ed.) (1973) *Gifts and poison*. Oxford: Blackwell.

—— (ed.) (1975) *Debate and compromise*. Oxford: Blackwell.

Barth, Fredrik (1965) *Political leadership among Swat Pathans,* LSE Monograph −19. London: Athlone Press.

Bauman, Zygmunt (1987) *Legislators and interpreters: on modernity, post-modernity and intellectuals*. Cambridge: Polity.

—— (1992) *Intimations of Postmodernity*, London: Routledge.

Becattini, Giacomo (1992) 'The marshallian district as a socio-economic notion'. In F. Pyke, G. Becattini and W. Sengenberger (eds), *Industrial districts and inter-firm cooperation in Italy*. Geneva: International Institute for Labour Studies.

Bejar, Hector (1970) *Peru 1965: notes on a guerrilla experience*. New York: Monthly Review Press.

Benson, John (1983) *The penny-capitalists: a study of nineteenth-century working-class entrepreneurs*. Dublin: Gill and Macmillan.

Benton, Lauren (1990) *Invisible factories: the informal economy and industrial development in Spain*. Binghamton: State University of New York Press.

Berg, Maxine (1994) *The age of manufactures, 1700–1820: industry, innovation and work in Britain,* 2nd edn. London: Routledge.

—— Pat Hudson and Michael Sonenscher (1983) *Manufacture in town and country before the factory*. Cambridge: Cambridge University Press.

Bernabé, Josep María (1976) *Industria i subdesenvolupament al País Valencià: El calcat a la Vall del Vinalopó*. Mallorca: Editorial Moll.

Bernstein, Henry (1979) 'African Peasantries: a theoretical framework'. *Journal of Peasant Studies* 6(4).

Bhaskar, Roy (1978) *A realist theory of science*. Brighton: Harvester.

—— (1989) *Reclaiming reality: a critical introduction to contemporary philosophy*. London & New York: Verso.

Blim, Michael (1990a) 'Economic development and decline in the emerging global factory: some Italian lessons'. *Politics and Society* 18(1): 143–63.

—— (1990b) *Made in Italy: small-scale industrialization and its consequences*. New York: Praeger.

—— (1992) 'Small-scale industrialization in a rapidly changing world market'. In F. A. Rothstein and M. L. Blim (eds), *Anthropology and the global factory: studies in the new industrialization in the late twentieth century*. New York: Bergin and Garvey.

Bloch, Maurice (1991) 'Language, anthropology and cognitive science'. *Man* 26:183–98.

Bloch, Marc and Lucien Febvre (1929) 'A nos lecteurs' *Annales d'histoire economique et sociale*. Vol I. Jan.

Bobbio, Norberto (1989) *Democracy and dictatorship: the nature and limits of state power*. Minneapolis: University of Minnesota Press.

Boddy, Janice (1989) *Wombs and alien spirits: women, men, and the Zar cult in Northern Sudan*. Madison, WI: The University of Wisconsin Press.

Bourdieu, Pierre (1977) *Outline of a theory of practice.* Cambridge: Cambridge University Press.

—— (1984) *Distinction, a social critique of the judgment of taste,* trans. Richard Nice. Cambridge, MA: Harvard University Press.

—— (1990) *In other words: essays towards a reflexive sociology.* Stanford, CAP: Stanford University Press.

—— (1991) *Language and symbolic power.* Cambridge: Polity.

—— and Terry Eagleton (1994) 'Doxa and common life: an interview'. In S. Zizek (ed.), *Mapping ideology.* London: Verso.

—— and J.-C. Passeron (1977) *Reproduction in education, society and culture.* Beverley Hills, CA: Sage.

—— and L. J. D. Wacquant (1992) *An invitation to reflexive sociology.* Chicago: University of Chicago Press.

Brandes, Stanley (1980) *Metaphors of masculinity: sex and status in Andalusian folklore.* Philadelphia: University of Pennsylvania Press.

Braudel, Fernand (1949) *La Méditerranée et le monde mediterranée à l'époque de Philippe II.* Paris: Colin.

—— (1958) 'Histoires et sciences sociales: la longue durée'. *Annales ESC* 13: 725–53.

Braverman, Harry (1974) *Labor and monopoly capitalism.* New York: Monthly Review.

Brubaker, Rogers (1985) 'Rethinking classical sociology: the sociological vision of Pierre Bourdieu'. *Theory and Society* 14(6): 745–75.

Brusco, Sebastiano (1982) 'The Emilian model: productive decentralization and social integration'. *Cambridge Journal of Economics* 6: 167–84.

Bryant, Christopher G. A (1993) 'Social self-organization, civility and sociology: a comment on Kumar's *Civil society'. British Journal of Sociology* 44(3): 397–401.

Burawoy, Michael (1985) *The politics of production: factory regimes under capitalism and socialism.* London: Verso.

Caceres, Andres Avelino (1973) *La guerra de 79: sus campañas.* Lima: Editorial Milla Bartres.

Calhoun, C., E. LiPuma and M. Postone (eds) (1993) *Bourdieu: critical perspectives.* Chicago: Chicago University Press.

Camus, Albert (1956) *The rebel: an essay on man in revolt.* New York: Knopf.

Capecchi, Vittorio (1989) 'The informal economy and the development of flexible specialization in Emilia Romagna'. In A. Portes, M. Castells and L. Benton (eds), *The informal economy: studies in advanced and less developed countries.* Baltimore: Johns Hopkins University Press.

Carbonella, August (1992) 'Historical memory, class formation, and power: a central Maine papermaking community, 1920–1988'. *Focaal* (Nijmegen) –19.

Carney, J., R. Hudson and J. Lewis (1980) *Regions in crisis: new perspectives on European theory.* London: Croom Helm.

Carstens, Peter (1991) *The queen's people: a study of hegemony, coercion, and accommodation among the Okanagan of Canada.* Toronto: Toronto University Press.

Castells, Manuel (1977) *The urban question.* London: Edward Arnold.

—— and Alejandro Portes (1989) 'World underneath: the origins, dynamics and effects of the informal economy'. In A. Portes, M. Castells and L. Benton (eds), *The informal economy: studies in advanced and less developed countries.* Baltimore: Johns Hopkins University Press.

Cento Bull, Anna (1996) 'Ethnicity, racism and the Northern League'. In Carl Levy (ed.), *Italian regionalism: history, identity and politics,* Oxford: Berg.

Cenzatti, Marco (1992) 'From dualism to territorial problematic in Italy: a restructuring of industry and theory'. In Michael Peter Smith (ed.), *After modernism: global restructuring and the changing boundaries of city life,* Comparative Urban and Community Research Vol 4. New Brunswick, NJ: Transaction Publishers.

Chayanov, A. V. (1966) *A. V. Chayonov on the theory of peasant economy,* ed. Daniel Thorner, B. Kerblay and R. Smith. Homeward, Illinois: American Economics Association.

Cohen, Anthony (ed.) (1982) *Belonging, identity and social organization in British rural cultures.* Manchester: Manchester University Press.

Cohen, Anthony (ed.) (1986) *Symbolizing boundaries: identity and diversity in British cultures.* Manchester: Manchester University Press.

Cohen, Jean (1985) 'Strategy or identity: new theoretical paradigms and contemporary social movements'. *Social Research* 52(4): 663–716 .

Cohen, Miriam and Michael Hanagan (1995) 'Politics, industrialization and citizenship: unemployment policy in England, France and the US, 1890-1950'. In C. Tilly (ed.), *Citizenship, identity and social history.* International Review of Social History, Supplement −3.

Cole, John W. and Eric Wolf (1974) *The hidden frontier: ecology and ethnicity in an Alpine valley.* New York: Academic Press.

Comaroff, Jean and John Comaroff (1991) *Of revelation and revolution: Christianity, colonialism and consciousness in South Africa.* Chicago: Chicago University Press.

—— and —— (1992) *Ethnography and the historical imagination.* Boulder, CO: Westview.

Connolly, William E (1982) *Appearance and reality in politics.* Cambridge: Cambridge University Press.

Cooke, Philip and Kevin Morgan (1991) 'The network paradigm: new departures in corporate and regional development'. *Regional Industrial Research,* Report −8

Cooper, R. and G. Burrel (1988) 'Modernism, postmodernism and organizational analysis: an introduction'. *Organization Studies* −9: 91–112.

Corrigan, Philip and Derek Sayer (1985) *The great arch: English state formation as cultural revolution.* Oxford: Blackwell.

Cowen, M. P. and R. W. Shenton (1996) *Doctrines of development.* London and New York: Routledge.

Cross, G (1983) *Immigrant workers in industrial France: the making of a new laboring class.* Philadelphia: Temple University Press.

Crush, Jonathan (ed.) (1995) *Power of development.* London and New York: Routledge.

Cucó i Giner, Josepa (1990) 'Asociaciones y cuadrillas: un primer avance al análisis de la sociabilidad formal valenciana'. In J. Cucó and Joan J. Pujadas (eds), *Identidades colectivas: etnicidad y sociabilidad en la peninsula ibérica.* Valencia: Generalitat Valenciana.

Culler, Jonathan (1997) *Literary theory: a very short introduction.* Oxford: Oxford University Press.

DaMatta, Roberto (1994) 'Some biased remarks on interpretivism: a view from Brazil'. In Robert Borofsky (ed.), *Assessing cultural anthropology.* New York: McGraw-Hill.

D'Andrade, Roy and Nancy Scheper-Hughes (1995) 'Objectivity and militancy: a debate (1. Moral models in anthropology; 2. The primacy of the ethical'). *Current Anthropology* 36(3) (June): 399–440.

Davis, John (1977) *People of the Mediterranean.* London: Routledge and Kegan Paul.

Deleuze, G. and F. Guattari (1984) *Anti-Oedipus: capitalism and schizophrenia.* London: Athlone Press.

de Soto, H (1986) *The other path.* New York: Harper & Row.

di Leonardo, Micaela (1998) *Exotics at Home.* Chicago: Chicago University Press.

Dunk, Thomas W (1991) *It's a working man's town: male working-class culture in Northwestern Ontario.* Montreal and Kingston: McGill Queens University Press.

Elias, Norbert (1976) *The civilizing process: sociogenetic and psychogenetic investigations,* in 2 vols. 1. *The history of manners; 2. State formation and civilization.* Oxford: Blackwell.

—— (1991) *The society of individuals,* ed. Michael Schröter, trans. Edmond Jephcott. Oxford: Blackwell.

Emmanuel, Arrighi (1972) *Unequal exchange.* New York: Monthly Review Press.

Ennew, Judith. K., P. Hirst and K. Tribe (1977) '"Peasantry" as an economic category'. *Journal of Peasant Studies* 4(4).

Escobar, Arturo (1992a) 'Culture, practice and politics: anthropology and the study of social movements'. *Critique of Anthropology* 12(14): 395–432.

Escobar, Arturo (1992b) 'Culture, economics and politics in Latin American social movements: theory and research'. In Arturo Escobar and Sonia Alvarez (eds), *The making of social movements in Latin America: identity, strategy and democracy.* Boulder, CO: Westview.

—— (1995) *Encountering development: the making and unmaking of the Third World.* Princeton, NJ: Princeton University Press.

—— and Sonia E. Alvarez (eds) (1992) *The making of social movements in Latin America*. Boulder, CO: Westview.

Esping-Andersen, Gøsta (1990) *The three worlds of welfare capitalism*. Cambridge: Polity.

Etzioni, Amitai (1997) *The new golden rule: community and morality in a democratic society*. London and New York: Profile Books.

Fentress, James and Chris Wickham (1992) *Social memory: new perspectives on the past*. Oxford: Blackwell.

Ferguson, James (1990) *The anti-politics machine: 'development', de-politicisation and bureaucratic power in Lesotho*. Cambridge: Cambridge University Press.

Firth, Raymond (1958) *Elements of social organization*. Boston, MA: Beacon.

Foucault, Michel (1980) *Power/knowledge: selected interviews and other writings 1972–1977*, ed. Colin Gordon. New York: Pantheon.

Fox, Richard G (1989) *Gandhian utopia: experiments with culture*. Boston, MA: Beacon.

Friedland, Roger and A. F. Robertson (eds) (1990) *Beyond the marketplace: rethinking economy and society*. New York: Aldine de Gruyter.

Friedmann, Harriet (1980) 'Household production and the national economy: concepts for the analysis of agrarian formations'. *Journal of Peasant Studies* 7(2) (July).

Fuá, G. and C. Zacchia (eds) (1983) *Industrializzazione senza fratture*. Bologna: Il Mulino.

Galeski, Boguslaw (1972) *Basic concepts of rural sociology*. Manchester: Manchester University Press.

Garcia, Soledad (1994) 'The Spanish experience and its implications for a citizens' Europe'. In Victoria A. Goddard, J. R. Llobera and Cris Shore (eds), *The anthropology of Europe: identity and boundaries in conflict*. Oxford: Berg.

Geertz, Clifford (1973) *The interpretation of cultures: selected essays*. New York: Basic Books.

George, Glynis (1996a) 'Contested meanings and controversial memories: narratives of sexual abuse in Western Newfoundland'. In Paul Antze and Michael Lambek (eds), *Tense past: cultural essays in trauma and memory*. New York: Routledge.

—— (1996b) Grass-roots feminist practice and the politics of culture in Bay St. George, Newfoundland. Ph.D. dissertation, Department of Anthropology, University of Toronto.

Gertler, Meric. S (1992) 'Flexibility revisited: districts, nations-states and the forces of production'. *Transactions of the Institute of British Geographers,* NS 17.

—— (1995) 'Manufacturing culture: the spatial construction of capital'. Paper presented to the Annual Conference of the Institute of British Geographers, Newcastle-upon-Tyne.

Gilmore, David D (1987) *Aggression and community: paradoxes and Andalusian culture*. New Haven: Yale University Press.

Giralt, Emili (ed.) (1978) *Dos estudios sobre el País Valenciano*. Valencia: L'Estel.

Godelier, Maurice (1972) *Rationality and irrationality in economics*. New York: Monthly Review Press.

Goffman, Erving (1977) *Asylums*. Harmondsworth: Penguin.

Goody, Jack (1993) 'Culture and its boundaries: a European view'. *Social Anthropology* 1(1).

Gough, Kathleen (1967) 'Anthropology and imperialism' [Pamphlet]. Ann Arbor, MI: Radical Education Project.

Gould, Jeffrey (1990) *To lead as equals: rural protest and political consciousness in Chinandega, Nicaragua 1912-1979*. Chapel Hill, NC: North Carolina Press.

Grabher, G. (ed.) (1993) *The embedded firm*. London: Routledge.

Gramsci, Antonio (1971) *Selections from the prison notebooks*, ed and trans. Q. Hoare and G. Nowell Smith. New York: International Publishers.

— (1977) *Selections from political writings 1910-1920*, ed. Q. Hoare, trans. J. Matthews. Minneapolis: University of Minnesota Press.

Granovetter, Mark (1985) 'Economic action and social structure: the problem of embeddedness'. *American Journal of Sociology* 91(3) (Nov.): 481-510.

— and Richard Swedberg (eds) (1992) *The sociology of economic life*. Boulder, CO: Westview.

Grimshaw, Anna, and Keith Hart (1994) 'Anthropology and the crisis of the intellectuals'. *Critique of Anthropology* 14(3): 227-62. 'Forum' response by David M. Schneider. *Critique of Anthropology* 14(4): 419-24.

Guha, Ranajit (ed.) (1981-7) *Subaltern studies,* Vols I-V. Delhi: Oxford University Press.

— (1988 [1981]) 'On some aspects of the historiography of colonial India'. In G. K. Spival and R. Guha (eds), *Selected subaltern studies*. New York & Oxford: Oxford University Press.

Gupta, Akhil (1992) 'The song of the nonaligned world: transnational identities and the reinscription of space in late capitalism'. *Cultural Anthropology* 7(1): 63-79.

Gupta, Akil and James Ferguson (eds) (1997) *Anthropological locations: boundaries and grounds of a field science*. Berkeley: University of California Press.

Gupta, Dipankar (1985) 'On altering the ego in peasant history: paradoxes of the ethnic option'. *Peasant Studies* 13(1): 5-24.

— (1997a) *Rivalry and brotherhood: politics in the life of farmers of Northern India*. Delhi: Oxford University Press.

— (1997b) 'Civil society or the state: what happened to citizenship?' MS, Centre for the Study of Social Systems, Jawarharlal Nehru University, New Delhi.

Habermas, Jürgen (1979) *Communication and the evolution of society*, trans. T. McCarthy. Boston, MA: Beacon.

—— (1981) 'Toward a reconstruction of historical materialism'. In K. Knorr-Cetina and A. V. Cicourel (eds), *Advances in social theory and methodology*. Boston, MA: Routledge. [Expanded and revised from *Theory and Society* 2 (1975).]

—— (1984) *The theory of communicative action, Vol. I: Reason and the rationalization of society*, trans. T. McCarthy. Boston, MA: Beacon.

Hadjimichalis, Costis (1986) *Uneven development and regionalism: state, territory and class in Southern Europe*. London: Croom Helm.

—— and Nicos Papamichos (1990) '"Local" development in Southern Europe: towards a new mythology'. *Antipode* 22(3): 181–210.

Hall, Stuart (1983) 'The problem of ideology: Marxism without guarantees'. B. Matthews (ed.), *Marx: 100 years on*. London: Lawrence and Wishart.

—— (1988) 'The toad in the garden: Thatcherism among the theorists'. In C. Nelson and L. Grossberg (eds), *Marxism and the interpretation of culture*. Urbana: University of the Illinois Press.

—— (1996 [1986]) 'Gramsci's relevance for the study of race and ethnicity'. In D. Morley and K-H. Chen (eds), *Stuart Hall: critical dialogues in cultural studies*. London and New York: Routledge.

—— and Martin Jacques (eds) (1990) *New times: the changing face of politics in the 1990's*. London: Verso.

Harvey, David (1973) *Social justice and the city*. London: Edward Arnold.

—— (1982) *The limits to capital*. Chicago: Chicago University Press.

—— (1985) 'The geopolitics of capitalism'. In Derek Gregory and John Urry (eds), *Social relations and spatial structures*. London: Macmillan.

—— (1989) *The condition of postmodernity*. Oxford: Blackwell.

—— (1991) 'Flexibility: threat or opportunity?' *Socialist Review* 21:1.

—— (1993) 'From space to place and back again: reflections on the condition of postmodernity'. In J. Bird, B. Curtis, T. Putnam, G. Robertson and L Tickner (eds), *Mapping the futures: local cultures, global change*. London: Routledge.

—— (1995) 'The conceptual politics of place, space and environment in the work of Raymond Williams'. *Social Text* 42 (Vol. 13 –1) 69–94.

Held, David and J. B. Thompson (eds) (1989) *Social theory of modern societies: Anthony Giddens and his critics*. Cambridge: Cambridge University Press.

Herzfeld, Michael (1985) *A place in history*. Princeton, NJ: Princeton University Press.

—— (1997) *Cultural intimacy: social poetics in the nation-state*. London: Routledge.

Himmelweit, S. and S. Mohun (1977) 'Domestic labour and capital'. *Cambridge Journal of Economics* 1.

Hinton, William (1964) *Fanshen: a documentary of revolution in a Chinese village*. New York: Vintage.

Hirst, P. and J. Zeitlin (eds) (1989) *Reversing industrial decline? Industrial structure and policy in Britain and her competitors.* Oxford: Berg.

Hobsbawm, E. J (1959) *Primitive rebels: archaic forms of social movements in the 19th and 20th centuries.* Boston, MA: Beacon.

—— (1969) *Bandits.* New York: Delacorte Press.

—— (1971) 'Class consciousness in history'. In Istvan Meszaros (ed.), *Aspects of history and class consciousness.* London: Routledge and Kegan Paul.

—— (1973) 'Peasants and politics'. *Journal of Peasant Studies.* 1 (1).

—— (1974) 'Peasant land occupations'. *Past and Present.* 62(Feb.).

—— (1984a) 'Notes on class consciousness'. In idem, *The worlds of labour: further studies in the history of labour.* London: Weidenfeld and Nicolson.

—— (1984b) 'The formation of British working-class culture'. In idem, *The worlds of labour: further studies in the history of labour.* London: Weidenfeld and Nicolson.

—— (1984c) 'The making of the working class 1870–1914'. In idem, *The worlds of labour: further studies in the history of labour.* London: Weidenfeld and Nicolson.

—— (1990) *Nations and nationalism since 1780: programme, myth, reality.* London: Canto.

Holmes, Douglas (1989) *Cultural disenchantments.* Princeton, NJ: Princeton University Press.

Hudson, Ray and David Sadler (1986) 'Contesting works closures in Western Europe's old industrial regions: defending place or betraying class?' In A. J. Scott and M. Storper (eds), *Production, work, territory: the geographical anatomy of industrial capitalism.* Boston, MAP: Allen and Unwin.

Jameson, Fredric (1994 [1991]) 'Postmodernism and the market' Ch. 8 of *Postmodernism, or the cultural logic of late capitalism. London:* Verso. [Reprinted in S. Zizek (ed.), *Mapping Ideology.* London: Verso, (1994).]

Jelin, Elizabeth (ed.) (1987) *Ciudadanía e identidad: las mujeres en los movimientos sociales latino-americanos.* Geneva: UNRISD.

Jenkins, Keith (1997) 'Introduction: on being open about our closures'. In idem (ed.), *The postmodern history reader.* London: Routledge.

Joyce, Patrick (1990) *Visions of the people: industrial England and the question of class, 1840–1914.* Cambridge: Cambridge University Press.

Kahn, Joel (1980) *Miñangkabau social formations: Indonesian peasants and the world- economy.* Cambridge: Cambridge University Press.

Kearney, Michael (1996) *Reconceptualizing the peasantry: anthropology in global perspective.* Boulder, CO: Westview Press.

Keating, Michael and J. Loughlin (eds) (1997) *The political economy of regionalism.* London: Frank Cass.

Keesing, Roger (1981) *Cultural anthropology*: a contemporary perspective, 2nd edn. New York: Holt, Rinhart and Winston.

—— (1987) 'Anthropology as interpretative quest'. *Current Anthropology* 28(2): 161–76.

—— (1994) 'Theories of culture revisited'. In Robert Borofsky (ed.), *Assessing cultural anthropology*. New York: McGraw-Hill.

Kerkvliet, B. J. T. and James Scott (eds), (1986) *Everyday forms of peasant resistance in South-East Asia*. Special Issue of *Journal of Peasant Studies* 13(2).

Kroeber, Alfred (1948 [1923]) *Anthropology*. New York: Harcourt, Brace.

Kumar, Krishan (1993) 'Civil society: an inquiry into the usefulness of an historical term'. *British Journal of Sociology* 44(3): 375–93.

Kurtz, Donald V. (1996) 'Hegemony and anthropology: Gramsci, exegeses, reinterpretations'. *Critique of Anthropology* 16(2): 103–35.

Laclau, Ernesto (1977) *Politics and ideology*. London: Verso.

—— and Chantal Mouffe (1985) *Hegemony and socialist strategy: towards a radical democratic politics*. London: Verso.

Lash, Scott and John Urry (1987) *The end of organized capitalism*. Oxford: Polity.

Law, J. (ed.) (1986) *Power, action and belief*. London: Routledge.

Lebovics, Herman (1992) *True France: the wars over cultural identity, 1900–1945*. Ithaca, NY: Cornell University Press.

Lefebvre, Henri (1974) *La production de l'espace*. Paris: Anthropos.

Lem, Winnie (1999) *Cultivating dissent: work and politics in Languedoc*. Binghamton, NY: State University of New York Press.

Lenin, V. I (1974) *The development of capitalism in Russia: the process of the formation of a home market for large-scale industry*. Moscow: Progress.

Linke, Uli (1990) 'Folklore, anthropology and the government of social life'. *Comparative Studies in Society and History* 32(1) 117–48.

Lloyd, David and Paul Thomas (1998) *Culture and the state*. London: Routledge.

Lluch, Ernest (1976) *La vía valenciana*. Valencia: Eliseu Climent.

Lockwood, David (1964) 'Social integration and system integration'. In George K. Zollschan and Walter Hirsch (eds), *Explorations in social change*. Boston, MA: Houghton, Mifflin.

Lomnitz Adler, Claudio (1992) *Exits from the labyrinth: culture and ideology in the Mexican national space*. Berkeley: University of California Press.

Long, Norman (1992) 'From paradigm lost to paradigms regained: the case of an actor-oriented sociology of development'. In N. Long and A. Long (eds), *Battlefields of knowledge*. London: Routledge.

—— and Bryan Roberts (eds) (1978) *Peasant cooperation and capitalist expansion in Peru*, Institute of Latin American Studies. Austin: The University of Texas Press.

—— and —— (eds) (1984) *Miners, peasants and entrepreneurs: regional development in the central highlands of Peru*, Cambridge Latin American Studies Series, No. 48. Cambridge: Cambridge University Press.

Lüdtke, Alf (1985) 'Organizational order or *Eigensinn*: workers' privacy and workers' politics in Imperial Germany'. In Sean Wilwentz (ed.), *Rites of power*. Philadelphia: Univerity of Pennsylvania Press.

—— (1986) 'Cash, coffee-break, horseplay: *Eigensinn* and politics among factory workers in Germany *c*.1900'. In Charles Stephenson (ed.), *Confrontation, class consciousness and the labour movement in proletarian class formation.* New York: Greenwood Press.

—— (n.d.) 'Hegemony or practices of domination? Aspects of compliance in "civil society".' Max Planck Institute. [Mimeo]

McDonald, Maryon (1989) *We are not the French!* London: Routledge.

MacEwen Scott, Alison (ed.) (1986) Rethinking petty commodity production. *Social Analysis, Special Issue Series,* No. 20 (Dec.).

Marcus, George (1986) 'Contemporary problems of ethnography in the modern world system'. In James Clifford and George Marcus (eds), *Writing culture: the poetics and politics of ethnography.* Berkeley: University of California Press.

—— and Dick Cushman (1982) 'Ethnographies as texts'. *Annual Review of Anthropology* 11: 29–69.

—— and Michael M. J. Fischer (1986) *Anthropology as cultural critique: an experimental moment in the human sciences.* Chicago and London: University of Chicago Press.

Marcuse, Herbert (1964) *One dimensional man: studies in the ideology of advanced industrial society.* Boston, MA: Beacon.

—— (1968) 'The affirmative character of culture'. In H. Marcuse, *Negations,* trans. J. J. Shapiro. Boston, MA: Beacon.

—— (1969) 'Repressive tolerance'. In H. Marcuse, B. Moore and K. Wolff, *A critique of pure tolerance.* Boston, MA: Beacon.

Marshall, T. H (1963 [1950]) 'Citizenship and social class'. In idem, *Sociology at the crossroads and other essays.* London: Heinemann Educational Books.

—— (1965) *Social policy in the twentieth century.* London: Hutchinson.

—— (1972) 'Value problems of welfare-capitalism'. *Journal of Social Policy* 1(1): 15–32.

Mar-Molinero, Clare and Angel Smith (eds) (1996) *Nationalism, and the nation in the Iberian peninsula: competing and conflicting identities.* Oxford: Berg.

Martinez-Alier, Joan (1977) *Haciendas, plantations and collective farms: agrarian class societies – Cuba and Peru.* London: Frank Cass.

Martínez Serrano, J. A., Ernest Reig Martínez and Vicent Soler Marco (1978) *Evolución de la economía valenciana, 1878–1978.* Valancia: Caja de Ahorros de Valencia.

Marx, Karl (1964) *The economic and philosophical manuscripts of 1844.* New York: International Publishers.

—— (1970) *The German ideology,* ed. and with an introduction by C. J. Arthur. London: Lawrence & Wishart.

—— (1971) *Early texts,* ed. David McLellan. Oxford: Oxford University Press.

—— (1976) *Capital,* Vol I, trans. Ben Fowkes. Harmondsworth: Penguin.

—— (1989) *Readings from Karl Marx*, ed. Derek Sayer. London: Routledge.

Mauss, Marcel (1969 [1920]) 'Nation, nationalité, internationalisme'. *Oeuvres*, Vol. 3, *Cohésion sociale et division de la sociologie*. Paris: Editions de la Minuit.

Melucci, Alberto (1980) 'The new social movements: a theoretical approach'. *Social Science Information* 19: 199–226.

—— (1982) *L'invenzione del presente: movimenti, identità, bisogni individuali*. Bologna: Il Molino.

—— (1989) *Nomads of the present: social movements and individual needs in contemporary society*. Philadelphia: Temple University Press.

—— (1996) *Challenging codes: collective action in the information age*. Cambridge and New York: Cambridge University Press.

Metcalfe, A.W (1988) 'The struggle to be human: the moral dimension of class struggle'. *Critique of Anthropology* 8(2): 7–41.

—— (1990) 'The demonology of class: the iconography of the coalminer and the symbolic construction of political boundaries'. *Critique of Anthropology* 10(1): 39–64.

Miller, D. (ed.) (1995) *Acknowledging consumption*. London: Routledge.

Mingione, Enzo (1991) *Fragmented societies: a sociology of economic life beyond the market paradigm*. Oxford: Blackwell.

Mintz, Sidney (1973) 'A note on the definition of peasantries'. *Journal of Peasant Studies* 1(1): 91–106.

—— (1985) *Sweetness and power: the place of sugar in modern history*. New York: Viking.

Mitchell, Timothy (1990) 'Everyday metaphors of power' *Theory and Society* 19: 545–77.

Molyneux, Maxine (1979) 'Beyond the domestic labour debate'. *New Left Review* 116.

Moore, Jr., Barrington (1966) *Social origins of dictatorship and democracy*. Boston: Beacon.

Morgan, G (1986) *Images of organization*. Beverly Hills: Sage.

Morris, A. D and C. M. Mueller (eds) (1992) *Frontiers in social movement theory*. New Haven: Yale University Press.

Mouffe, Chantal (1979) 'Hegemony and ideology in Gramsci'. In C. Mouffe (ed.), *Gramsci and marxist theory*. London: Routledge and Kegan Paul.

Muratorio, Blanca (1991) *The life and times of Grandfather Alonso*. New Brunswick, NJ: Rutgers University Press.

Murray, Fergus (1983) 'The decentralization of production – the decline of the mass-collective worker?' *Capital and Class* 19:74–99.

Myrdal, Gunnar (1968) *Asian drama: an inquiry into the poverty of nations*, 3 vols. New York: 20th Century Fund.

Nadal, Jordi (1990) 'El desarrollo de la economía valenciana en la segunda mitad del siglo XIX: una vía exclusivamente agraria?' In J. Nadal and A. Carreras (eds), *Pautas regionales de la industrialización española (siglos XIX y XX)*. Barcelona: Ariel.

Nairn, Tom (1964) 'The English working class'. *New Left Review* 24 (Mar.–Apr.).

Narotzky, Susana (1989) 'Ideas that work: ideologies and social reproduction in rural Catalunya and beyond'. Ph.D. Thesis, New School for Social Research, New York.

—— (1990) 'Not to be a burden: ideologies of the domestic group and women's work in rural Catalonia'. In J. Collins and M. Gimenez (eds), *Work without wages*. Binghamton, NY: SUNY Press.

—— (n.d.) 'The political economy of political economy in Spanish anthropology'. Paper presented at the joint meetings of the Canadian Anthropology Society/Société canadienne d'anthropologie and the American Ethnological Society, May, 1998. To appear in Belinda Leach and Winnie Lem (eds), *The new political economy in anthropology* (forthcoming).

Noiriel, Gerard (1996) *The French melting pot: immigration, citizenship and national identity*. Minneapolis: University of Minnesota Press.

Nugent, Daniel (1993) *Spent cartridges of revolution: an anthropological history of Namiquipa, Chihuahua*. Chicago: University of Chicago Press.

O'Brien, P. and Keyder, C (1978) *Economic growth in Britain and France: two paths to the twentieth century*. London: Allen and Unwin.

O'Hanlon, Rosalind (1988) 'Recovering the subject. *Subaltern Studies* and histories of resistance in colonial South Asia'. *Modern Asian Studies* 22(1): 189–224.

Ortner, Sherry (1984) 'Theory in anthropology since the sixties'. *Comparative Studies in Society and History* 26(1): 126–66.

—— (1995) 'Resistance and the problem of ethnographic refusal'. *Comparative Studies in Society and History* 37(1): 173–193.

Palafox, Jordi (1987) 'Exports, internal demand, and economic growth in Valencia'. In Nicolás Sánchez-Albornoz, (ed.), *The economic modernization of Spain, 1830–1930*. New York: New York University Press.

Peet, Richard and Michael Watts (eds) (1996) *Liberation ecologies: environment, development, social movements*. London and New York: Routledge.

Piore, Michael and C. Sabel (1984) *The second industrial divide*. New York: Basic Books.

Pitt-Rivers, Julian (1957) *People of the sierra*. Chicago: University of Chicago Press.

—— (ed.) (1963) *Mediterranean countrymen*. The Hague: Mouton.

Pizzorno, Alessandro (1978) 'Political exchange and collective identity in industrial conflict'. In C. Crouch and A. Pizzorno (eds), *The resurgence of class conflict in western Europe since 1968*. London: Macmillan.

Polanyi, Karl (1957) *The great transformation*. Boston, MA: Beacon.

—— (1968) *Primitive, archaic and modern economies: essays of Karl Polanyi*. Boston, MA: Beacon Press.

Pollert, Anna (1988) 'Dismantling flexibility'. *Capital and Class* 34: 42–75.

Portelli, Alessandro (1985) *Biografia de una città: storia e racconto: Terni 1830–1985*. Turin: Einaudi.

—— (1990) 'Uchronic dreams: working class memory and possible worlds'. In R. Samuel and P. Thompson (eds), *The myths we live by*. London: Routledge.

—— (1991) *The death of Luigi Trastulli and other stories: form and meaning in oral history*. Albany, NY: State University of New York Press.

Postone, Moishe (1993) *Time, labor, and social domination: a reinterpretation of Marx's critical theory*. Chicago: University of Chicago Press.

Pred, Allan and Michael Watts (1992) *Reworking modernity: capitalisms and symbolic discontent*. New Brunswick, NJ: Rutgers University Press.

Putnam, Robert (1993) *Making democracy work*. Princeton, NJ: Princeton University Press.

Pyke, F., G. Becattini and W. Sengenberger (eds) (1990) *Industrial districts and inter-firm cooperation in Italy*. Geneva: International Institute for Labour Studies.

Rebel, Hermann (1989) 'Cultural hegemony and class experience: a critical reading of recent ethnological-historical approaches', Parts I and II. *American Ethnologist* 16(1): 117–36; 16(2): 350–65.

Redfield, Robert (1940) *The folk culture of Yucatan*. Chicago: Chicago University Press.

Rogers, Susan Carol (1991) *Shaping modern times in rural France*. Princeton, NJ: Princeton University Press.

Rosanvallon, Pierre (1988) 'The decline of social visibility'. In John Keane (ed.), *Civil society and the state*. London: Verso.

Roseberry, William (1983) *Coffee and capitalism in the Venezuelan highlands*. Austin: University of Texas Press.

—— (1988) 'Political economy'. *Annual Review of Anthropology* 17.

—— (1989) *Anthropologies and histories: essays in culture, history and political economy*. New Brunswick, NJ, Rutgers University Press.

—— (1993) 'Beyond the agrarian question in Latin America'. In F. Cooper, A. Isaacman, F. Mallon, W. Roseberry and S. Stern (eds), *Confronting historical paradigms*. Madison, WI: Wisconsin University Press.

—— (1994) 'Hegemony and the language of contention'. In G. M. Joseph and D. Nugent (eds), *Everyday forms of state formation: revolution and the negotiation of rule in modern Mexico*. Durham: Duke University Press.

—— (1996) 'Hegemony, power and the languages of contention'. In Edwin N. Wilmsen and Patrick McAllister (eds), *The politics of difference: ethnic premises in a world of power*. Chicago: Chicago University Press.

—— (1997) 'Marx and anthropology'. *Annual Review of Anthropology* 26: 25–46.

—— (1998) 'Political economy and social field'. In Alan Goodman and Thomas Leatherman (eds), *Building a new biocultural synthesis: political-economic perspectives in biological anthropology*. Ann Arbor, MI: University of Michigan Press.

Rosenberg, Harriet (1988) *A negotiated world*. Toronto: Toronto University Press.

Sabel, Charles F. (1982) *Work and politics: the division of labour in industry.* Cambridge: Cambridge University Press.

—— (1989) 'Flexible specialization and the re-emergence of regional economies'. In P. Hirst and J. Zeitlin (eds), *Reversing industrial decline? Industrial structure and policy in Britain and her competitors.* Oxford: Berg.

—— (1991) 'Moebius-strip organizations and open labor markets: some consequences of the reintegration of conception and execution in a volatile economy'. In P. Bourdieu and J. S. Coleman (eds), *Social theory for a changing society.* Boulder, CO: Westview.

—— and Jonathan Zeitlin (1985) 'Historical alternatives to mass production: politics, markets and technology in nineteenth century industrialization'. *Past and Present* 108.

Sachs, W. (ed.) (1992) *The development dictionary: a guide to knowledge as power.* London: Zed Books.

Samuel, Raphael (1977) 'Workshop of the world: steam power and hand technology in mid-Victorian Britain'. *History Workshop* 3: 6–72.

—— (ed.) (1981) *People's history and socialist theory.* London: Routledge & Kegan Paul.

Sanchis, Enric (1984) *El trabajo a domicilio en el País Valenciano.* Madrid: Ministerio de Cultura.

Sarkar, Sumit (1997) 'Renaissance and Kaliyuga: time, myth and history in colonial Bengal'. In G. Sider and Gavin Smith (eds), *Between history and histories.* Toronto: University of Toronto Press.

Sayer, Derek (1979) *Marx's method: ideology, science and critique in 'Capital'.* Brighton: Harvester.

—— (1987) *The violence of abstraction: the analytic foundations of historical materialism.* Oxford: Blackwell.

Sayer, Andrew and Richard Walker (1992) *The new social economy: reworking the division of labor.* Cambridge, MA: Blackwell

Schneider, Jane and Peter Schneider (1976) *Culture and political economy in Western Sicily.* New York: Academic Press.

Schumacher, E. F. (1974) *Small is beautiful: a study of economics as though people mattered.* London: Abacus.

Schumpeter, Joseph. (1970 [1944]) *Capitalism, socialism, democracy.* London: Allen & Unwin.

Schutz, Alfred (1971a) *Collected Papers,* Vol. I. The Hague: Nijhoff.

—— (1971b) 'The well-informed citizen: as essay on the social distribution of knowledge'. In *Collected Papers,* Vol. II. The Hague: Nijhoff.

Scott, James 1976) *The moral economy of the peasant: rebellion and subsistence in Southeast Asia.* New Haven and London: Yale University Press.

—— (1985) *Weapons of the weak: everyday forms of peasant resistance.* New Haven: Yale University Press.

—— (1986) 'Everyday forms of resistance'. In J. Scott and Kerkvliet (eds), 'Everyday forms of resistance in South-East Asia, Special Issue'. *Journal of Peasant Studies* 13(2).

—— (1990) *Domination and the arts of resistance*. New Haven: Yale University Press.

Sennett, Richard and Jonathan Cobb (1972) *This hidden injuries of class*. New York: Knopf.

—— (1995) 'Something in the city: the spectre of uselessness and the search for place in the world'. *Times Literary Supplement* 4825 (22nd Sept.).

Shanin, Teodor (ed.) (1987 [1971]) *Peasants and peasant societies*. Oxford: Blackwell.

Sider, Gerald (1984) 'The ties that bind: culture and agriculture property and propriety in the Newfoundland fisher'. *Social History* 5: 1–39.

—— (1986) *Culture and class in anthropology and history*. Cambridge: Cambridge University Press.

—— (1993) *Lumbee Indian histories*. Cambridge: Cambridge University Press.

Silver, Hilary (1993) 'National conceptions of the new urban poverty: social structural change in Britain, France and the US'. *International Journal of Urban and Regional Research* 17(3).

—— (1996) 'Culture, politics and national discourses of the new urban poverty'. In E. Mingione (ed.), *Urban poverty and the underclass*. Oxford: Blackwell.

Silverman, Sydel (1975) *Three bells of civilization: the life of an Italian hill town*. New York: Columbia University Press.

Silverman, Marilyn and P. H. Gulliver (1992) 'Historical anthropology and the ethnographic traditions: a personal, historical and intellectual account'. In M. Silverman and P. M. Gulliver (eds), *Approaching the past: historical anthropology through Irish case studies*. New York: Columbia University Press.

Slater, David (ed.) (1985) *New social movements and the state in Latin America*. Amsterdam: CEDLA.

Smith, Carol (ed.) (1976) *Regional analysis*, 2 vols. New York: Academic Press.

—— (1984) 'Local history to global context: social and economic transitions in Western Guatemala'. *Comparative Studies in Society and History* 26: 193–228.

Smith, Gavin (1975) 'The account of Don Victor'. *Journal of Peasant Studies* 2(3).

—— (1976) 'Movimientos de campesinos en la region central'. *Churmichasun* (Peru) 1(3).

—— (1977) 'Contemporary peasant folk history: some preliminary observations'. *Bulletin of the Society for Latin American Studies* 3(3).

—— (1979a) 'Fieldwork, Part 3) Writing about it afterwards'. In Gavin Smith and David H. Turner (eds), *Challenging Anthropology: a critical introduction to social and cultural anthropology*. Toronto: McGraw-Hill, Ryerson.

—— (1979b) 'The use of class analysis in social anthropology'. In Gavin Smith and David H. Turner (eds), *Challenging Anthropology: a critical introduction to social and cultural anthropology*. Toronto: McGraw-Hill, Ryerson.

—— (1984) 'Confederations of households: extended domestic enterprises in city and country'. In Norman Long and Bryan Roberts (eds), *Miners, peasants and entrepreneurs: regional development in the Central Highlands of Peru.*. Cambridge: Cambridge University Press.

—— (1985) 'Reflections on the social relations of simple commodity production'. *Journal of Peasant Studies* 13(1).

—— (1989) *Livelihood and resistance: peasants and the politics of land in Peru.* Berkeley: University of California Press.

—— (1990) 'Negotiating neighbours: livelihood and domestic politics in central Peru and the País Valenciano'. In J. Collins and M. Gimenez (ed.), *Work without wages: domestic labor and self-employment within capitalism.* Binghamton: SUNY Press.

—— (1991a) 'The production of culture in local rebellion'. In J. O'Brien and William Roseberry (eds), *Golden ages, dark ages: imagining the past in anthropology and history.* Berkeley: University of California.

—— (1991b) 'Writing for real: capitalist constructions and the constructions of capitalism'. *Critique of Anthropology* 11(3).

—— (1993) 'Toward a framework for the study of informal economies in western Europe'. Paper presented to the Graduate Program in Anthropology, City University of New York, March.

—— (1994a) 'Western European informal economies in historical perspective'. In Henri Lustiger-Thaler and Daniel Salée (eds), *Artful Practices: the political economy of everyday life.* Montreal: Black Rose.

—— (1994b) 'Comment on Starn: Rethinking the politics of anthropology: the case of the Andes'. *Current Anthropology* 35(1): 32–3.

Smith, Neil (1984) *Uneven development: nature, capital and the production of space.* Oxford: Blackwell.

Soja, Edward (1989) *Postmodern geographies: the reassertion of space in critical social theory.* London: Verso.

Somers, Margaret and Gloria Gibson (1994) 'Reclaiming the epistemological "other": narrative and the social constitution of identity'. In C. Calhoun (ed.), *Social theory and the politics of identity.* Oxford: Blackwell.

Starn, Orin (1994) 'Rehinking the politics of anthropology: the case of the Andes'. *Current Anthropology,* 35(1): 13–26.

Stavenhagen, Rodolfo (ed.) (1970) *Agrarian problems and peasant movements in Latin America.* New York: Anchor Books.

Stedman Jones, Gareth (1983) *Languages of class: studies in English working-class history 1832–1982.* Cambridge: Cambridge University Press.

Stephen, Lynn (1997a) 'The Zapatista opening: the movement for indigenous autonomy and state discourses on indigenous rights in Mexico, 1970–1996'. *Journal of Latin American Anthropology* 2(2): 2–42.

—— (1997b) 'Redefined nationalism in building a movement for indigenous autonomy in Southern Mexico'. *Journal of Latin American Anthropology* 2 (1): 72–101.

Stern, Steve (1987) 'New approaches to the study of peasant rebellion and consciousness: implications of the Andean experience'. In S. J. Stern (ed.), *Resistance, rebellion and consciousness in the Andean peasant world, 18th to 20th cultures.* Madison: University of Wisconsin Press.

Stolcke, Verena (1995) 'Talking culture: new boundaries, new rhetorics of exclusion in Europe'. *Current Anthropology* 36(1): 1–24.

Storper, Michael and R. Walker (1989) *The capitalist imperative: territory, technology and industrial growth.* Oxford: Blackwell.

Swindells, Julia and Lisa Jardine (1990) *What's left? women in culture and the labour movement.* London: Routledge.

Taussig, Michael (1980) The devil and commodity fetishism in Latin America. Chapel Hill, NC: University of North Carolina Press.

Taylor, Charles (1989) *Sources of the self: the making of modern identity.* Cambridge, MA: Harvard University Press.

—— (1991) *The malaise of modernity.* Concord, Ontario: Anansi.

—— (1993) 'To follow a rule . . .'. In C. Calhoun, E. LiPuma and M. Postone (eds), *Bourdieu: critical perspectives.* Chicago: Chicago University Press.

Terradas, Ignasi (1995 [1979]) *La qüestió de les colònies industrials: l'exemple de l'Ametlla de Merola.* Manresa: Centre d'Estudis del Bages.

Thompson, Edward (1968) *The making of the English working class: the origin of the Black Act.* Harmondsworth: Penguin.

—— (1975) *Whigs and hunters.* New York: Pantheon

—— (1978a) *The poverty of theory and other essays.* New York: Monthly Review Press.

—— (1978b) 'Eighteenth-century English society: class struggle without class?'. *Social History.* 3(2): 133–65.

—— (1993) *Customs in common.* London: Merlin Press.

Thompson, John B (1990) *Ideology and modern culture: critical theory in the era of mass communication.* Stanford, CA: Stanford University Press.

Tilly, Charles (1986) *The contentious French.* Cambridge, MA: Belknap, Harvard University Press.

Tilly, Louise (1983) 'People's history and social science history'. *Social Science History* 7(4): 457–74.

Todorov, T (1993) *On human diversity: nationalism, racism and exoticism in French thought.*
Minneapolis: University of Minnesota Press.

Touraine, Alain (1992) 'Beyond social movements'. In Mike Featherstone (ed.), *Cultural theory and cultural change.* London: Sage.

Turner, Bryan (1990) 'Outline of a theory of citizenship'. *Sociology* 24(2): 189–217.

Vincent, David (1981) *Bread, knowledge and freedom: a study of nineteenth-century working-class autobiography.* London: Methuen.

Wallerstein, Immanuel (1974) *The modern world system. Capitalist agriculture and the origins of the European world economy in the sixteenth century.* New York: Academic Press.

Walzer, Michael (1989) 'Citizenship'. In Terence Ball (ed.), *Political innovation and conceptual change.* Cambridge: Cambridge University Press.

Watson, Graham (1991) 'Rewriting culture'. In R. G. Fox (ed.), *Recapturing anthropology: working in the present.* Santa Fé, NM: School of American Research Press.

Weber, Max (1978) *Economy and Society.* 2 Vols. Berkeley: University of California Press.

Williams, Raymond (1961) *Culture and society 1780–1950.* Harmondsworth: Penguin.

—— (1973) *The country and the city.* London: Hogarth.

—— (1977) *Marxism and literature.* Oxford: Blackwell.

—— (1988) *Keywords: a vocabulary of culture and society* (revised edition). London: Fontana.

—— (1989) *Resources of hope.* London: Verso.

Williams, Karel, Tony Cutler, John Williams and Colin Haslam (1987) 'The end of mass production?'. *Economy and Society* 16(3).

Williamson, Oliver and William Ouchi (1981) 'The markets and hierarchies and visible hand perspectives'. In A. Van de Ven and W. Joyce (eds), *Perspectives in organizational design and behavior,* pp. 347–70. New York: Wiley.

Willis, Paul (1977) *Learning to labour: how working-class kids get working-class jobs.* London: Saxon House.

Wolf, E. R (1955) 'Types of Latin American peasantry: a preliminary discussion'. *American Anthropologist* 57(2).

—— (1956) 'Aspects of group relations in a complex society: Mexico'. *American Anthropologist* 58: 1065–78.

—— (1959) *Sons of the shaking earth.* Chicago: Chicago University Press.

—— (1966) *Peasants.* Englewood Cliffs: Prentice-Hall.

—— (1978) 'Remarks on *The people of Puerto Rico*' *Revista/Review Interamericana* 8(1): 17–25.

—— (1969) *Peasant wars of the twentieth century* . New York: Harper & Row.

—— (1982) *Europe and the people without history.* Berkeley: University of California Press.

—— (1987) 'On peasant rebellions'. In Teodor Shanin (ed.), *Peasants and peasant societies* (2nd edn). Oxford: Blackwell. [Originally published in *International Social Science Journal* 21, 1969.]

—— (1990) 'Facing power – old insights, new questions'. *American Anthropologist* 92: 586–96.

—— and Sidney Mintz (1957) 'Haciendas and plantations in Middle America and the Antilles'. *Social and Economic Studies* 6: 386–412.

Womack, John (1969) *Zapata and the Mexican Revolution.* New York: Knopf.

Worsley, Peter (1970 [1957]) *The trumpet shall sound,* 2nd edn New York: Shocken.
—— (1984) *The three worlds: culture and world development.* London: Weidenfeld & Nicolson.
Wright, Susan (1993) '"Working class" versus "ordinary people": contested ideas of local socialism in England'. In C. N. Hann (ed.), *Socialism: ideals, ideologies, and local practice,* ASA Monograph 31. London: Routledge.
Ybarra, Josep-Antoni (1986) 'La informalización industrial en la economía valenciana: un modelo para el subdesarrollo'. *Revista de treball* 2.
Zdatny, Steven M (1990) *The politics of survival: artisans of 20th century France.* Oxford: Oxford University Press.

Index

Abrams, Philip, 235-236
Agency, 101-102, 104-105, 113,
  121, 130, 181, 184, 232-233,
  238, 244, 251, 256, 265, 268
Anthropology, 10, 22, 27, 46, 53
  88-90, 92-94, 98, 105, 107, 114,
  116, 127, 133, 135, 138-139,
  147-150, 169, 181, 186, 189,
  190, 197, 199, 201-208, 213,
  218, 220, 222-228, 230,
  233-238, 243, 252-254, 255,
  257, 265-267, 270
Appadurai, Arjun, 4-5, 7, 164,
  251
Artisans, 145, 147, 175, 177, 190
Augé, Marc, 136, 163

Bagnasco, Arnaldo, 139, 142, 145,
  155, 167
Bailey, F.G., 144, 164
Bajo Segura, 135, 139, 147, 157,
  160, 163, 191, 196, 199, 220
Bauman, Zygmunt, 24, 27, 148,
  197
Becattini, Giacomo, 142, 145, 156,
  158, 160
Bloch, Maurice, 202-203, 208
Bobbio, Norberto, 209-210
Bourdieu, Pierre, 10, 15, 22, 103,
  171, 187, 191, 228, 242, 252,
  257, 265, 268
Brusco, Sebastiano, 167, 168, 170

Buroway, Michael, 46, 103, 167,
  169, 187, 189

Capital-labour relations, 143, 151
Cenzatti, Marco, 158-159
Citizenship, 196-198, 202, 213,
  217-218, 221
  and citizen, 220
  social, 213, 216, 219, 222, 227
  universal, 216-217
Civil society, 202, 207-212, 216,
  220, 222, 225, 236, 239, 265
Class, 92, 100, 106, 118, 150, 152,
  155, 183-184, 205, 225, 229,
  211, 240-241
  and class-system, 206
  and experience, 191
  and struggle, 146, 152
  theory, 237
Cohen, Anthony, 197, 224
Cohen, Miriam, 216-217
Collective expression, 46, 90, 92,
  94, 121, 126, 231, 181, 190,
  195, 198, 203, 206, 216, 218,
  225, 231, 236, 266
  and action, 180
  and agency, 23, 31, 126, 261
  and culture, 205, 207, 214
  movements, 120
  and organization, 34-40, 45,
  183
  and social subjects, 240, 266

and struggle, 116, 123, 204, 216, 220
Comaroff, Jean, 203, 242, 228, 245, 255, 268
Comaroff, John, 203, 242, 228, 245, 255, 268
Community, 56, 62, 68, 72–73, 77, 79, 82, 83, 85, 108, 109, 110, 111, 147, 156, 177, 183, 195, 198, 201–202, 206, 209–211, 220–223, 234, 254
local, 198, 201, 213–214
national, 220
rural, 175
Confederations of households, 62, 67, 86, 109, 165
Consciousness, 118, 181, 248, 269
consciousness-identity-praxis, 184
and false consciousness, 247
and peasants, 125,
political, 80–81, 84, 116
working class 32, 106
Cooperation, 142, 145, 165, 179, 180
Cultural critics, 22
Culture, 46, 90, 105–106, 112, 121, 126, 133,137, 144, 146, 149, 152, 154–155, 158, 160–161, 197, 199, 202–204, 206–208, 211–212, 216, 219–220, 222–224, 229, 233–236, 238, 242–243, 246, 248, 263, 257–258, 270
of collective resistance, 157
forms of, 268
and identity, 84, 90
as ideology, 161
interpretation of, 266
local, 146, 153, 159, 161, 163, 197–199, 212–213, 222, 224
notion of, 56, 81, 149, 160, 202–204, 250
and practice, 196

processes of , 242
production of, 63, 146, 172, 183, 187–188
regional, 157, 160
rural, 186, 225

Development, 89–90, 106, 156, 160, 174, 184, 217
scholarship on, 89
Domestic labour, 169–170
and family, 142
household, 109
non-wage, 170
Durkheim, Emile, 23

Economics, neo-classical, 141, 148, 150, 155
Eigensinn, 37–40, 103
Elias, Norbert, 33, 48
Empiricism, 148, 241
Engels, Friedrich, 183, 209
Entrepreneurs, 92, 139, 142, 145, 168, 179
local, 160
Escobar, Artruro, 90, 91, 121
Étatisation, 215–216
Ethnography, 1–4, 7–8, 10, 84, 89, 107, 134–138, 166, 169, 181–182, 184, 196, 204, 221–222, 228, 238, 243, 264–265
Exploitation, 150, 152
'Expressivism', 91, 92, 97, 117, 120, 124–126

Firms, 141, 142–144, 147, 158, 160, 167, 180
networked, 148, 185
Foucault, 24, 197, 237

Giddens, Anthony, 10, 15, 171
Gramsci, Antonio, 13, 15, 22, 27, 42–45, 46, 49, 53,104, 112, 118–120, 197, 207, 210–211,

223, 228, 229, 231–249,
252–256, 258, 260, 265–268,
270
and hegemony, 239–246
Gough, Kathleen, 93, 96
Guerilleros, 75–76, 78, 87
Guha, Ranajit, 98, 100, 101, 106,
118
Gupta, Akhil, 195–197, 209, 224
Gupta, Dipankar, 103, 104, 106,
133

Habermas, Jürgen, 172, 182–184
Habitus, 202
Haciendas, 57–60, 65, 66, 67, 68,
70–71, 74–78, 109, 111, 112,
230, 234–235, 248, 253–254,
267
Hale, Charles, 121, 122
Hall, Stuart, 122, 240, 246–248,
253–254, 263, 269
Hanagan, Michael, 216–217
Harvey, David, 85, 127, 140, 149,
150, 152–154, 158–159,
160–162, 164–166, 184, 196,
240
Hegel, 209, 232
Hegemony, 22, 39, 80, 99, 113,
117, 119, 123, 155, 169, 173,
191, 208, 211, 220, 226,
228–229, 231, 232–240,
245–250, 252–258, 259–270
and counter-hegemony, 236, 254
cultural, 252, 264, 266, 267
and fieldwork, 233, 238
neo-liberal, 264
Hegemonic processes, 49, 120,
231, 232, 238–248, 252,
255–258, 262
hegemonic fields, 229, 264
hegemonic projects, 246, 253,
263, 267
Herzfeld, Michael, 196, 224, 227
Heterogeneity and difference,

61–63, 67, 79, 82, 85
Historiography, 98, 99, 100, 104,
106
Historical materialism, 96, 107
Historical realism, 1, 4, 15, 122,
124, 160
Hobsbawn, Eric, 13, 26, 28–29, 42,
60, 77, 84, 87, 93–96, 98–99,
100, 106–107, 113, 125, 127,
206
Homework, 168, 169, 177, 199,
200
Huasicanchinos, 60–87, 109,
111–114, 116, 127, 135–136,
147, 162–164, 224, 230–231,
234–235, 248, 253–254, 258,
261, 264, 267

Identity, 78, 91, 113, 117,
126–127, 181, 204, 217, 219,
245, 262
collective identity, 183, 230
and community, 136
and diversity, 197
politics of, 122
regional, 186
shared, 172,186–187
social, 244, 264
Images of society, 20, 23

Kumar, Krishna, 207, 211

Labour, 40, 47,150, 151, 156, 158,
142, 168, 169, 171–173, 177,
180, 183, 185–189, 205, 212,
217, 220, 253
commodification of, 115
division of, 23, 145, 176, 181
and labour power, 150–151
local 152, 159–160
organized, 141–142, 217
processes of, 170, 187
social labour, 172, 180–181,
183, 185, 187–188

Labour markets, 155, 168, 190,
217
Land, 75–77, 109, 145, 133–134,
253
ownership of, 63, 65, 79, 135
recuperation of, 58, 70
struggle over, 54, 81
Land invasions 59, 70, 77, 112,
248
Leadership, 56, 74, 82, 87, 95,
110, 175, 226, 229, 267–268,
248
Livelihood, 173, 175–176, 187,
216, 220, 232, 261, 264
forms of, 170, 184, 188–190,
199
reproduction of, 181, 186, 221,
224
Locality, 134, 139, 155, 159–160,
162–163, 169, 176, 178, 196,
200, 203–206, 211, 216–217,
220–221, 135, 161, 168, 195
and community, 209, 217, 219,
226
and culture, 142, 148, 209, 217,
219, 225
Lüdtke, Alf, 35–40, 53, 103

Markus, George, 204–205
Marshall, Alfred, 140, 148, 150,
154, 155, 176
Marshall, T. H., 213, 214, 218
Marx, Karl, 10, 12, 14–15, 23–25,
27, 43, 49, 63, 120, 127, 153,
160, 172, 186, 195, 204, 210,
228, 239, 241, 245, 249,
251–253
Marxism, 89, 97, 161, 191, 205,
237, 246, 252, 269
Mass collective worker, 180, 183
Materialism, 21, 121–122
'cultural materialism', 251, 270
Mauss, Marcel, 203, 206
Migrants, 61–62, 65–68, 71–74,
78, 111, 200

Mingione, Enzo, 171–172, 189
Mintz, Sidney, 93, 137
Mobilization, forms of, 89, 100,
104
Modernism, 24, 90, 121, 144, 148,
175, 185, 205, 266–267
Mouffe, Chantal, 240, 246, 253,
258, 263, 270
Multi-occupationality enterprises,
61, 109, 175, 135, 139, 165

Neo-liberalism, 123, 126
Neo-modernism, 90, 148, 161
Networks, 136, 142–143, 147–148,
176–177, 185, 199, 221, 226,
237

Objectivist approach, 95, 98, 101,
124
Organic intellectuals, 241,
260–264, 270
Ortner, Sherry, 115, 134, 166, 226

Peasants, 54, 56–57, 66, 69, 73,
75–79, 80, 87, 89, 91, 93–97, 99,
101–103, 105–107, 113,
115–116, 123–124, 175, 219,
234
Petty commodity production,
60–61, 63, 72, 108, 109, 110
Phenomenology of practice, 255
Place, 136–137, 149, 163, 211
sense of, 135–137, 162
social constitution of, 136, 150
Polanyi, Karl, 93, 144, 155, 173
Political economy, 204, 221
Portelli, Alessandro 6–7
Postmodernism, 21–22, 121, 154,
170, 182, 205, 265
Power, 24, 92–93, 100, 106,
115–117, 119, 121, 123, 137,
154, 158–159, 166, 175, 211,
223, 226, 228–229, 233–236,
239, 241, 244, 246–248, 254,
256, 260, 265, 269

coercive, 210–211
fields of, 252
role of 236, 265
social, 158, 187, 261
Praxis, 181, 216, 229, 241–242,
    256
    collective, 261
    political, 232
    philosophy of, 244
Production, 20, 23, 120, 124, 134,
    137, 141–142, 145, 150, 152,
    159, 167, 172, 175–176, 180,
    199, 211, 221, 240, 244
    artisan production, 174–175
    relations of, 46, 92, 102, 127,
    134, 138, 145, 153, 158, 167,
    189, 251, 267
Putnam, Robert, 145, 164, 225

Rebellion, 92, 95, 102, 126
Regional diversity, 152, 174, 219
Regional economies, 140,
    144–146, 165, 182, 187, 191
Regional identity, 175
Regional politics, 146
Regional studies, 148, 166, 169
Regional institutions, 137, 140,
    146–147, 149, 152, 155–156,
    159–163, 176, 180–184, 196
    and development, 151
    and production, 141
    and regional economies, 138,
    140, 144–146, 165, 182, 187,
    191
    regional success, 156
Resistance, 46, 60–61, 76–77,
    83–84, 91, 93–94, 97–100,
    102, 104–107, 109–116, 124,
    127, 156, 208, 220, 226, 230,
    236, 264, 267
    domination and, 88, 90–92,
    94–95, 98, 105, 116, 120,
    124–125
    everyday forms of, 270
    and rebellion, 108, 125–127

Sabel, Charles, 140–144, 146–147,
    153–155, 164–167, 185
Sayer, Andrew, 149, 210, 222
Schutz, Alfred, 256–257, 259–260,
    266, 270
Scott, James, 84, 98, 99, 101–108,
    116–120, 124–127
Sider, Gerald, 177–178, 189
Silver, Hilary, 216–217
Social economy, 184
Social market, 154
Social movements, 90–91, 94, 121,
    124, 127
Social regulation, 158
Social relationships, 95, 97, 101,
    104, 107, 111, 124, 135,
    150–152, 160, 162, 177, 201,
    210, 220, 237, 248
Social Reproduction, 23, 66, 80,
    92, 96, 100, 105–106, 109,
    122, 134, 157–158, 169, 183,
    186, 267, 110, 120, 124, 127,
    150, 187–188, 229, 244, 249,
    251–253, 263–264, 225, 250,
    252
    of capitalism, 90, 225, 232, 137,
    240, 243, 247–251, 253–254,
    267, 269
Social space, 185, 187, 198, 217,
    255–256
Social subjects, 46, 156, 197, 212,
    244, 250, 253, 262, 266
Sociology, 46, 167–171, 173, 182,
    185, 187, 189, 207, 223, 233,
    240, 244, 262
Space, 90, 106, 117, 127, 136–137,
    152–153, 171, 161, 166, 188,
    195, 196, 201, 207–208, 210,
    212, 216, 225, 261
State, 197–199, 200, 202, 204,
    207–227, 239
    and welfare, 199–200, 209,
    212–213, 216, 219, 220–221,
    224, 226
Subcontracting, 168–169, 177

Tacunan, Elias, 65-68
Taylor, Charles, 33, 48-49, 90,
    187, 259, 264, 270
Third Italy, 139, 141-143, 145,
    155, 160, 165-167, 178, 185
Thompson, E .P., 11, 19, 26-28,
    42, 49, 100-104, 122, 126, 204,
    214, 270
Thompson, J.B., 191
Todorov, Tzvetan, 195, 197, 223
Touraine, Alain, 32-33

Unions, 141, 152, 168, 206, 218

Weber, Max, 23, 120, 187, 237,
    239, 265, 172
Welfare, 199-200, 219-221
    welfare state,
        and policies, 213,

projects, 224
provision, 224
regimes, 216
state, 209, 212-213
system, 226
Williams, Raymond, 9-10, 13, 28,
    40-42, 46, 48, 53, 85, 100, 112,
    114, 122, 162-164, 187-188,
    205-206, 216, 226, 229, 240,
    246-247, 251-253, 257-258,
    269
Wolf, Eric, 13, 19, 56, 84, 87,
    94-96, 98, 106-107, 113, 123,
    125, 127, 137-138, 164
Working class, 25, 94, 100, 105,
    118, 126, 172, 183, 220
    and culture, 27, 28, 30, 42, 45,
        100, 101
    formation of, 173
Worsley, Peter, 94, 96, 203